EAST LOOE.

TOPOGRAPHICAL

AND

HISTORICAL SKETCHES

OF THE

BOROUGHS

OF

EAST AND WEST LOOE,

IN THE

County of Cornwall;

WITH

AN ACCOUNT OF THE NATURAL AND ARTIFICIAL CURIOSITIES

AND

PICTURESQUE SCENERY OF THE NEIGHBOURHOOD.

BY THOMAS BOND.

LONDON:
PRINTED BY AND FOR J. NICHOLS AND SON, 25, PARLIAMENT STREET;
AND SOLD BY THE BOOKSELLERS AT EXETER, PLYMOUTH,
DOCK, TRURO, AND PENZANCE.

1823.

INTRODUCTION.

The Looes being frequently resorted to in the Summer season by strangers, either in pursuit of health or pleasure, the Writer thinks it may be of service to these places, and to the publick, to give some short account of these antient Boroughs.

Looe recommends itself as a bathing-place, or situation for invalids, or for parties of pleasure, on account of its convenient beach, fine mild air (being considerably farther South than most of the watering-places in the kingdom), beautiful walks, rides, and views, short distance from Plymouth, and lowness of house-rent.

The greatest part of this work the Author had sketched out some years ago, merely for his private amusement, without the least idea of publishing it; he must now apologize for its imperfections, and request those who can suggest improvements, supply defects, and make corrections, so to do.

As there is nothing in the performance of this work which can merit applause, so the Writer hopes there is nothing to be found in it which deserves censure. Books of this description are certainly of some use in informing and directing travellers, strangers, and indeed even residents; and they tend to perpetuate facts which would otherwise be buried in oblivion by the desolating hand of Time. These considerations introduce this book to the Publick, and, it is hoped by the Author, will sanction it from calumny.

Dec. 1, 1822.

HISTORY

OF

EAST AND WEST LOOE.

THE Boroughs of EAST and WEST LOOE are situated in the South-east part of the County of Cornwall, in the Hundred of West.

EAST LOOE.

East Looe is by far the largest, best built, and most flourishing town, but whether more antient than the other I cannot learn; though from its being antiently called Loo only, without the adjunct, I think it likely to have been a town before West Looe was in existence. East Looe is certainly an antient town; for in the reign of Edward I. Henry de Bodrigan, then Lord thereof, certified his claim to a Market and Fair at Looe, and view of Frank Pledge, a Ducking-stool, a Pillory, and Assize of Bread and Beer [*].

---

[*] Placita Jur. et Assis. apud Launceston, anno 30 Edw. I.

It does not appear that Looe is mentioned in Domesday Book.

Carew, in his "Survey of Cornwall," says, that "East Looe voucheth less antiquity (than West Looe) as lately incorporated, but vanteth greater wealth, as more commodiously seated."

From the "History of the Boroughs of Great Britain," &c. published anonymously in 1792, it appears that East Looe was first summoned, I apprehend to return Members of Parliament, the 14th of Edward III.; discontinued the same year, and restored in the 13th of Queen Elizabeth (1571).

In the 14th year of the reign of Elizabeth (1572) Thomas Stone and Thomas West were returned Members for East Looe *. It also appears by the aforesaid publication, that West Looe was first summoned to return Members 6th of Edward VI. Nothing is said about being discontinued or restored. Both these Boroughs were first incorporated by Queen Elizabeth; East Looe by the name of "Major et liberorum Burgensium Burgi de East Lowe in Comitatu Cornub."

Nine Chief Burgesses were appointed by Queen Elizabeth's Charter to East Looe. This Charter is dated the 14th of June, in the 29th year of her Majesty's reign (1587). Their names were,

---

* See copy of the indenture of this election, printed in the Appendix. The original record is in the Chapel of the Rolls.

Walter Conner,   Thomas Spurr,
Philip Mayo,   Thomas Collin,
Philip Hooper,   Martin Connor,
Philip Fitzwilliams, John White.
John Hicks,

The above-named Walter Conner was the first Mayor, and Sir William Mohun, Knt. was by this Charter appointed first Recorder.

At the time of the last Inquisition (Heralds' Office) 12 October 1620,

John Egar was Mayor of East Looe.
Sir Reginald Mohun, Knt and Bart. Recorder.

Philip Fitzwilliams,
Edmund Fitzwilliams,
Henry Cloake,
Thomas Egar,   } Burgesses.
Denis Fitzwilliams,
Daniel Chubb,
William Parvis,
Philip Williams,

Joseph Bastard, Steward and Town-clerk.

Before this Charter of Elizabeth there was a Portreeve.

To this Charter James I. granted a supplemental one, the 7th of July, 1623, in the 21st year of his reign. In the reign of James II. these Charters were surrendered up*, and a new Charter granted

---

* The surrender was intended to have been made to Charles II. The Corporation, by deed under their common seal, dated Oct. 20, 1684, appointed John Earl of Bath their attorney for this purpose; but before the Earl arrived in London, the King was dead.

by him the 28th of March, in the first year of his reign (1685).

By this Charter Twelve Chief Burgesses were appointed, and 36 Free Burgesses. Their names were,

Capital Burgesses.

John Natt, first Mayor,	Henry Eager,
Reginald Hawkey,	Philip Hicks,
Thomas Blight,	John Chubb,
John Pope,	Philip Stephens,
Nathaniel Ambrose,	Nicholas Reed,
Richard Pope,	John Oben.

Free Burgesses.

Bernard Granville,	Nathaniel Michell,
Jonathan Trelawny, bart.	Richard Hamley,
Charles Trelawny,	John Helston,
Henry Trelawny,	Richard Scadgell, sen.
Joseph Sawle,	Bernard Cleere,
Thomas Vivian,	Nicholas Short,
John Vyvian, jun.	Richard Scadgell, jun.
Henry Vincent,	Francis Scadgell,
Francis Kelly,	William Scadgell,
Thomas Achym,	John Haven,
John Arundell, jun.	Daniel Chubb,
Thomas Kelly,	Thomas Jewell,
William Martyn,	William Merick,
Philip Pope,	Francis Langston,
John Natt, jun.	John Baker,
Christopher Chubb,	John Cunning,
Thomas Bond,	Richard Hicks,
John Arnoll,	John Williams.

By this Charter, John Earl of Bath, Lord Lieutenant of the County of Cornwall, was appointed Recorder.

The Mayor is elected annually from the Chief Burgesses, by their votes, and the votes of the Free Burgesses, on the Court-day immediately preceding Michaelmas-day, and on Michaelmas-day is sworn into office *.

The Mayor, last Mayor, and Recorder, are Justices of the Peace. The Mayor and Recorder have a power of appointing deputies during absence, and such deputies are Justices of the Peace; there is a non-intromittant Clause in the Charter as to County Justices.

The Jurisdiction of the Borough extends to about one hundred acres, so says the Charter, and the boundaries thereof are therein particularly expressed.

There is a fee-farm rent of twenty shillings *per annum*, paid by the Corporation for the Borough. To whom it now belongs I do not exactly know. In the year 1736 it belonged to one James Cox, Esq. and perhaps formerly belonged to the Duchy of Cornwall or to the King.

Each of these Boroughs sends two Members to Parliament. In the 14th year of the reign of Edward III. East Looe and Fowey sent one and the same Merchant, then called a ship-owner, to a Coun-

---

* Vide a Table of Mayor-chusing Days from 1800 to 1899, hereafter, in the Appendix.

cil at Westminster (not to Parliament). See the original Writ, Prynne, Brev. Parl. vol. IV. p. 186, where J. Shackcloch was returned at the same time for Polruan only, and these Members allowed for forty-four days in going to, staying at, and returning from Westminster, four pounds twelve shillings!

At the commencement of the Protectorate of Cromwell, an Act was passed, whereby Cornwall was to be represented as follows:

For the Borough of Dunishevet, otherwise
   Launceston - - - - One
For the Borough of Truro - - One
For the Borough of Penryn - - One
For the Boroughs of East and West Looe One
For the County of Cornwall - Eight.

In pursuance of this Act, in the year 1653, a writ was issued by Oliver Cromwell, Protector of the Common-wealth of England, &c. for electing eight Knights for the County of Cornwall, one Burgess for Launceston, one Burgess for Truro, one for Penryn, and one for the Boroughs of East Looe and West Looe. Who was returned for East and West Looe I do not know; but in 1654, on the 3d of July, Antonie Rous was elected for East Looe and West Looe, and on the 12th of the same month Robert Bennett was elected for East Looe and West Looe*.

---

* The writ, together with the Sheriff's precept, by virtue of which these two returns were made, required the election of only one Burgess for the two Boroughs; and it seems, from the

In Richard Cromwell's first and only Parliament the renowned Sir William Petty, Knt. sat for the Borough of West Looe, elected, I apprehend, in 1658 *. See Barlow's Peerage, under title Lord Wycombe.

---

returns, that some misunderstanding at that time subsisted between the said two Corporate Bodies; for the Mayor of West Looe, with other parties particularly named, and two persons styled Capital Burgesses of East Looe, are parties to the indenture which has the priority of date, and the Mayor of East Looe is not included or even mentioned as a party; and so, *vice versa*, with respect to the second return, in which the Mayor of East Looe is expressly named as a party. See copies of this writ and indentures hereafter, in the Appendix. The originals are in the Tower of London.

* This distinguished character was the son of Anthony Petty, a clothier at Rumsey in Hampshire, and was born there May 25, 1623. At a very early age, as stated in his will, he evinced a peculiar "genius for mechanics." He acquired the rudiments of education in his native village, whence he went to the University of Oxford. Here he obtained a comprehensive knowledge of the Latin, Greek, and French languages, and likewise of those branches of geometry and astronomy most requisite to the practice of navigation, dialling, &c. Thus qualified he served for several years in the Royal Navy; but, on the breaking-out of the grand rebellion, he quitted the sea, and studied medicine at different universities on the Continent. During this period of his life he became acquainted with the celebrated Hobbes, of Malmesbury, whose friendly instructions contributed much to his advancement in philosophy and knowledge. In 1647, returning to England, he procured from the Parliament a patent for his invention of double writing, and began to practise his profession at Oxford. In 1649 he was admitted doctor of physic

THE BRIDGE.

The Boroughs of East and West Looe are separated from each other by a river, over which is a narrow stone Bridge of about 384 feet long, with originally fifteen arches, including two square open-

---

and deputy professor of anatomy in that university. About the same time he was elected a fellow of Brazen Nose College; and in December 1650 became noted from being instrumental in the recovery of Ann Green, who had been hanged at Oxford on an unjust charge of child-murder, and who afterwards married, and had several children. Soon after this he was chosen a member of the Royal College of Physicians, London, and was also appointed lecturer on music in Gresham College. In 1652 he visited Ireland as physician-general to the Army; and being long resident in Dublin was constituted clerk to the Council, and secretary to Oliver Cromwell, who was styled Lord Lieutenant. About two years after his arrival in that kingdom he engaged in his Political Survey of Ireland, which obtained for him both fame and fortune. This work was compiled with the most scrupulous exactness, and was illustrated with several maps. How long he was employed in its execution we are uncertain; but in 1658 we find him conspicuous and much famed in Richard Cromwell's first and only Parliament. On the deposition of the Protector by the Rump Parliament, Petty returned to Ireland, where he remained till the Restoration, when he again came back to England. In 1661 he received the honour of knighthood, and was returned one of the Burgesses of Enniscorthy, in the County of Wexford, to the Parliament convened at Dublin May 9th in that year. He was one of the first members of the Royal Society, and likewise an original member of the College of Physicians, as incorporated by patent in 1667. Sir

ings, made for the more commodious passing of boats laden with wood; but the first arch on East Looe side was filled up within time of memory. The Bridge is apparently very old, and is at this time in a ruinous condition. What is odd enough in such a work, you can scarce meet with two arches on the same scale. Messrs. Lysons, in their "Magna Britannia," say, that this Bridge was built about the year 1400 (but give no authority for this), and that there was formerly a Chapel or Oratory on this Bridge, dedicated to St. Anne. Within time of memory one of the recesses on the piers, about the centre of the Bridge, had a wall athwart it different from all the other recesses, and I suppose this was the place where the little Chapel or Oratory stood. Inscriptions on granite at each end of the Bridge state that it was repaired by the County in the year 1689. I find by some old writings in my possession, that in this year the Bridge

---

William was twice married, and left behind him several children at his death, which happened Dec. 16, 1687, when he was interred in the church at Rumsey, and over him was placed a flat stone with this inscription:

"HERE LIES SIR WILLIAM PETTY."

Besides the Survey above mentioned, Sir William was author of a treatise on "Political Arithmetic," which shews great depth of capacity, and will be of lasting service to posterity. He was likewise the inventor of several useful mechanical instruments, and suggested many important improvements in natural philosophy. Among his inventions was that of a double-bottomed ship, the mould of which is still preserved in the repository of Gresham College.—*Beauties of England and Wales.*

was in general decay, and was then thoroughly repaired. At the County Sessions, held at Bodmin the 7th of October, in the 25th year of the Reign of Charles II. Nicholas Glynn, one of the Justices of the County, presented Looe Bridge as being ruinous and in great decay for want of reparations, so that the Lieges of the Lord the King could not use the Bridge without running into great danger, and that the inhabitants of the Boroughs of East Looe and West Looe the said Bridge ought to repair, as they were accustomed to do. This presentment was traversed, and tried at the Sessions held at Bodmin the 24th of July, in the 26th year of the Reign of the said King, before Sir John Carew, bart., Sir John ————, bart., Sir Walter Moyle, knt., &c. and the Jury gave their verdict, that the inhabitants of the said Boroughs ought not to repair the said Bridge, but that the same ought and was accustomed to be repaired by the County [*].

CHAPEL.

There is a Free Chapel within the Borough of East Looe; it has a tower of about fifty feet high, with one bell and a clock in it. Service, till of late years, used to be performed in this Chapel

---

[*] A copy of the Record of Sessions is in West Looe Townchest. See also hereafter in the Appendix.

twice on Sundays, and Prayers on Wednesdays, but now only once on Sundays, and none at other times.

Sir Jonathan Trelawny, formerly Lord Bishop of Exeter, afterwards Lord Bishop of Winchester, by deed poll, bearing date the 9th of October 1716, settled certain lands in trust for raising two thousand pounds, reciting that he had taken into consideration the state and condition of the inhabitants of the several Boroughs and Towns of East Looe and West Looe, in Cornwall, and their being so remote from their respective Parish Churches, so as that in bad weather it was very inconvenient for the inhabitants of the said towns to repair to their Parish Churches; and that there was in the said town of East Looe a very large and handsome Chapel erected, but no revenue or allowance settled for the maintenance of any Chaplain or Minister to officiate in the same Chapel; the Bishop, therefore, by the said deed declared, ordered, and appointed, that the Trustees therein-named should, with all convenient speed after his death, out of the yearly rent, fines, and other profits of the lands therein-mentioned, raise and levy two thousand pounds in trust, to and for the only use, benefit, and behoof of his heirs or assigns. And as to one thousand pounds, part of the said two thousand pounds, he directed the same to be laid out by his Trustees, by and with the consent and approbation of his heirs and executors, in the purchasing the inheritance of some sheaf tythes or other hereditaments; and that the same, when purchased, should, by his said Trustees, with such consent and approbation as aforesaid, be conveyed to ten or some greater number of honest and trust-worthy persons, and their heirs, upon trust to apply four parts in five parts to be divided of the annual rent, issues, and profits for ever, to and for the maintenance of a Chaplain or Priest of the Established Church of England, constantly to officiate in the said Chapel of East Looe, to read prayers every day of the week, and to preach every Lord's-day there; and upon trust to apply one-fifth part of such annual rents and profits to and for some person who shall teach school within the said town of East Looe, or within the said town of West Looe, and who shall teach gratis, and without any other reward, ten poor children of each of the said towns of East Looe and West Looe; which said Chaplain or Minister and Schoolmaster shall severally and respectively, from time to time, and at all times thereafter, be nominated and appointed by his heirs. And as to the other one thousand pounds, the Bishop directed the same when raised, to be paid or laid out as his trustees and his heirs and executors should seem best, for carrying on the charitable design of the Society for promoting Christian Knowledge. Provided that if he should in his life-time give or settle the sum of two thousand pounds aforesaid, to the pious and charitable uses before mentioned, then his said trustees should stand seised or possessed of the said premises, in trust, only for him, his heirs, and assigns; and if he in his life-time should pay or lay out any sum or sums of money for the uses aforesaid, and should not pay or lay out the whole two thousand pounds, then his said trustees should not pay or lay out the whole two thousand pounds for the purposes aforesaid, but only so much thereof as with the money as should by him be laid out would make up the two thousand pounds; and gave full power to said trustees, by and with the consent of his heirs or executors, after they had received the said one thousand pounds for finding a Chaplain, or Minister, and Schoolmaster, to lay out the same money or any part thereof in the public funds, or in India bonds, Exchequer bills, or Bank notes, until such times as they might have an opportunity of laying the same out in the purchase of a sheaf-tythe, or other hereditaments as aforesaid.

This money originally produced fifty pounds a year, but the stock (for the principal was never laid out in tythe-sheaf or other hereditament) having from time to time had its interest reduced, now produces only thirty pounds *per annum,* and which sum is now paid to the Chaplain for the time being. And the Chaplain is appointed by Sir Harry Trelawny and James Buller, Esq. of Dounes, as the representatives of Bishop Trelawny. Before this endowment was made, the Chaplain was appointed and paid by the Corporation, to whom the Chapel belongs, and is by them kept in repair; and the

Corporation might still if they chose appoint their own Chaplain, but he would not be entitled to the above endowment.

Capgrave (Legenda, fol. 204) speaking of the Chapel says, "'Tis dedicated as I guess to St. Kayne, by which name the parish of St. Martin's (within which East Looe is) is also called, from St. Kayne or Kenna, a holy virgin of the Blood Royal, daughter of Braganus Prince of Brecknockshire. She is said to have gone a pilgrimage to St. Michael's Mount, in this county, and was in great esteem here and in Somersetshire, as may be seen in Camden, who derives Keynsham from her. An account of her and her well may be seen in Carew, fol. 130. She lived about the year 490, and her festival is celebrated September 30, on the eve of which day is yet held a fair at this town — which seems to strengthen my conjecture, there being nothing more usual in towns than to perpetuate the memory of the Saint the Church was dedicated to in this manner, as appears by antient charters, which being generally granted for three days, though now reduced to one; the eve and morrow being in few places observed, makes me conclude this grant was so, and that Michaelmas, being so well noted, occasioned it to be then kept as it is now."

To which Mr. Willis, in his "Notitia Parliamentaria," adds: " Here is a poor Battery of four guns, and a little Chapel of Ease, kept up by buttresses, in which the Minister of St. Martin's, the Mother

Church and Burial-place to this town, should preach once in three weeks."

In the year 1805, the old Chapel at East Looe being in a very decayed state, it was determined on by John Buller, Esq. M. P. and Recorder of the Borough, with consent of the Corporation, to have it taken down, and to build a new Chapel on the same spot. The old Chapel consisted of two ailes, the Northern one much wider than the other, divided by pillars and five circular arches, and was not plastered over head. On the 5th of March the workmen began to demolish it. Two piscinas, or receptacles for holy water, were found closed up in the walls, one of them in the Eastern part of the South wall, and the other in the East part of the wall dividing the two ailes. About the middle of the North wall, immediately behind where the Aldermen of East Looe's seat stood, and now stands, a low and narrow sharp-pointed arch door-way was discovered, which led to a narrow flight of winding steps in the wall, which ascended to a hollow place in the wall, not unlike a stopped-up window. It has been conjectured that this was a rood-loft, or led to one. The remains of an arch walled up were found on the South side of the tower, which appeared very antient, but its original use could not be ascertained. The old Chapel had two roofs, with a lead gutter between them. When the last lead gutter was placed there, about a century since, the former decayed one was ordered, by the person who paid for the new one, to be carried out to sea, and thrown overboard, that it might not be used for profane purposes.

On the 7th of April, 1805, the first stone of the new Chapel was laid by Captain, now Vice-admiral Sir Edward Buller, Bart. It was the foundation-stone of the North-east corner, under which were placed, by those who attended the ceremony, some of the King's coin, &c. The new Chapel was finished so as to have divine service performed in it about September 1806, as the following inscription in gold letters on the front of the gallery states:

"This Chapel was rebuilt at the sole Cost of JOHN BULLER, Esq. Recorder and M. P. for this Borough; the Foundation-stone of which was laid, and the Chapel ornamented and painted, by his brother, Captain EDWARD BULLER, also Recorder and M. P. for this Borough. Divine Service was first performed Sept. 28, 1806, in the Mayoralty of THOMAS BOND, Esq."

The new Chapel cost upwards of £1500; is about the same size as the old one as to its exterior, but the walls being less thick, it is somewhat larger inside; and it is built to a few inches (to make it in square, which the old one was not) on the exact spot where the old one stood. The old tower was not taken down, but remains, and declines from the perpendicular, owing, perhaps, to its being built on sand.

There were two tablets in the old Chapel, with the following inscriptions, erected, probably, in gratitude of the facts they were intended to communicate:

Over the seats in which the wives of the Aldermen of East Looe sat:

This Chapel was repaired
at the sole Cost of the Hon[ble]
Sir HENRY SEYMOUR, Bar[t].
and the Hon[ble] Brigadier
TRELAWNY, Burgesses in Parlia[t]
for this Corporation.
THOMAS BOND, Maior,
1700.

Over the seats in which the wives of the Aldermen of West Looe sat:

These Seats were
built, and this Chapel
beautified, at the sole Cost
and Charge of the Hon[ble] and
Right Rev[d] Father in God Sir
JON[N]. TRELAWNY, Bar[t]. Lord Bishop
of Winchester, Prelate of y[e] most
Noble Order of the Garter,
1715.

There were no sepulchral monuments of any kind.

St. Martin's is the burial-place for the town. Marriages are not solemnized in the Chapel. Children are frequently christened there, though sometimes objéctions have been made to this by the Rector of St. Martin's.

The only Chapel Register of Christenings in existence commences in the year 1709.

The inhabitants of West Looe are allowed to sit in the Chapel by courtesy. Though Bishop Trelawny's endowment was for their benefit in common with the inhabitants of East Looe, he could not grant the right to the Chapel also.

ST. MARTIN'S PARISH.

East Looe, as before stated, is within the parish of St. Martin's; in which parish, tradition says, there was formerly a Nunnery, probably at Bucklauren, which place belonged to the Priory of Launceston, before it was suppressed by Henry VIII.

REV. JONATHAN TOUP.

This parish had Jonathan Toup for its Rector a few years since. He was famous for his great knowledge of Greek. There is in the Church (which is about a mile from Looe) a small but neat marble monument to his memory. There is also a round brass plate, presented to his representatives from the University of Oxford. The inscriptions on the monument and plate are as follow:

Near this place lie the remains
of JONATHAN TOUP, A. M.
Rector of this Parish xxxiv years,
Vicar of St. Merrin's,
and Prebendary of Exeter.
His abilities
and critical sagacity
are known to the learned throughout Europe.
His virtues,
from the retired privacy of his life,
were known but to few.
To those few
they have endear'd his memory.
J. T. was born Dec. MDCCXIII.
Died Jan. XIX. MDCCLXXXV.

The Tablet above
was inscribed to the memory of her Uncle
by PHILLIS BLAKE;
the charge of it was afterwards defrayed
by the Delegates of the Oxford Press,
as a small testimony
of their respect for the character of Mr. TOUP,
and of their gratitude
for his many valuable contributions.

Mr. Toup was born at St. Ives in Cornwall; took his degree of Bachelor of Arts at Exeter College, Oxford; and in 1756 took his Master's degree at Cambridge. The rectory of St. Martin's was procured for him by his uncle, Mr. Busvargus. For the vicarage of St. Merrin, in Cornwall, and a prebend in the Cathedral Church of Exeter, he was indebted to his zealous patron and friend, Bishop Warburton, at whose solicitation both preferments were bestowed on him by Dr. Keppel, Bishop of Exeter. "His Annotations on Suidas and on Theocritus, his edition of Longinus, and the notes which he contributed to almost every distinguished work of classical criticism published during his time, evince (says a recent author) deep learning, and, in general, great ingenuity. He censured freely, and praised sparingly; but by a peculiar felicity in discovering the places to which the author alludes or quotes, he has explained difficulties, and illustrated obscurities with greater plausibility, and more undoubted success, than any of his predecessors."

Most of Mr. Toup's Greek manuscripts were presented by his representative to the University of Oxford.

The Delegates of the Oxford Press, as before stated, paid the charges for the monument, and also presented Miss Blake, Mr. Toup's personal representative, with an Edition of Shakspeare's Works.

MONUMENTS.

There is also in St. Martin's Church a large and elegant Monument to the Langdon family, who formerly lived at Kevéril, in this parish. It has the following inscription:

This monument was
erected in memory of WALTER
LANGDON, of Keveril, Esq. being
the last of the male line of that
loyal, antient, and honourable
family, and RHODA his wife, the
daughter of William Martin, of
Linridg, in the County of Devon,
Esquire, he died the 16th day of
February, in the year of our
Lord 1676, and was buried
under this marble.

There is likewise an altar-tomb on Philip Maiowe:
Here lyeth the Bodye of PHILIPPE MAIOWE, of East Looe, Gentleman; who deceased this Lyfe the 27th day of August, in the year 1590, being then of the age of 72 years:

Here under this great carved stone
Is PHILLIPPE MAIOW entombde,
Who in his life for Merchandice
Was through this land renown'd.
His trade was great, his dealins just,
The poor did feel his bountie,
Great cost he put for sea and land,
In buildyng verye plentie.

There is a mural monument on the Rev. Stephen Medhope:
In memory of the late Reverend and faithful Pastor of this Church of St. Martin's, STEPHEN MED-

HOPE. He died in the Lord the sixth day of January, Anno Dom. 1636.

This marble clad in mourning seems to say,
Come do bewail with me, lament the day
On which you lost this worthy, call to mind,
The man of God, you that are left behind.
This Abel being dead, yet speaks, and we
May read ourselves in his life's history,
How meek was he, yet how majestic all,
His grave discourse seem'd apostolical.
His sermons were new Threnes *, as if in him
The soul of Jeremy transfus'd had been,
Each part did preach his heart, his tongue, his eye,
Will you have more, his life was not a lie,
And when his body did his soul outlet,
Was heard a cry—our western sun is set.

The following is copied from an old paper found in the late Mr. Clement Jackson's closet, perhaps written by his Father, who was a Baptist Minister, or his Father.

The account of Mr. Midhope's leaving his benefice, to embrace and stick by what he found to be truth.

"Mr. Stephen Midhope was famed in his time for a man of good learning, a good liver, and a good preacher, and deservingly enjoy'd ye Benefice of St. Martyn's in Cornwall as the minister for several

---

* Perhaps from Threnodia — a mourning song — a song of lamentation.

years, which is worth at least £.200 *per annum*;
but in searching aft^r truth, he found th^t ye Baptist
Religion was nighest the primitive institution and
practice, he took up wth y^t, freely parting with his
benefice for the love of truth, and the necessary de-
pendance on it, to witt, peace and satisfaction in his
own mind, which are the natural produce of a good
conscience toward God, willing to live honestly, and
liv^d a Minist^r to the Baptist Church in Looe, which
is a Corporation in ye Parish of St Martyn's, for
several years aft^r, and departed this life in peace,
and with a good conscience, February 24, 1652 *.

"Many of his parishioners, as I have been credibly
informed, came over to the Baptist wth (or just after)
him. And if all the rest of the Clergy of the Church
of England had ye like knowledge, integrity, and
courage as he had, they will doe ye same, but in
common they are deficient in one or the oth^r of
these things.

"One of the Clergy y^t serv^d the said Parish of S^t
Martyn's not many years since, attacked me vigor-
ously for not baptising our children; I told him y^t
we had no precept nor precedent for it in the Scrip-
tures, and y^t it was not likely to be practised by
the Apostles and Primitive Church, because we read
of men and women baptized, but no children. Upon
which ye parson told me that we never read of a woman's being baptiz'd; and if I could produce any

---

* He must therefore have been a son of the former Rector,
whose epitaph is before given.

such text he would turn Baptist y^t moment. I askt him whether he was reall in what he proposed, he said he was, on which I produced him the accounts we have of it in ye Acts of the Apostles; but the parson was sooner confounded by than converted to the truth; he wanted some of the above-mentioned integrity or courage."

On the north side of St. Martin's * Church is a door near the Tower, which has a peculiar arch (a Saxon receding one), there are but few of the same kind in Cornwall. There is one at St. Germans, and I think I saw one walled up in the north-wall of St. Cleer Church.

FORTIFICATIONS.

But to return to East Looe.—This Borough is fortified towards the Sea by a parapet-wall with embrazures, and formerly ten long six-pounders, and on the hill towards Plymouth were four more cannon of the same calibre. During the French Revolution four eighteen-pounders with a full supply of ammunition, and every other requisite for their use, were

---

* St. Martin was a native of Hungary, and for some time followed the life of a soldier, but afterwards took orders, and was made Bishop of Tours in France, in which see he continued for twenty-six years. Martin died about the year 397, much lamented, and highly esteemed for his virtues. His festival is the 11th of November.

sent to Looe; and a volunteer company of artillery being established here, and furnished with seventy muskets, these Boroughs had no great reason to fear depredations from privateers.

When Looe was first fortified with cannon I do not know; but by a memorandum in one of the Corporation books I find, that the inhabitants subscribed towards the maintenance of a gunner for the town of East Looe, previous to the year 1607.

SCHOOLS.

John Speccott, Esq. of Penhale, in the parish of Egloskerry, Cornwall, by his will, dated the 19th of August, 1703, gave to Sir Jonathan Trelawny, then Bishop of Winchester, and to the Hon'ble Charles Trelawny, of Hengar, in the said county of Cornwall, and other Trustees, one thousand pounds, to be applied by them and the survivors to some public use and benefit for the county of Cornwall, for which no provision was then before made. Bishop Trelawny and his brother the General being the surviving Trustees, and thinking that the establishment of a Public School was most consonant to the wishes of the Donor, by their deed, dated the 9th of November, 1716, founded a Mathematical School at East Looe, and appointed Mr. Samuel Haines, whom the learned Walter Moyle, in his letter to Dr. Tancred Robinson, giving an account of a wonderful meteor which he saw from Bake in 1718-9, speaks of as a very sensible and ingenious young man, and who was about to give his friend Dr. Halley an account of this meteor (as seen by him from Looe) the first master thereof, under the apprehension that Colonel Speccott himself, had he lived, would have appointed him to that situation. By the said deed of foundation, the Master is to reside in one of the Looes *, to instruct poor children, of the county of Cornwall, in the mathematics, particularly in those branches which relate to navigation.

The appointment of the Master after the death of the original Trustees was vested in the Heirs of Charles Trelawny, and the proprietors of Trelawny-house. The interest of the endowment was appropriated as a salary for the Master, except such part as the Trustees should think requisite for the purchase of books, globes, and mathematical instruments. This School is now kept at West Looe by Mr. Rundle.

In the 12th year of the reign of Queen Anne, John Buller, of Shillingham, in the county of Cornwall, Esq. laid out one thousand pounds in the purchase of a Government annuity of £.100 *per annum*

---

* Some writers have stated that this School was first established at Penryn; from whence this mistake could have originated I know not.

for 99 years, commencing the 25th of December, 1705, and vested the same in Trustees for the purpose of establishing five Schools in the county of Cornwall, in the towns following, Saltash, Liskeard, one of the boroughs of Looe, Penzance, and Grampound; the Masters to be paid £.10 each *per ann.* and forty shillings *per annum* to be allowed to the Trustees towards the expences of their meetings, the remainder to be laid out in buying bibles, prayer-books, and other books of piety, and also in binding and putting out one of the most hopeful poor boys of every of the said five Schools to some trade, calling, or honest employment, or service, &c. &c.

This annuity having ended by efflux of time, the Schools are consequently broken up. The boys who went to this School at East Looe, used to be dressed (at the expence of the Charity) in a light blue coat, with a cap of the same coloured cloth, and went by the name of the Blue Boys. Mr. Clement Triggs was the last Master. The following is a copy of a Hand Bill which he published:

"*East Looe, Cornwall.*

" C. Triggs having taken a roomy and commodious House, intends taking a few more Boarders at Midsummer next, for the purpose of instruction in Writing in the various Hands. Merchant's Accompts by the Italian method of Double Entry, Arithmetic in all its branches, Algebra, &c. Plain and Spherical Trigonometry and Geometry, Dialling, Navigation, the Use of the Globes, Planisphere, &c. &c.

" Pupils intended for Nautical Learning, will be shewn to take Observations of the Sun, Moon, and Stars, so expeditiously and accurately, as if actually at Sea; Looe having the advantage of the Horizon thereof upwards of 110 degrees.

" No care or attention will be wanting to facilitate the Learning, and improve the Genius of Youth placed under his care.

" *8th of June*, 1801."

LOOE ISLAND.

About one mile from this Borough to the Southward lies an Island, called by Carew St. George's Island, by others St. Nicholas's, and I observe in the map of Cornwall, in Camden's Britannia, it is called St. Michael's; but whatever its tutelar Saint might have been called, it is now known to the inhabitants of Looe by no other name than that of Looe Island. It is more than half a mile in circumference, and has been inhabited by one family of the name of Finn (who before resided on the Mewstone [*], Plymouth) for about forty years past.

---

[*] The Mewstone is a small insulated spot in or near Plymouth Sound.

There is no tree on the Island: Sir Harry Trelawny, the owner, sometime since had some firs planted there, but they did not grow *. This Island is the largest on the cost of Cornwall, except some of the Scilly Islands. On the top of it are the remains of some building, which goes by the name of the Chapel. Some years since a remarkably large human skeleton was found in it. This Island is hardly half a mile from the nearest land, and upon the ebbs of the equinoctial tides may be termed a peninsula, as at those times people frequently walk over to it dry shod. There is a dangerous range of rocks called the Ranny, which runs out into the Sea from the Eastern part of this Island. Before the present inhabitants took possession of this domain, it abounded with rabbits and rats. As to the rats they came from a ship, that many years since ran foul of and was wrecked on the Ranny; before which time, tradition says, there were no rats on this place. The rabbits and rats are now much decreased, by the inhabitants of the Island catching and eating them. A rat smothered with onions must no doubt be a delicate dish †. These are the only wild quadrupeds, and there are no reptiles. Carew speaks of " great abundance of sundry sea-

---

* Tufts of trees on this Island would have a beautiful effect, and I am told the most likely mode of procuring them would be by raising them from seed on the spot, not by planting young trees produced in another soil.

† He was a bold man who first ate a raw oyster.

fowl breeding upon the Strand, where they lay and hatch their eggs without care of building any nests. At which time, repairing thither, you shall see your head shadowed with a cloud of old ones, through their diversified cries, witnessing their general dislike of your disturbance; and your feet pestered with a large number of young ones, some newly and some not yet disclosed; at which time, through the leave and kindness of Master May (Mayow) the owner, you may make and take your choice." At present few if any birds frequent the Island. Before the present inhabitants lived there, the writer remembers great numbers of choughs there, and that they used to make their nests in the rabbit-holes. The only houses on the Island are a small dwelling-house and an out-house, which are situated at the lowest part of the Island, and appear antient buildings. Just below the houses is a spring of fresh water.

SEA BEACH. — BATHING. — SALUBRITY.

There is a fine beach of sand and pebbles between the town of East Looe and the Sea, well adapted for the use of bathing-machines. In the year 1800 a bathing-machine was established here by subscription, but few persons ever used it, and it was suffered to fall into decay. In the evening of the day it was completed for use (August 20), a party of ladies and gentlemen drank tea in it, with much mirth and merriment; and musick being called for, one of the party wrote with a pencil on the door the following verses:

> Bring the harp, and bring the flute,
> Let none be silent, none be mute;
> Sing the song, and chant the air,
> That Bathing will the Health repair.
> Success attend our present measure;
> Health below's the greatest treasure.
> What is Freedom, what is Wealth,
> Compar'd to thee, sweet blooming Health!
> May those who want thee dip and find
> Freedom, Wealth, and Thee combin'd!

The Boroughs of East and West Looe are remarkable for their healthiness and the longevity of the inhabitants. Gilbert, in his History of Cornwall, says, that from November 1814 to May 1815 there died in East Looe eleven persons, the youngest of whom was eighty-three years of age; and that Mrs. Bray, one of them, was 100 *. I remember a man called Cowling, who died at East Looe many years since, who was said to be of the age of 110. I think Mr. Gilbert's account is not quite correct,

---

* A few months before this old woman died, she almost made the writer's hair stand on end with astonishment. He had been told, a twelvemonth before, that she was dead; but on turning a corner in a lane he and the old woman almost came in contact. She had been taking a walk in the country.

though certainly a great many very old persons died at East Looe about the time he mentions.

HOUSES, STREETS, FORTIFICATIONS, &C.

The houses at East Looe are almost all built on sand, as mentioned by Carew, the town in fact being built on the antient bed of the river. The ground-plot being confined, the streets are rather narrow, and more numerous than occasion requires. Most of the houses have two doors, one leading into one street, and the other into another; and some of them have three doors, leading into as many different streets. Most of the old houses were built with a cellar under; and the dwelling part above reached by a flight of stone steps from the street, the landing-place covered over by a continuance of the roof, and which covering and upper landing-place is called an Orley, perhaps a corruption of O'erlop. Most of the antient ground-floors are three or four feet below the street. Whether this happened by the streets being raised, or that the houses were originally so sunk in the sand, I cannot ascertain. The houses are mostly built with stone, and covered with slates, though the fronts of most of the best of the old houses are, or were within a few years past, of stout and very heavy oak timber, with large bow-windows; the exposed part of the timber carved into a variety of figures, and the plastering adorned likewise with griffins, mermaids, &c. &c. Some of these houses have dates in their fronts; the writer's own dwelling-house has 1632.

The names of the streets in East Looe are, Fore Street, Castle Street, Higher Market Street, Middle Market Street, Lower Market Street, Chapel Street, Lower Chapel Street, Middle-gate Street, Lower Street, formerly King Street; and there are other streets and alleys, intersecting those named.

FORTIFICATIONS.

Though there is no tradition of there ever having been a Castle at Looe, yet there is a street called Castle Street, which leads to a place called Tower Hill, where the roads from Plymouth and Liskeard unite, or cross each other, and form the two Eastern entrances into the town — one road descending into the Eastern part of the town, and the other, through Castle Street, to the Western part. At this cross of the roads the buildings commence, and descend as the roads descend. The place where the said two roads cross may be about thirty or forty feet above the ground-plot of the town; and were there no houses below this spot, it would, I conceive, assume the appearance of a perpendicular rock or cliff, just above the centre of the town. And I think it by no means improbable that Tower Hill formerly jutted out further into the town, and a tower or small castle then stood on it. At a short distance from

Tower Hill, on the Liskeard road, is a place called Barbican Rocks, and near it a place called Cold Harbour *, and, a little further on, a village called Barbican †, and near Barbican Rocks some fields called the Warrens (possibly a corruption of War Rings) — names which have some reference to fortified places. About half a quarter of a mile from Tower Hill, on the Plymouth road, there is (or rather lately was) a battery of four guns; but as Castle Street has been so called for a great number of years, as appears by entries in the Corporation Books, and other documents, and as there is a tradition of this four-gun battery having been made by Mr. Eager, when Mayor of Looe, and as this battery was, as I have been told, formerly called Eager's Battery, and is, comparatively, a modern work, Tower Hill and Castle Street did not take their names in consequence of leading to this battery, but from some other cause which time has buried in oblivion.

The ground-plot on which East Looe stands was, in all probability, first formed by the sea throwing up a bank of sand and shingle at the mouth of the

---

* Cold Harbour is a name which frequently occurs in the line of Roman roads. It may possibly be derived from the Celtic or Old British Coll and Harbour, the Head of the Entrenchment. Har-bourhs Field signifies the Area of a Military Station.

† Barbacan, or Barbican, properly denotes an outer defence or fortification to a city or castle; used especially as a fence to the gates or walls.

river, and this bank afterwards secured by friths and walls. The first houses, no doubt, were built on the banks of the river, or side of the valley; and by degrees the river being, by the shingle and sand, thrust Westward, a ground-plot sufficiently firm for houses to be built on was formed. The quays were built up and down as the river ran; and at the mouth of the valley, towards the sea, a wall appears to have been built from the foot of East Looe Hill, across the valley, to the river, and perhaps adjoined to the quay; but the quay extended farther out towards the sea, and ends in a jutty called Looe Quay Head. Some parts of this wall across the valley I remember in existence; it ran about thirty feet without the Eastern end of the chapel. In this wall were three openings or gateways towards the sea. Houses running parallel to this wall, and annexed to it, were afterwards built; but the gateways remained, which led to the place called Churchend. These openings still retain the names of Higher Gate, Middle Gate, and Lower Gate. There is also another gateway, called Dung Gate, which is about a hundred feet within the others, and leads from the quay to Churchend. The shingle being thrown by the sea against this wall formed another bank outside it, which goes by the name of Churchend; and then another wall was built outside this bank; and outside this last-mentioned wall, at the lower end of Churchend, outside the Linney or Shed called The Walk, was a square spot, inclosed with a wall (within memory of old people), where four guns were planted for defence of the town; and there was a larger gun, which went by the name of The Thundering Mug, placed on a platform formed in the rock near the pound at the higher end of Churchend.

In the year 1744 Churchend Wall (the outer one) was, in a violent gale of wind (the same time the Victory man of war was lost), washed down by the sea, and soon after the present wall was built, at the expence, I believe, of the then Members of Parliament for East Looe. This wall was built with ten embrazures in it; and Government, on the 9th of July 1747, supplied this place with ten long six pounders cannon, and four more for the battery on the hill. On August 8, 1778, fourteen new six-pounders were sent, and the old ones returned. In the year 1803 four eighteen pounders were sent down, with an ample supply of ammunition; and all the old guns were directly after sent to Plymouth.

VOLUNTEER CORPS.

In the year 1803, a Volunteer Company, under the title of the East and West Looe Volunteer Artillery, was established and kept in pay from Government for six years. They learned the exercise of the great guns, and also of small arms; seventy stand of small arms, and every requisite for their use being supplied by Government. The Company on an average consisted of from sixty to seventy men, and were commanded by a Captain and two Lieutenants of their own choosing. The dress was a dark blue coat and pantaloons, with red facings, and yellow wings and tassels, and a white waistcoat. Not a single man of the company died during the six years, which is certainly very remarkable. The men, except seven or eight of them from the neighbouring parishes, belonged to East and West Looe, as did also the officers. A list of the Volunteer Corps of Cornwall will be given in the Appendix.

There is a place at East Looe called Pennyless Bench. It took its name, I apprehend, from a bench being placed there adjoining to a public-house, the owner of which, as a taunt to those who sat on the bench, gave it this name, in order to induce them to spend their money in his house.

MAY-POLE.

In the centre of the town is an open place called the May. Till within a few years past, in the centre of this spot was a sort of a raised platform, about three feet high and twelve or fourteen wide, covered over with flat stones, on which the market-people used to expose their wares for sale. Most likely this spot used to have the May-pole erected on it, from whence the name. "The leisure days after seed time were chosen by our Saxon Ancestors for Folkmotes or Conventions of the People. Nor till after the Norman Conquest was the Pagan Festival of Whitsuntide fully melted into the Christian Holiday of Pentecost; its original name is Wittentide, the time of chusing the Wits or Wisemen to the Wittenegemotte. It was consecrated to Hertha, the Goddess of Peace and Fertility, and that no quarrel might be maintained, no blood shed during the truce of the Goddess, each village, in the absence of the Baron at the Assembly of the Nation, enjoyed a kind of saturnalia. The vassals met upon the Common Green around the May-pole, when they elected a Village Lord or King, as he was called, who chose his Queen: he wore an oaken, and she an hawthorn wreath, and together they gave laws to the rustic sports during these sweet days of freedom. The May-pole then is the English Tree of Liberty.*

No May-pole has been erected at East Looe within time of memory I believe. I remember one at West Looe many years since, which had been taken from Morval woods without consent of the owner, and that the depredators had been threatened with imprisonment for so doing.

On May-day (the first of May) the boys of East and West Looe dress their hats with flowers and hawthorn, and furnish themselves with bullocks' horns in which sticks of about two feet long are

---

* Cornish Gazette, May 21, 1806.

fixed, and with these instruments filled with water they parade the streets all day, and dip all persons who pass them if they have not what is called May in their hats, that is, a sprig of hawthorn.

FREEMEN.—FOREIGNERS.

From a document in the Augmentation Office, bearing date between 1512 and 1524, it appears that Henry Calys was then Dñs Burgi de Loe (Query, whether this means Mayor or Lord of the Manor). The return of Aliens in the Record is, one barber, eighteen fishermen, one shearman, and two taylors. Perhaps the aliens were people not admitted to the freedom of the place—for in old presentments made by the Jury at the Court-Leet, I have found several instances where the Jury present several persons, whom they called foreigners, for living and carrying on trade in the town not being free so to do—or in other words, not being freemen of the said borough.

ANTIENT SUIT.

" In the 27th year of the Reign of Queen Elizabeth, there was a suit commenced in the Exchequer Chamber by the Portreeve and Burgesses of the Borowe of Lowe al's East-loowe, against one Frauncis Courtney, Esquiere, and one Walter Vahan." As the Bill and Answer are curious, and afford some information respecting the place, I shall give the following abridgment thereof:

"To the Right Honble Sir Wm. Cecill, Kn^t. Lord Burleigh, Lord High Treasurer of England, Sir Walter Mildmay, Kn^t. Chauncellor of Thexchequer, Sir Roger Manwood, Kn^t. Ld Chief Baron, and the rest of the Barons.

"Cornub. In most humble wise complayninge, sheweth unto your honors your poore and dayly Orators the Portreeve and Burgesses of the Borowe of Loowe al's East Loowe, in the Countie of Cornwall.

"That where the said Borowe ys, and tyme out of mynde hath bin an auntient Borowe, and charged to find Burgesses to the P'liment scytuat fast to the sea bancke, open to all forein hostilitie, subject ev'y daye to the violent inrode and force of the meane sea, which in fewe tydes wold eate out and spoyle the whole towne, were yt not for the continual chardge which the inhabitants of the same bestow and imploy in frith pyles, stakes, and in like defences, to withstand the chissel and preble cast in by the force and rage of the sea; and so in effect the said towne is and hath byn preserved and kept by continual labor and charge of the poor inhabitants of the same towne, being for the most parte poor maryners, fyshers, and seamen, for within the same towne there are twentye fyshinge-boates, twenty cock-boates, and nine serviceable shippes and barkes, which, according to their several qualityes, be furnished with men of the said towne, and ymployed continuallie, to the greate benefitt and help of the towne and countrie. And furder may yt please your honors, that your said Orators and their predecessors are, and tyme out of mynd have been, lawfullie and quietly seised of a weekly market, holden upon the Saturday, within the said towne, and of other franchises, as yt shall appear to this honorable Court by matter of record, and of certain burgag* and houses builded by your said Orators and their predecessors upon certain void grounds within the said towne, belonginge to your said Orators and their predecessors; the profitt of all which hath byn, from tyme to tyme, and yet is, used and bestowed towards the defence of the said towne, as aforesaid. But now so yt ys, yf yt may please your honors, that one Frauncis Courtney, Esquier, and one Walter Vahan, upon untrue surmyse and informac'on to your honors, and procured to themselffs and to one John Gylpyn, Gentleman, by her Maj^{ts} l'res pattents under the seale of Thescheker, bearing date the last day of October, in the sixe and twentieth yere of the Quenes Majesties reigne, a lease of the said markett and of a faire within the said towne, and of all courts and other fraunchises belonginge to the said towne, for one and twentie yeres, yeldinge xjs. 1d. ob.; and likewise the said burgage, yeldinge a verye small rent: by coler whereof the said Fraunceis Courtney and his confederates have and do offer weekely disturbance in most outragious manner to the inhabitants of the said towne, &c. and the Quenes Majesties subjects that do use to come to the said markett for their necessary relief, so that they do refuse to come to the said markett, and are forced to go to other marketts, seven or eight miles distant from their dwellinge places, for their necessarys. By reason of which disturbance ther is like to growe and arise great tumult and brawles, and had byn before this time yf the same had not byn stayed by the great labor, travell, and p'swasion of your said Orators. May it therefore pleas your Honors, &c. to grant subpœna, and that the s^d letters patent be repealed, &c. &c. &c."

"The Aunswere of Franceis Courtenay, Defendant, to the Bill of Complaynt of the Inhabitants of Eastlowe, within the County of Cornwhall, Complaynant.

"The sayed Defend^t, by p'testac'on, &c. &c. &c. sayeth, that the sayed towne or village of Eastlowe, in the sayed Bill of Complaynt menc'oned, as ye sayed Defendant doth verilye thincke and beleve, and which he hopeth hereafter to prove very plainly, is not, nor ever was, any auntiente Boroughe Towne; nor is or ev^r was at any tyme to be charged lawfullye to fynd any Burges or Burgesses to any Parlem^t to be holden, as he thinketh. But he confesseth yt to be true y^t of late he hath harde, rather by usurpac'on than of any lawful right or authority, as he thinketh, Burgesses have bynn sent to divers Parlim^{ts} for the sayed towne; and he is induced so to think for that he never coulde learne, knowe, or ever did see any letters patents concerninge ye incorporac'on of ye sayed towne or village, or y^t is or ev^r was incorporated, either by the Quenes Matie or any of her predecessors Kings or Quenes of Englande. But he confesseth that ye sayed towne is situated faste by the sea shore or banke. But doth utt'lye denye, to his judgment, y^t it is subject to all forein hostility or violent inrode or force of the mayne sea, or y^t yt ys likely to be eaten out or spoyled with the sea, except yt were defended wth pyles and stakes, in such manner as in the sayed Bill of Complaynt is most untruly alledged, declared, and set forth. And the chyfest reason and cause wch moveth him so to denye it is, for y^t the haven there or creeke is a barred haven or creeke, defended with mighty huge and vaste heaps of saynde and other rubbyshe y^t ye sea doth cast up there, wch is a wonderful defence for the sayde towne, for that at a lowe water no shippe or other vessell of any great burthen can come neare the sayde towne. And the sayed sand and other rubbyshe, wch ye sea doth so cast up there, doth breake the cheifest force of the waves of the sea a great way from the sayed towne, so that they neede not to bestowe any such great paynes, labor, or coste in fryth pyles or stakes for defence of the chissell or preble cast in by the force of the sea, as in the sayed Bill is most untruelye alledged. And the sayed Defend[t] sayeth, that, by coller of the makyne of the sayed fryth pyles and stakes, they do cut, fell, and carye away much and great stores of the Quenes woods there growinge, wch they do employ about other occasions, and verye seldome to such purposes as in the sayed Bill is alledged; and this he hath heard by very good and crédible reporte. And further sayeth, that the sayed towne is inhabited by men who, allthoughe some of them use fishinge and are mariners, yeat ye most p'te of the inhabitants are marchants, weavers, shoemakers, taylors, smithes, and of other occupac'ons, and y[t] greate part of them not poore but grown to greate and mightye wealth; and that there are divers fishinge-boats, cocke-boats, barges, and shippes, belonging to the sayed village, as the sayd Complaynants do alledge and set downe, the number of them this Defend[t] knoweth not. And the s[d] Defend[t] doth verylye think and beleve y[t] lesser coustome or p'fit her Ma[tie] hath not so manie barkes and shippes thorow all her dominions, for y[t] y[e] sayed Complaynants, or the moste part of them, as this Defendant thinketh, do carrye thence into forren p'tes beyond the seas all sorts of p'hibited wares and merchandice, as corne, tallow, lether shooes and hindes, bell metal, scroff, and such other p'hibited wares, wch they commonlye and very secretlye conveye over, the Custom Searcher and Controler either winking at it or else compounded wth all, or else beinge p'ty owners of the sayed murchandice, &c. as this Defend^t doth verylye beleeve and thinketh, whereby they or the most of the sayed Complaynants are grown into such greate and excessive wealth, by defraudinge of the Queens Matie and the undoinge of y^t p'te of the sayed Country of Cornwhall, by conveying secretlye away, as aforesayed, such victualles and other necessaries wherewith their poor neighbers and countrymen should lyve withall; a matter lamentable and to be regarded, and wch the poor people thereabout do much lament and bewayle daylye, &c. &c. &c."

To this Answer there was a Replication, and to the Replication a Rejoinder; but whether the cause came to hearing I am not informed.

SITUATION OF EAST LOOE.

The hill at the foot of which East Looe lies, is perhaps about two hundred feet in height, and falls back in a slope, and is occupied with gardens and orchards, which are formed like those on the mountains of Palestine, by different platforms raised one above the other, and supported by stone walls. These orchards and gardens have a fine effect in Spring and Summer, particularly just as the apple-blossom expands itself.

RIVER.

The river comes in and goes out in spring-tides with prodigious rapidity. Vessels of between two and three hundred tons burthen can come to the quays of either East or West Looe. The river which branches off into two arms about a quarter of a mile from Looe Bridge, is navigable with boats and flat-bottomed barges of about twenty tons burthen, as far as Sandplace on one branch, about two miles up, and about the same distance on the other branch. Sandplace is so called from the sand dredged up by these barges for manure being usually carried there. The barges are in fine weather constantly dredging up this manure at a short distance from Looe Beach. The sand, however, is not of a fine quality, as it contains but few fragments of shells, and chiefly consists of schist and quartz.

DULO.

Borlase, in his Natural History of Cornwall, says, " One mile below Sandplace the Looe is joined by another Stream from the West called Dulo, that is the Black Loo or Water. The district through which it mostly runs is called Dulo or Duloo parish, as it is reasonable to conjecture from some apparent darkness in colour, sufficient to distinguish it from the adjoining stream of East Loo, whose whole course is at a medium not two miles distant. This water rises in the Parish of St. Pinnock, and coasting nearly South, becomes navigable at Trelawn Wear, about two miles from the Sea, a mile after it joins the East Looe, and they both pass the Stone Bridge before-mentioned into Loo Creek, its whole course being about seven miles."

Hals says, the modern name of Dulo is taken from the Church, and is compounded of Du-Lo, Du-Loe, or Loo, i. e. God's Lake, or River of Water, either referring to the Looe river, on which it is situate, the original fountain whereof, *viz.* in Loue Douns in Liskeard, was undoubtedly consecrated by our ancestors the Britons, as well as other rivers, or so called from God's Lake, *viz.* the Font Waters of the Church, or Baptism and Regeneration, freely dispensed with to all comers, after a spiritual manner.

In the Domesday Roll the 20th of William I. 1087, this parish was rated under the jurisdiction of Treworgye. At the time of the Inquisition of the Bishops of Lincoln and Winchester, 1294, into the value of Cornish Benefices, Ecclesia de Dulo in Decanatu de Westwellshire was taxed £7. 6s. 8d. Vicar ejusdem £1. 10s. In Wolsey's Inquisition it was rated £22. The Vicarage £8. 11s. The Patronage in Seyntaubyn and Arundell alternately. The Parish rated to the 4s. *per lib.* Tax the 3d of William III. 1696, £246. 4s.

About the last century a Mr. Finsher was incumbent of this parish, and expecting to purchase the patronage of the same, had built a pretty good house on the glebe; but Sir John St. Aubyn and Mr. Arundell sold the same to Baliol College in Oxford, in the year 1701; which circumstance as Hals says, so dismayed Mr. Fincher, that he forthwith grew melancholy, and the grief thereof so depressed his spirits, that he broke his heart, and departed this life the 26th of November, 1703, at night, and so went to Heaven in that great tempest and hurricane that then happened, with many others. The Vicar has now all the tythes, paying £.40 yearly to the Master or one of the Fellows of Baliol College.

In Usher de Brit. Eccl. Primord. p. 560, it appears that the Church of St. Theliaus in Wales is called Lhau Deilo Vaur, the Church of Great Theliaus. And the change of Deilo to Dulo is so easy, says a recent writer, that St. Theliaus seems to have the best title to this Parish, as the patron and owner of it. In confirmation of this conjecture, says the same writer, we find on the Barten of Tresidern in St. Burien, a Chapel dedicated to St. Dillo, who is undisputably the Theliaus.

DERIVATION, AND ANTIENT NAMES.

Never having observed or heard of any apparent darkness in the colour of the water of the West

DERIVATION, AND ANTIENT NAMES. 49

river, as Borlase conjectures, and not being satisfied with the other derivations of the name Dulo; and as the Cornish words Deu and Deau signified Two, I think the Parish took its name from the circumstance of its being a tongue of land lying between two rivers or waters, Du two, Lo water. Carew conjectures these Boroughs to have taken their names from the river which rises in St. Cleer parish, and is called Lo or Loe River*, and that the river might have taken its name from running so low under the hills. Lo is the Cornish name for a Pool, and if I may hazard a conjecture, the expanse of water between and above these Boroughs, might have given them their names, or at least one of them its name, and the other from its relative situation to the first town. Tradition says, that East Looe was formerly called St. Mary's in the Marsh, and that the Chapel was dedicated to St. Mary. It also says that the first town was at a place called Shutta or Shoota, about a quarter of a mile up the river, but I know of no authority for this supposition; there certainly, however, was a small town at Shutta antiently, as will appear hereafter from the Charter of Otho de Bodrigan.

---

* Also Loow and Loowe, Leland, vol. VII. p. 113; and Low, p. 14; and vol. III. p. 26. Wallicè, Lhûch; Cornu. Brit. Lich; Ir. Lough; Scot. Lock. Anglicè, Lake, Pond, or Pool.

E

WEST LOOE.

West Looe (though generally now so called) also goes by the name of Portbyhan, sometimes spelt Portbyham, and in the Writs to the Sheriff for the Election of Members of Parliament Portpigham *. On the Corporation Seal it is called Portuan †. The impression of the Seal is a man holding a bow in his right hand, and an arrow in the left, with the legend Por * tu * an, * other * wys * called * Westlo.

Browne Willis ‡ says, " The first Record I have seen of West Looe or Portpigham is the following: Ann. 22 Hen. III. Hugh de Treverbin Plaintiff, and Odo Treverbin and his wife Defendants, levied a fine of the manor of Portloe." Portpigham and

---

* A corruption, probably, of Port Bighan or Bican; Cornish, Little Port.

† Port Vean; Cornish, Little Port.   ‡ Page 90.

Portloe are, however, two distinct manors, but adjoin each other. 'Tis likely, however, that both manors belonged to the Treverbyn family.

The following document, which I have lately met with, throws more light on the History of West Looe than any other I have ever seen. It is either a copy or translation from the original; I rather think the latter. It has no date, but its antiquity may in some degree be ascertained by the facts, that the family of Treverbyn the grantor, and of Killigath one of the witnesses (or at least their names), were extinct in the reign of Henry VI.

"To all X^{can} people by whom this writinge shall be seen or heard, Hugh of Treverbyn * sendeth

---

* Treverbyn, of Treverbyn, in St. Austell; name extinct in the reign of Henry VI. The coheiresses married Courtenay and Trevanion. The arms of Treverbyn, as quartered by Prideaux, who married an heiress of this family at an early period, are, Per pale, Argent and Gules, three castles counterchanged.

"The manor of Treverbin, in St. Austell, belonged to an antient family of that name [Walter Treverbyn was Sheriff in 1223]. This family became extinct in the reign of Henry VI. when the estate was divided into moieties, having passed by coheiresses to the families of Courtenay and Trevanion, of Carhayes. Treverbyn Courtenay having been forfeited to the Crown by the attainder of the Marquis of Exeter, was, with other manors, annexed by Henry VIII. in 1540 to the Duchy of Cornwall, in lieu of the honor of Wullingford. The manor of Portpigham, no doubt, came to the Courtenay family in the same manner, and was forfeited also, and annexed to the Duchy." *Lysons, Mag. Brit.*

greetin [or ' health' as is inserted in the margin]. Knowe yee that I for me and my heirs doe quit claime unto all my Burgesses of the Borough of Portbyghan and their heires, the sum of sixpence, wch s^{d} sixpence, Odo, my father, did use to receive of the severall . . . . . . w'hin the s^{d} Boroughe, p'served for me and my heires wth ye forfeitures and amercem^{ts}, wch other ye free burgesses for Cornwall doe make of o^{r} assise of sellinge beere, and so that I the said Hugh and my Heires the s^{d} sixpence of ye s^{d} Burgesses in the s^{d} Boroughe of Portbyhan, or of their heires, for the future may not have.

" And I the said Hugh and my heires doe grant unto the Burgesses of the Borough of Portbyghan and their Heirs, all the libertyes and antient customs wch other the free Burgesses in Cornwall have, *viz.* Helstone and Lanceston. And that this may remain sure, I have hereunto put my seale. These witnesses, Jo. de Killigath, Ango de Tregenor, David de Kilminiat, Nichol de Tallan, &c. &c."

Within a few months past (written May 1822) a document has been found in the Tower of London, which is supposed by some Antiquaries to relate to the Borough of West Looe; but I cannot help doubting whether it may not relate to the antient Borough of Portruan, or Polruan (near Fowey), for the name in the document seems to me more like Portruan than Portbican, being there written Porbuan. And, besides, Richard Earl of Cornwall kept his Court at Restormell Castle, which stands at the head of the river which descends to Polruan, which is at the mouth of it. And as this river is navigable from Polruan to near Restormel Castle, it is by no means unlikely but that the Earl frequently made excursions down this beautiful river, and occasionally landed at Polruan from the heights near which some of the most extensive sea prospects could be seen; and he might have bestowed on the owner of the place his royal enfranchisement in consequence. Now Richard Earl of Cornwall and King of the Romans, who was brother to King Henry III. died in the year 1272; and I find that Polruan had also the name of Portruan [Roman Pool, Roman Port, having probably been a Roman station]; and that, as early as the year 1291, and till the year 1420, it belonged to the Daubeny family, commonly called Dauney or Danney; and that John Dauney actually married one of the coheiresses of Odo de Treverbyn. I also find that the manor of Lantegles by Fowey adjoins Polruan, and in the reign of Henry III. belonged to Ralph de Sulloia. And I observe that Ralph de Sulling was one of the witnesses, and Robert Fitzwilliams and Walter Fitzwilliams (who lived at Hull, close to Polruan) were two others of the witnesses, who attested Richard Earl of Cornwall's grant to Odo de Treverbyn. The manor of Polruan was formerly held with the manor of Faweton; which manor of Faweton, in the reign of Henry III. belonged to

Andrew de Suleny (this family seems to have written their names De Sulling, De Sulloia, De Suleny, De Solenny); on whose death without issue it devolved to his uncle Jeffery, and he dying without issue it was inherited by his sisters in moieties; and afterwards one moiety passed by marriage to the Treverbyns.

The translation of this document is as follows:

"Amongst the Records of the Court of Chancery, preserved in the Tower of London, to wit, in the Roll of Letters Patent of the 18th year of the reign of King Edward the Second after the Conquest of England, part 1, membrane 22, is thus contained:

"For Roger Prideaux and Elizabeth his wife, and others. &c. The King, to whom, greeting. We have inspected the Charter which Richard heretofore Earl of Poictou and Cornwall made to Odo de Treverbyn, in these words:— To all to whom this present writing shall come, Richard Earl of Poictou and Cornwall greeting, Know ye, that I have granted, and by this my Charter have confirmed, for me and my heirs, to Sir Odo de Treverbyn and his heirs, that his Borough of Porbuan shall be a free Borough, and that the Burgesses of the same Borough shall be free and quit of all customs, and they may buy and sell all merchandizes in markets and fairs, and in all places throughout the whole County of Cornwall. Also I. have granted to the same Odo and his heirs, that if any one shall reside for a year and a day in the same Borough without just claim, he shall, according to the law of other free Burgesses, be quit of all neifty and slavery. Also I have granted to the said Odo and his heirs, for me and my heirs, that they shall have in the same Borough a market on Wednesday in every week, and a fair once in the year, to continue for three days, to wit, on the eve, on the day, and on the morrow of Saint Michael; so that the aforesaid Odo and his heirs shall receive and have all issues and all advantages pertaining to the said fair; saving every where all pleas which pertain to the Crown of the Lord the King. Wherefore we will that the same Odo and his heirs shall entirely and peaceably hold the aforesaid liberties for ever. And that their Grant shall be preserved, ratified, and unshaken, I have testified this present writing by the affixing of my seal, these being witnesses: Hugh de Saint Philiberto, Ralph de Sulling, Robert Fitzwilliam, Walter Fitzwilliam, and Richard de Kilvard, Auger de Tregorioz, and many others. — Now we, the Grants and Confirmation aforesaid ratifying and confirming the same, for us and our heirs, as much as in us lieth, do grant and confirm to Roger Prideaux and Elizabeth his wife, the cousin and one of the heirs of the aforesaid Odo, and to John Danny and Sibilla his wife, the cousin and other heir of the same Odo, and to the heirs of the same Elizabeth and Sibilla, as the Charter aforesaid reasonably testifieth, and as the same Roger, Elizabeth, John, and Sibilla, and the ancestors of the same Elizabeth and Sibilla, the liberties aforesaid, from the time of the Grants and Confirmation aforesaid, have hitherto reasonably used and enjoyed. In witness whereof, &c. Witness the King, at Porchester, the 22^d day of September," For a fine of four marks.

DUCHY OF CORNWALL.

Henry VIII. in the 32d year of his reign, severed the honor and castle of Wallingford, in Oxfordshire, from the Duchy of Cornwall, being moved thereunto, for that the said castle and honor was near adjoining the manor of Newelme, which was by said Act of Parliament made an honour, and, therefore, for the commodious situation and vicinity thereof, the said King did sever the same from the said Duchy, and made it parcel of the said manor of Newelme, whereof he was then seised in right of his Crown*; and in lieu thereof, there was given and annexed to the said Dukedom the manors of

---

* Carew says, that, not long after, the same King passed away this castle unto Christ's College in Oxford, who use it as a place of retreat when the University is visited with any contagious sickness.

Westanton, Portlow, Northhill, Portpigham, Lawdren, Treloweia, Treganse, Trelogan, Crofthole, Trewitherne, Courtney, Landulph, Leighdurant, and Tinton, in the County of Cornwall; and all other the lands in the said places which came to the King by the attainder of treason of Henry Courtney, Marquiss of Exeter *. Also the manors of Austell, Fentregan, Tremaynalls, Tremagwon, Fowey, Credyowe, and Portnaprior, in the said County of Cornwall, which came to the said King's hands by the dissolution of the Priory of Trawardreth in the said County of Cornwall. Also all the manors of Bradford, Curveden, Clymesland, Pryor, Treworgye, Stratton, Eastway, Bowyton, Bradrissey, Bucklawrne †, and Benyalvey, which came to the said King's hands by the surrender and suppression of the Priory of Launceston. All which manors so newly granted unto the said Duchy, were by the said act so annexed thereto, as were the said castle and honor of Wallingford and the members and parcels of the same, before the making of the said act, any act, law, usage, or custom to the contrary notwithstanding ‡.

Sir John Dodridge's Account of the Antient and Modern State of the Duchy of Cornwall.

---

* Carew says, these lands were afterwards, by Queen Mary, restored in tayle to his son the Earl of Devon, and, upon his issueless decease, received them again.

† A place near Looe.

‡ The manor of Wallingford was granted by Richard the First

From this source springs the Modern Duchy of Cornwall, as it is called. The tenants of these manors hold their estates on lives. The tenants of the Antient Duchy have a descendible freehold interest in their tenements, though the tenure is, strictly speaking, copyhold. The Antient Duchy descends to the customary heir-at-law.

---

to his brother John, whose second son, Richard, King of the Romans, Earl of Cornwall, repaired the castle, and celebrated his wedding in it with considerable splendour, his guests consisting of Henry the Third, his Queen, and many of the Nobility. On the death of Richard it devolved to his son Edmund, together with the advowsons of all the churches. When he died his estates became the property of King Edward, whom he had chosen for his heir. Edward II. bestowed it, together with his Duchy of Cornwall, to which it had been annexed, on Piers Gaveston, and afterwards on Hugh de Spencer the elder, his unfortunate favourites, both of whom were beheaded. Edward next presented it to his Queen, Isabella, from whom it descended to Edward III. who gave it, with other manors, for the support of the Dukedom of Cornwall, a title first conferred on his son, Edward the Black Prince, in the year 1355. It remained vested in the Royal Family till the reign of Henry VIII. when that Monarch granted it to Wolsey, for the use of the magnificent College of Christ Church, Oxford, which the Cardinal had founded. On Wolsey's disgrace the castle appears to have been separated from the manor, the latter being annexed to Ewelm, or New Elm, in Oxfordshire, and afterwards given by James I. to Prince Charles; the former remaining in possession of the College.

WEST LOCK.

SITUATION.—GUILDHALL.

West Looe consists but of one street, and a few scattered houses (very picturesquely situated) on the quays and sides of the hills of the ascending valley in which the principal part of the town lies; and has nothing remarkable to notice, except its Guildhall*, which tradition says, was formerly a Chapel

---

* Adjoining the stairs of this hall are still to be seen the remains of a cage for scolding women; but, to the credit of the sex, it has not been used of late years. East Looe had a similar cage within a few years since. The only instance within memory of its ever being used is the following: Hannah Whit and Bessy Niles, two women of fluent tongues, having exerted their oratory on each other, at last thought it prudent to leave the matter in dispute to be decided by the Mayor. Away then they posted to his Worship. The first who arrived had scarce begun her tale when the other bounced in in full rage, and began hers likewise, and abuse recommenced with redoubled vigour. His Worship (Mr. John Chubb) ordered the constables to be called, and each of the combatants thought her antagonist was to be punished, and the event proved each thought right. When the constable arrived, his Worship pronounced the following command to him: "Take these two women to the cage, and there keep them till they have settled their dispute." They were immediately conveyed thither, and, after a few hours confinement, became as quiet and inoffensive beings as ever breathed; and were then liberated to beg Mr. Mayor's pardon.

Cages for scolding women are not, I believe, very common. Indeed I never saw or heard of any but in these towns; nor do I

of Ease or place of Worship, dedicated to St. Nicholas, the patron of mariners or fishermen. It has a turret with a bell and clock in it, but instead of apertures being left for the sound to come forth, they are blocked up with glass windows, so that the clock is of very little service. Round the railings of the bench for the Mayor and Burgesses to sit on is this inscription:

"Erected in the Mayoralty of Colonel JOHN TRELAWNY, 1679."

This inscription must refer to the bench. The fabric has the appearance of considerable antiquity.

TALLAND.— LEMAIN.

West Looe is situated in the parish of Talland, within which parish is a hamlet called Lemain, and part of West Looe lies in this hamlet. On the barton of Portlooe in the parish of Talland, just opposite Looe Island, was a cell of Benedictine Monks, called Lammana, subject to the Abbey of Glastonberry, to which the site appears to have been given by the ancestors of Hastulus de Solenny; there are

---

recollect of ever reading of this mode of punishment. The Tribucket, or Ducking-stool, seems to have been the general chastisement formerly; and each of these towns had one of these instruments also. Since writing this, I find the ladies of Penzance were formerly privileged with the like comparatively-elegant mode of punishment, a cage.

some remains of the Chapel still in existence *. In Hearne's Appendix to Adam de Demerham, is a grant of Hastulus de Solenny, confirming the Island of St. Michael de Lammana (most probably that of St. George opposite Looe) to the Monks of Glastonbury; a grant of Roger Fitzwilliam quitting claim to the lands of Lammana, which he held for life under the Church of Glastonbury (reserving the house which Mabil his sister occupied), and one of Richard Earl of Cornwall, granting the Monks a licence to farm out the Church, and the Island of Lammana. It appears that Abbot Michael, about the middle of the thirteenth century, leased it to the Sacristary of the Convent. The Free Chapel of La Mayne in Cornwall, was granted to Edward Bostock, 5th Jac.—*Lysons's Mag. Brit.*

MIDMAIN ROCK.—PORTNADLER BAY.

Between the main land and Looe Island stands a rock, higher than the surrounding ones, which is

---

* I measured this Chapel on the 13th of April 1815, and found it, within the walls, about forty-seven feet long by twenty-four wide. About three or four hundred yards to the Eastward of the Chapel are the remains of some antient building, perhaps that in which the Monks dwelt. The remains of the Eastern end wall thereof, at present eight or ten feet high, have two very narrow windows, or openings, still in being. The situation of this chapel and house is very pleasant; they lie in a sort of natural amphitheatre, sheltered from the North winds by high land.

called Midmain or Magmain. Small vessels frequently pass between the island and the main land when the tide is in. An imaginary line drawn from Looe Island Westward, to a high rock called Horestone or Orestone * about a mile distant, would form the outer boundary of a piece of water called Portnadler Bay; from whence the name is derived I know not.

---

* Query, from whence is the word Hore or Ore derived, and what is its signification? There are many places along shore and elsewhere which have this adjunct. There is a place near Plymouth called Orestone. St. Michael's Mount was formerly called the Hore Rock in the Wood; and the circle of stones in St. Cleer's parish is called the Hurlers. Borlase says, Harz signifies a bound, limit, or hindrance, derived from the Armoric; as Men-hars, a Boundstone. Hamper, in his recent " Observations on certain antient Pillars of Memorial called Hoar-stones," says, the Greek Horos, the Latin Ora, the Celtic and Welsh Or and Oir, the Armoric Harz, the Anglo-Saxon Or, Ord, and Ora, the obsolete British Yoror, and the obsolete Irish Ur and Or, have all, to a certain degree, one and the self-same meaning, viz. a Bound or Limit; and the Hoar-stone is, consequently, nothing more than the Land-mark, or Stone of Memorial, describing the boundary of property, whether of a public or private nature, as it has been used in almost all countries, from the patriarchal era to the days of the present generation. " The conic, pyramidal, and cylindric stones, perpendicularly raised, which are to be seen in the British Islands, were, in Pagan times, generally to ascertain the boundaries of districts." This is the remark of Mr. Astle, in the "Archæologia," vol. XIII. p. 211; and in like manner Borlase observes, in his " History of Cornwall," p. 167, that " Stones were erected by the antients as boundaries, either national or patrimonial. Laban and Jacob's monument was partly of the

CORPORATION.

Queen Elizabeth incorporated West Looe 14th February 1574, in the sixteeth year of her reign, by the name of Mayor and Burgesses of the Borough of Portbyhan, otherwise West Looe, in the County of Cornwall. Twelve Chief Burgesses were appointed by this charter. The Mayor is elected from the Chief Burgesses, by their votes and the votes of the Free Burgesses, on Michaelmas-day annually, between nine and twelve of the clock in the forenoon, and then sworn into office. The Mayor is also a Justice of the Peace, as is likewise the Steward. The Mayor has no power to appoint a Deputy. The Steward, however, has such an authority; but his Deputy is not a Justice of the Peace.

---

patrimonial kind: 'This heap be witness, and this pillar be witness, that I will not pass over this heap to thee, and that thou shalt not pass over this heap and this pillar unto me, for harm.' Genesis xxxi. 52. As to national boundaries, the Israelites, where no city, sea, lake, or hill, offered itself, made a stone their boundary, as in the limits of the kingdom of Judah; ' And the border went up to the Stone of Bohan, the son of Reuben.' ibid. xviii. 17. The Northern Nations had also the same way of marking out the boundaries of districts. Olaus Magnus, p. 11."

WEST LOOE DOWN.—GIANT'S HEDGE OR MOUND.

Just above the houses (the intermediate space filled up with gardens and orchards) is a common or down, called West Looe Down, of near a hundred acres, on which are the remains of a mound of earth that runs many miles across the country, and is noticed by Borlase, who, from its extent and other circumstances, supposed it to be a Roman work. His account of it is as follows: "That the Romans had ways in the Eastern parts of the county about Loo and Lostwithiel, the following antient work, shewn me by the Rev. Mr. Howell, Rector of Lanreath (June 25 and 26, 1756), will abundantly confirm. It is called The Giant's Hedge, a large mound, which reaches from the valley in which the Boroughs of East and West Looe are situated to Leryn, on the river Fowey. It is first visible on West Looe Down, about two hundred paces above the Mills; whence it runs to Kilminarth Woods; from and through them to Trelawn Wood, about three hundred paces above Trelawn Mill; then through Little Larnick to the Barton of Hall, in which there are two circular encampments, about four hundred paces to the North of it; thence quite through the said Barton, making the Northern Boundary of Fields to the Glebe of Pelynt Vicarage, called Furze Park; then cross the Barton of Tregarrick; and thence, through the North Grounds of

Tresassen and Polventon, to the Glebe Lands of the Rectory of Lanreath, where I measured it seven feet high and twenty feet wide at a medium; thence it stretches through the Tenement of Wyllacombe to Trebant Water; whence it proceeds, through the Barton of Longunnet and some small tenements, to Leryn; from which there is a fair dry Down, called St. Winnow Down, leading North along to Lostwithiel. This Risbank, or Mound, ranges up hill and down hill indifferently; has no visible ditch continued on any brow of a hill, as intrenchments always have; there is no hollow, or foss, on one side more than the other; it is about seven miles long, and tends straight from Looe to Leryn Creek, in the direct line from Looe to Lostwithiel. By all these properties, its height and breadth, in wanting the fosses of fortification, its straightness and length, the grandeur of the design, and the labour of execution, I judge that it can be nothing less than a Roman work. In this supposition I am the more confirmed, first, because several Roman coins have been found on the banks of Foway river (as see "Antiquities of Cornwall," p. 282), and, as I have been informed, also in the run of this notable work; secondly, by its tendency to the first ford over the navigable river of Fowey; for it must be observed that the Romans, thoroughly sensible of the delay and hazards of crossing friths and arms of the sea, and the danger of bridges getting into the possession of the natives, were equally averse both to bridges and passing large rivers, they had therefore in constant view the nearest and most commodious fords of rivers, and directed their roads accordingly. Now near Leryn Creek, where the work ends, there is a ford, and no where below is the river Fowey fordable; which plainly accounts for their conveying this road so high up the country, that it might at once convey their troops towards their station at Lostwithiel, and afford them a safe passage over the river Fowey into the Western parts, through Grampont and Truro."

Borlase also, in his Natural History, says, "There are the remains of a Causey between Liskeard and Looe, near Polgover, the seat of Mr. Mayow, which, as well as the Cross Road from Dulo to Hessenford, vulgar tradition makes to be Roman." This Causey I have never been able to find out.

The above-mentioned Mound is first visible directly above Looe Bridge; so that, if a line was drawn West, as the Bridge tends, it would come to it at the head of a field called Bridgend Meadow, where a small orchard is planted. There is a very visible ditch all along West Looe Down to the North of the rampart. On the Barton of Hall, however, the ditch is to the South of the rampart. This rampart on the Barton of Hall is at least fifteen feet high and about twenty feet thick at the base. About four hundred paces North of it, as Borlase says, there are two apparently (though not perfectly, as I was informed by Captain Dawson, who assisted in taking the Trigonometrical Survey, under Colonel Mudge) circular encampments, situated in a field called Berry Park. Berry Park contains about eighteen acres, and may be termed a tongue of land. It has a valley on each side, and also at the bottom. Across the isthmus, if I may so term it, of this tongue of land, runs the mound, protecting that part of the field which the valleys do not extend to. The circles (or rings, as they are now called by the tenant) consist of one entire circle of about 122 paces diameter, surrounded with a rampart, ditch, and breast-work; the height of which rampart, from the bottom of the ditch, is, I imagine, upwards of fifteen feet, and must originally have been much higher. This circle has but one gateway into it, which is guarded by mounds without ditches, running upwards of fifty feet into the circle. The part of this circle where the gateway is, is surrounded by about three fourths of another circle, whose sweep, had it been continued, would have intersected the inner circle; but the Southern part of this outermost circle, when it comes within twenty or thirty feet of the inner, falls into the segment of another circle, which runs parallel to the inner circle, leaving a platform of about fifty feet breadth between the two ditches, and surrounding about a third part of the inner circle. From the gateway of the inner to the opposite point of the outward circle, is about 144 paces, which may be about three fourths of the diameter. The outer circle has a similar rampart, ditch, and breast-work with the inner circle, and one gateway, which is not quite opposite that of the former. These circles command very fine prospects both of land and sea. Rame Head and the entrance into Plymouth are visible from Berry Park. You can see these circles from Bindown Hill with the naked eye; and from the elevation of that hill you look down on them so as to see their areas.

In a field a short distance South-west of Polynt Church-town, and about half a mile in a direct line from the said circles, are many Barrows. The field in which they are is, I believe, called The Five Barrows. At the bottom of this field is a highway, leading from Pelynt Church-town to the Fowey road. In this highway, just at the bottom of the said field, a few years since, a grave was discovered by some men mending the highway. It was formed by four stones on their edges, and a covering stone. In this kestvaen was an urn, with burnt ashes in it; and round the urn were piled, in a regular manner, the unburnt remains of human bones. I went to Pelynt purposely to see this curiosity, but found the grave had been filled up, and its contents buried. The urn was described to me by a man who saw it as having ornaments of flowers and leaves on its outside, and that it fell into sheards when touched. I could not learn that any coin or other thing was found in the urn or grave; indeed, I fancy there was a lack of curiosity in all concerned.

Part of the mound on West Looe Down has been from time to time dug down, to obtain earth for building and plastering. I have several times desired the labourers, in case of their finding any coin or other thing curious to preserve it; but have never heard of any thing being found of late years. A celt (commonly called in this neighbourhood a thunder-bolt *) was some years ago found on this Down; and it was given by the late Mr. Bawden, of Looe, to Mr. James, of St. Kevern. I have a celt, made of a hard black stone, which was found in pulling down an old house at East Looe a few years since; it is between six and seven inches long, and very perfect. I lately saw some like it in shape and stone, but not so large, in the British Museum.

I also remember seeing a celt that was found, about thirty years ago, at Kilminarth, near the run of the said mound: about which time a gold chain and several instruments of brass were found in a decayed hedge, or side of a highway, near Little Larnic, by an apprentice-girl. Her mistress described them to me as being somewhat like hatchets, and said "she believed they were things which the warriors used in antient times." I applied to the mistress, in hopes of getting a sight of them; but

---

* The common people believe these celts to be produced by thunder, and thrown down from the clouds; and that they shew what weather will ensue by changing their colour. Possibly "thunder-bolt" may be a corruption of "the under-bolt." Qu. what was their use?

her apprentice had sold them to a buyer of old brass. The hedge formed one side of the high road, not far from the said mound. The apprentice told me that the gold chain was about a foot and a half in length — that when she found it, not thinking it was gold, she tied it to the end of a stick, and made a sort of whip of it to drive home the cows. She, some time after, discovered that it was gold, and kept it by her for several years, when she gave it to her brother, who sold it to a Mr. Patrick, a jeweller at Dock, for three pounds. The brother told me that Mr. Patrick said it was Corsican gold; and he (the brother) also told me that he well remembered the brass instruments, and that some of them were like the tops of spontoons.

POLVELLAN.

On West Looe Down the late John Lemon, Esq. (M. P. for Truro, and who died April 5, 1814), about the year 1787 erected a small but extremely neat house in the cottage style, and inclosed some ground round it by virtue of a grant from the Corporation. He gave it the name of Polvellan, and laid it out with great taste. Pol, in Cornish, signifies a Pool, and Vellan a Mill; and below the house are a mill and pool, inclosed by a stone wall of about half a mile sweep, in a circular direction. I cannot describe the contrivance and use of this pool better than in the words of Mr. Carew, in his "Survey of Cornwall."—"Amongst other commodities afforded by the sea, the inhabitants make use of divers his creekes for grist mills, by thwarting a banke from side to side, in which a flood-gate is placed, with two leaves; these the flowing tide openeth, and, after full sea, the waight of the ebb closeth fast, which no other force can doe; and so the imprisoned water payeth the ransome of driving an under shoote wheel for his enlargement." I apprehend the mill and pool-wall were built by one of the Arundells of Tremodart, in Duloe parish. The wall is about six or eight feet high, and almost broad enough for a coach to pass over it, and must have cost a great deal of money. It appears, by a deed which I have seen, that the Mayor and Burgesses of West Looe, on the 30th of May, in the twelfth year of the reign of James the First (1614), granted all that parcel, quantity of ground, oze, or water, now surrounded by the said mill-pool-wall, to Thomas Arundell, of Tremodart, in the parish of Duloe, Esq. for 500 years, from thence next ensuing; that afterwards the said Thomas Arundell built a mill-house, and four grist-mills, and other houses, and also the mill-pool-wall. On November 3, 1648, the said Thomas Arundell made his will; and I believe the mills and mill-pool-wall were built by him before he made his will. Afterwards this term in these premises were assigned over by the Arundells (father and son) and one Drew (perhaps a mortgagee) to Sir Jonathan Trelawny, for the remainder of the said term. I am apprehensive, however, that there was a mill at this place previous to the aforesaid grant.

INCLOSURE OF THE DOWN DESIRABLE.

It is much to be regretted that West Looe Down is not wholly inclosed; the soil is very good, as is apparent from the fine state of the grounds of Polvellan. The Looes being bounded by the sea on one side, and by rivers and woods on the other, arable land is much wanted. The objection raised against this inclosure is, that the poor of West Looe would be deprived of gathering furze and fearn for firing. But does not the labour wasted and cloaths worn out in gathering this fuel more than counteract the gain? If an inclosure were to be made, in a year or two the hedges would produce greater quantity and more substantial fuel than can now be obtained. The Down belongs to the Corporation; but various tenants of houses and fields claim a right of putting what is called Breaths (cattle), some more, some less, to depasture on it. To such as are entitled to put breaths on this, common allotments should be made in proportion to the number of breaths they are entitled to; and an allotment to the poor might be made in lieu of their claim (if it is a legal one) to take furze and fearns for firing. The many advantages which would arise to the poor in particular from an inclosure should be considered. Exclusive of the numerous productions which would follow, labour would be demanded, hedges must be made, manure procured, land ploughed, corn tilled, cut, &c. &c. Milk, potatoes, &c. &c. would be obtained at a much more moderate price than at present; and, no doubt, the poor rate would soon find the beneficial effect of an inclosure. In short, the advantages arising herefrom would be very great; and I sincerely hope the prejudices of the interested will soon be done away, and that the commoners will get an Inclosure Act passed. Formerly the Corporation used to let out certain parts of this Down for tillage. There are several memorandums of such lets in the Town Books. In 1621 that part of West Looe Down which lieth on the West part of the Homer Well, was let to rent, for two crops, at 6s. 8d. per acre.

TRADE.

Formerly a pretty considerable Trade was carried on at Looe, and many ships belonging to this port used to go from thence to France, Spain, and up the Streights, &c. Even so late as the beginning of the last century there were several ships kept here, principally employed in foreign voyages; but, for seventy or eighty years last past, few, if any, have been so employed.

PILCHARD FISHERY.

The exports consisted of tin, serges, &c. but chiefly of fish, particularly Pilchards and Conger Douce. The pilchards were then caught (at Looe) in drift-nets; now seans are used for taking them. The first pilchard sean was established at Looe in the year 1778. At present nine seans are put out from Looe. A sean is a net of about 220 fathoms long, and about fifteen fathoms deep*. Three boats belong to each sean; the first and largest boat is called the sean-boat, as it carries the sean and seven men. The next boat is called the vollier (follower, so corrupted, probably, or the French *voilier*), and carries another sean, called the tuck-sean, which is about 100 fathoms long and eighteen deep; this boat carries seven men. The third boat is called the lurker, and carries three or four men. The master seaner or chief commander is usually in this boat. A new sean concern, with the boats, &c. costs about one thousand pounds. The pilchard season usually commences in July, and continues for about eight or ten weeks. The method of

---

* Most of the Cornish pilchard-nets are made at Bridport, in Dorsetshire. As the spinning-jennies have of late years deprived a great number of poor women and children in Cornwall of getting a maintenance by their usual employ of carding and spinning wool, it would be no bad policy to introduce the manufactory of twine and fishing-nets into Cornwall as a substitute.

taking them is as follows: — the boats, with their seans on board, are put to sea so as to get to their births, as it is called, by three or four o'clock in the afternoon. When they get to their birth or station, at a short distance from the land, and where the place is free from rocks at bottom, the sean boat and vollier remain at anchor, at a short distance from each other, and the lurker boat at a little way off from them; the fishermen in all the boats constantly looking out to see if any pilchards are jumping out of the water near them. They call the jumping of the fish Stoiting. When a few fish are seen so stoiting, a signal is given, by waving the hat, that fish are seen; upon which the sean boat and vollier get on the spot, and the crew of the sean boat pass, as it is called, the wharp, that is, they throw a rope, which is fixed to the end of the sean, on board the vollier, and then they throw or shoot the sean overboard, which, having leaden weights at bottom, sinks, and the top is buoyed up by corks. The sean boat, while three men are throwing the sean overboard (which is usually accomplished in about eight or ten minutes), is rowed, in a circular course, round where the fish were seen stoiting; and then they arrive again at the vollier, and the spot where the fish were seen is inclosed. They then, if they find the fish taken, which is known by their stoiting in the sean, hem with a cord the two ends of the sean together, so as to prevent the fish getting out of it; and while this is doing, a man is constantly plunging down a stone, fastened to a rope, to frighten back the fish. This operation is called throwing the minnis (probably a corruption of menace, as the fish may be said to be threatened or menaced with danger if they come that way). When the two ends of the sean are thus hemmed together, the fish are surrounded with a circle of net, and grapes*, fastened with ropes to the sean, are let down to keep the sean expanded and in one place till after the fish are taken up. As soon as it grows dark, they begin to take up the fish from the sean in the following manner, which is called tucking the sean. The boat with the tuck-sean on board passes the wharp of that sean to one of the other boats, usually the vollier, or ties the end of the wharp to the stop-sean, and then throw out or shoot this tuck-sean within the stop-sean, and then draw up the same to the edge of the water, and dip up the fish with baskets into their boats. When the boats are filled, if any more fish remain in the stop-sean, this stop-sean is left in the water, till, by successive tuckings, night after night, all the fish are taken therefrom. When the fishermen conceive they have but a small catch, they do not tuck, but draw up the stop-sean at once, with all the fish in it. Sometimes the fishermen observe the fish by colour, as they call it; that is, the water appears, upon looking down into it, quite red, owing to the

---

* A grape or grapnell is a small anchor, generally used for mooring boats.

great quantity of fish below. Indeed, in some parts of Cornwall, though not at Looe, men are placed on the cliffs from whence this red appearance of the water is seen, in order to give the fishermen notice of the place where the fish are to be found. This is done by certain significant signs and odd gestures of the men on shore, and sometimes by hallooing. The men giving such signals are called Huers (probably from the French word *huer*, to hoot). In the mackarel fishery, huers are employed at Looe.—The pilchards are seen at times in large, at other times in small, quantities, playing on the surface of the water, and thereby rendering the spot of a darker colour than the surrounding water. Such fish, so appearing, are called Shirmers. In general the fishermen do not chuse to shoot the sean at shirmers, as few are supposed to be below water. The stoiting of a few fish out of the water is the principal sign of a large shoal. It sometimes happens, that instead of inclosing pilchards, other fish are caught, such as scads or horse-mackarel, young pullock, mackarel, long noses, or chads. A laughable circumstance happened, a few years since, at Polperro, near Looe. One sean inclosed a large body of fish, pilchards as was thought, and several hogsheads of them were taken up in the tuck, and the stop-sean left in the water, with some hundred hogsheads more, as was imagined. When the boats came to shore, an old woman of that place desired the men to give her some fish; which being refused, she poured a torrent of abuse on them for their unkindness, and vociferously wished that all the pilchards remaining in their sean might be turned into chads. The next night the seaners went to tuck again, and behold all the remaining fish proved to be chads indeed; and the old woman, of course, became a witch from that time forward. The pilchards taken at the first tuck, in all probability, had detached themselves from the shoal of chads imprisoned along with them, and kept nearer the surface. But whether this or the old woman's witchcraft was the true cause, the reader will determine on according to his own judgment.

Several hundred hogsheads of pilchards are often caught at one time *. A pilchard hogshead consists of fifty gallons, and contains from 2500 to 3000 fish. It frequently happens, at the commencement

---

* A sean belonging to the late Philip Rashleigh, Esq. of Menabilly in this county, once inclosed near the Gribbin (just under Menabilly) about 2500 hogsheads at one catch. This happened in the Winter season; but of late years few if any pilchards have been caught or seen but in the Summer. The Winter fish were larger than the Summer ones, but did not produce so much oil. Sixty thousand hogsheads of pilchards have been taken in Cornwall in one season. The lowest price I have ever heard them sold for was fourteen shillings *per* hogshead, and the highest £5. 2. 0., exclusive of bounty; lowest price of the oil fifteen pounds *per* ton, and the highest forty pounds. Upon an average about twelve hogsheads of fish produce a hogshead of oil of 63 gallons. In the year 1815, when the fish produced £5. 2. 0. *per* hogshead, one sean at Looe made a profit of more than £1200., few fish being that year taken at other places in the county.

of the fishery, that shoals of small fish are taken, and not being properly coated, *i. e.* scaled, for saving, are thrown away, or used for manure. If such fish were to be boiled, which might easily be done in the cauldrons in which the nets are usually barked, they would produce a quantity of oil, for they are as fat, if not fatter, than larger fish, and would amply repay the trouble. In Sweden, I am told, a great quantity of oil is extracted, by this method, from herrings. When the fish are brought on shore, they are carried into cellars (called Palaces at Looe, but from whence this name arises I do not know), and there a layer of salt of a large grain, usually French, is strewed on the floor under the shed, for these palaces are usually open courts in the middle, with sheds or linhays around. The fish are then placed on their sides by women, on this layer of salt, fish after fish, so as to cover the salt completely. They are thus placed the whole length of the cellar or sheds, and the first row may be about six feet deep to the wall. Another layer of salt is strewed over this layer of fish, so as just to cover them; and then another layer of fish is placed on this layer of salt; and thus they go on till the fish are four or five feet high. Each layer of fish is lessened in depth, in order that they may all remain firm, and not overtop the under layer, and thereby fall down. The last layer is also covered with salt, so that when you are in the cellar you only see the heads of the fish which are outermost; this is what they call bulking the fish. At the ends of the cellars are pits dug, with casks set in them, to receive the brine and train-oil which run from the fish. As the oil swims on the top of the brine, every now and then it is skimmed off, and put into casks kept for that purpose. After the fish have lain thus in bulk for some time, usually upwards of four weeks, they are taken out of the salt, which is called breaking bulk; are then put into hollow baskets, and by men shaken to and fro in the river, or in a large tub of water, to cleanse them from the salt and impurities of blood and oil *. After being so washed they are by women put into hogsheads made so as to admit the oil getting out at their bottoms; and the hogsheads, when filled, are placed on their ends, side by side, in the runs where the fish were bulked; the upper end of the hogsheads being left open, a round flat piece of wood, which is called a buckler (probably from its resembling one), a little less than the circumference of the cask, is placed on the top of the fish

---

* It is a pity this latter method is not constantly adopted, and the water, so highly impregnated with salt and oil, saved for manure. In some parts of Cornwall farmers know the value of this manure. In speaking of Manure it may be worthy to remark that in the Winter season immense quantities of Oreweed (commonly called at Looe Ore Mongel) are thrown on shore on the beach before East Looe; and that though the Mayor usually grants any one who asks leave to take it away, very little, comparatively speaking, is removed, except by the town's people, who carry it into their gardens. By far the greatest part (till very recently) has been left to decay, or to be carried away by the tides.

in each, and then a long pole, one end of which is thrust into a sort of pigeon-hole in the wall, crosses the buckler and so presses on it; and in order to increase this pressure, large stones are hung on the outward end of the pole, and as the fish and buckler on them sink, plugs are put on the buckler under the pole, so that with an immense weight the fish in the hogsheads are pressed together. When there is a vacancy in the hogshead by the pressure, more fish are added till the casks can hold no more. The oil issues out of the bottoms of the casks, and runs into the pits called the train-pits, from whence it is taken up as before-mentioned. After having been pressed for a certain time, the casks are taken out and headed up; the fish usually remain in press about nine days. A hogshead of fish takes about five or six guns or bushels of salt to cure them. A gun is fifty-six pounds weight avoirdupois, by 38 Geo. III. c. 89. About one-half of this salt is entirely consumed, but the remainder serves again, and is sometimes kept for the next year. A hogshead of fish, therefore, absolutely consumes about two or three guns of salt. By the Act of 38 Geo. III. c. 89, sec. 104, two hundred and eighty pounds weight of salt were allowed for every cask or vessel containing fifty gallons of pilchards or scads, and so in proportion for any greater or less quantity. By the same Act, sec. 3d, a bounty of seven shillings was allowed for every cask or vessel of pilchards or scads containing fifty gallons, which shall be duly exported from

Great Britain to parts beyond the sea. And by 39 Geo. III. c. 65, sec. 1, an additional bounty of one shilling and sixpence on every cask or vessel of pilchards exported immediately to any of the British West-India Islands, or to any port or place in the Mediterranean, to continue till 24 June 1805. A proportionable bounty is allowed by sec. 2 and 3 of the same Act for casks of thirty gallons, and casks commonly called pilchard hogsheads, containing less than fifty gallons. This bounty is continued by subsequent Acts.

The Pilchards, when cured as before mentioned, are called Fumadoes, though rather improperly; formerly the name was proper enough, for instead of their being cured as they now are, they used to be smoaked, somewhat probably after the manner of red-herrings. This practice has, however, been discontinued throughout the county for a great number of years, and few of the common people know from whence the name is derived, as they now call them Fair Maids *. They are a cheap and wholesome food, usually retailed at four or five for a penny, and broiled on the gridiron or boiled with a potatoe are extremely nice things. It is astonishing more of them are not consumed in this kingdom. If a

---

* At a trial at the Cornish Assizes some years ago, a witness being asked what he was doing at a particular place, very innocently puzzled his lordship and the council, by telling them he was there " eating Fair maids and drinking Mahogany."—Gin and Treacle so called!!

bounty was allowed for home consumption, it would be not only advantageous to the fishery, but to the kingdom at large.

The seans are frequently shot near Looe. Sometimes you may see three or four shooting at once within half a mile of the parade; from the hill this distance appears but just below; the motion of the boats, the activity of the fishermen, the joy of the adventurers collecting together to behold their increasing good fortune, contribute greatly to enliven the scene and exhilirate the spirits. Upon these occasions parties of pleasure are formed, and the most timid are induced to venture out alongside of the seans. Parties also go out to see the tucking or taking up the fish, which is usually commenced just as it grows dark, the fish being then not so apt to be frightened. Commonly about this season of the year the sea produces the luminous appearance which in Cornwall goes by the name of Brining, and is supposed to be produced by animalculi or phosphoric particles of some animal or vegetable matter floating in the water, the least motion of the water produces this appearance. Conceive then to yourself the effect the splashing of tens of thousands of fish must produce; the sea appears full of glow-worms of the most splendid lustre, the ropes hauling up from below appear like chains of fire, in short, the scene is beyond expression beautiful. A universal calm o'erspreads the sea, its waters are hushed, no noise is heard but from the fishermen and fish;

the land appearing with sombre hue, contrasted to the light of a summer evening sky, charmingly defines the visible horizon of the high hills around, and the spangled canopy of Heaven, and shooting meteors of the atmosphere, contribute to produce the utmost tranquillity of the mind, and the purest and finest of pleasures.

Conger Douce no doubt derives its name from the French Douce (sweet), so that it may be termed sweet Conger, in contradistinction to salt. These fish are caught with a hook and line at some distance from the shore; when they arrive they are split open and cleaned, and then five, six or more of them, according to their sizes, are sewn together and exposed on poles to the sun for many weeks, till their moisture is quite dried up, and then they are said to be cured. A quintal (112 pounds) of this fish so cured, used to sell for about thirty shillings. Some years, I have been told, about two hundred quintals have been sent off from Looe. Spain was the usual market for them. Of late years, however, line-fishing has much decreased at Looe, and Conger Douce is now no longer made.

RIOTS.

A few years since, large quantities of corn used to be bought up by cornfactors residing at Looe and its neighbourhood, and by them sent coastwise from thence. This trade, as it was a means of circulating much cash, was of course very beneficial to the place. In January 1793, corn being then rather of high price, between three and four hundred Tinners from the parish of St. Austell and neighbouring parishes, hearing there was a great quantity of corn in the granaries, came to Looe in order to compel the reduction of the price. The then Sheriff of Cornwall (Davies Giddy, Esq.) happened to be spending a few days at Looe. The Mayors and gentlemen of the two boroughs and neighbourhood of course waited upon him, and the Tinners were prevailed on to return to their homes the next day. In the beginning of the next month, however, a letter from St. Austell informed us, that near a thousand Tinners were collecting in that neighbourhood with intent to visit us about the corn again. The Mayors and gentlemen again waited on the Sheriff, and it was determined to resist force with force. An express was immediately dispatched to the Commander in Chief at Plymouth for a company of soldiers; and the Sheriff issued warrants for raising the posse comitatus, which brought here from the neighbouring parishes a great number of men; most of the inhabitants of the two towns also came forward, and all was bustle and preparation, expecting hourly the arrival of the enemy. The Tinners, however, hearing of our preparations, and being advised by the gentry in their neighbourhood, thought it prudent not to come on.

In the year 1796 a disturbance broke out again about the price of corn, when most of the lower order in these boroughs assembled in so riotous a manner, that the Riot Act was obliged to be read. The mob entered on board a vessel at the quay laden with corn, and cut the rigging and prevented her sailing. The Magistrates were again obliged to get a company of soldiers from Plymouth. These disturbances have occasioned considerable loss to these boroughs. When the corn was brought here, much money was left behind by the farmers and sailors at our shops, &c. and women and girls, employed in carrying the corn from the granaries to the ships, used to get two or three shillings a day, chiefly in the winter season when they had no other employ. With respect to the dearth of corn in Cornwall, I entirely agree with Mr. Carew, the Author of the Survey before-mentioned. He says, therein, on this subject, " I have been always prone to maintain a paradox that dearth of corn in Cornwall (for with other shires I will not undertake to meddle), so it go not accompanied with a scarcity, is no way prejudicial to the good of the country, and I am inclined thus to think for the reasons ensuing. There are no two trades which set so many handes to worke at all times of the year, as that one of tillage; the husbandman finding profit herein, is encouraged to bestow pains and charges for enclosing and dressing of waste grounds, which therethrough afterwards become also good for pasture;

with the readie money gotten by his weekly selling of corne, he setteth the artificer to worke, who were better to buy deare bread, being but a part of his meate, and which he countervaileth again by raising the price of his ware, then to sit idly knocking his heels against the wall. Their objection, who fear lest the transporting of much away, will leave too little at home, I answer with this observation: when the price of corn falleth men generally give over surplus tillage, and break no more ground than will serve to supply their own turne; the rest they employ in grazing, when through it falleth out, that an ill kerned or saved harvest soon emptieth their old store, and leaveth them in necessity to seek new relief from other places. Whereas on the other side, if through hope of vent they hold on their larger tillage, this retaineth one year's provision under hand to fetch in another, which upon such occasions may easily be left at home; and of this, what Cornishman is there that hath not seen the experience." There is certainly a great deal of sound sense in these remarks, and worthy to be reflected on when the high price of corn is apt to induce the unthinking lower class of people to act diametrically against their own interest.

IMPORTS.

The imports at Looe formerly consisted of fruit, wine, cloths, and Spanish iron. About a hundred and fifty years since, tradition says, that Looe supplied the whole county of Cornwall and great part of Devonshire with Spanish iron. I have heard that even Exeter used to be supplied from this place; the merchants here quite engrossing the whole of this trade, until, as tradition says, some Quaker of Bristol contrived to get connected with the Spanish merchants. Probably the export trade from Looe to Spain enabled the Looers to import at a cheaper rate than others; though the story runs, that other merchants did not know from whence the iron came, which is too absurd to be credited.

THE GEORGE OF LOOE.

In this place I cannot help mentioning that Mr. Carew, speaking of the shipping of Looe, says, "That one of them hath successively retained the name of The George of Loo ever since the first so called did a great while sithence, in a furious fight, take three French men of war." At present there is not the least tradition of this ship or the furious fight.

TOWN SEAL.

Whether the ship in the town seal was meant as a memorial I cannot say, but if so, the George of Looe must have been badly manned, only having two on board, unless we are to imagine the remainder of the crew were killed in this furious fight and thrown overboard. This ship in the town seal bears three escutcheons on her side, with the same arms on each, *viz.* three bendlets, colours not expressed, and its legend is, in very old characters, something like the Saxon letters "SI : COMMUNETATIS : DE : LOO." This seal is apparently very old, and when out of the knob or handle appears as if it had originally a hole to hang it to a chain, but this part is broken; it is made of a sort of bell-metal.

OTTO OF BODRIGAN.

I have lately accidentally discovered that the scutcheons on the seal bear the arms of Otto or Otes of Bodrigan, who by a deed I have lately met with, appears to have been lord of the manors of Pendrim and Loe in the reign of Edward II. (Pendrim manor surrounds Looe.) This Otto or Otes of Bodrigan, and his ancestors, granted several charters to the towns of Loe and Showta (now Looe and Shutta or Shoota). Hals, in his History of Cornwall, under title Gor-an Vicarage, mentions this place in that parish where this gentleman lived as follows: " Bo-drig-ham, alias Bo-trig-an (for in British *d* and *t* are indifferently used and pronounced for each other) is in this parish. The first name of which signifies the cows, kine, or cattle, sea-shore, or tide, home, habitation, or dwelling; the second, sea-shore, or tide, cows, kine, or cattle, or, more plainly, cattle that grazed on the tide or seacoast, according to the natural circumstances of the place*. In Carew's Survey of Cornwall, p. 47, it is called Bo-drugant, *i. e.* cows, kine, cattle, or steers. This Barton gave name and original to an old family of gentlemen surnamed De Bodrigham, or Bodrigan alias Botrighan (for so they wrote; see Ladock), who flourished here in great fame, wealth, and reputation, for several descents; and, in particular, here lived Otho de Bodrigan, temp. 17 Edward II. 1307, of whom we read in Carew's Survey of Cornwall, p. 51, *viz.* Otto de Bodrugan peregrinatus est ad San. Jacobum, Licentiâ Domini Regis, *i. e.* Otho de Bodrigan, by licence of our Lord the King, is gone a pilgrimage to St. James, that *is* to say, the Apostle St. James's Church at Compostella, in Spain, who had for his fellow-traveller Rodolphus de Bello Prato, qui peregrinatus est cum Ottone de Bodrigan, cum licentiâ regis, pro se et duobus valettis, that is to say, Ralph of the Fair Mea-

---

* See his Cornish Vocabulary.

dow, who by licence of the King for himself and two servants or young gentlemen is gone a pilgrimage with Otho of Bodrigan. And of these it follows in the same page, isti prænominati habent 40 libras terræ et redditus per annum, that is to say, held by the tenure of knight's service. This Otho de Bodrigan had issue Otho de Bodrigan, Sheriff of Cornwall, 3d Richard II. A. D. 1400, and gave for his arms (as appears yet in the door of this house) Argent, three bends or bendlets Gules.

I find by the deed before-mentioned, which bears date 14 Edward II. 1321, and is a charter of confirmation to the towns of Loe and Showta, by the said Otto or Otes, that charters had before been granted by the ancestors of this family to the said towns, and that a common seal (not unlikely the present town seal, from its antique appearance, and the circumstance of there being a very antient impression of it, as I am told,) was in existence at that time, as the deed is said to be sealed with the common seal of the Burgesses of the towns aforesaid, to wit, Loe and Showta. This deed * proves Looe to have been a very antient borough. Tonkin, in manuscript Hist. of Cornwall, says, that the manor of Bodrigan was antiently written Bodrugan, which he interpreted to mean, "The House on the Down

---

* See a copy of it hereafter, in this work. And also a copy of Eustacius de Grenville's grant to his men of Shete (Showta or Shoota).

of Oaks." The Barton of Bodrigan, as Tonkin says, was looked upon as the best in the county of Cornwall, containing between 5 and 600 acres, mostly very good land. On a point of this land was a chapel (almost demolished when Tonkin wrote), built by some of the Bodrigans, on some deliverance of which, and his estate, hear Leland: "This chapel, land, or point is in the park of Bodrugan, and in this park was the house of Sir Henry Bodrugan, a man of auntient stok, attaynted for taking part with King Richard III. against Henry VII. and after flying into Ireland, Syr Richard Egecombe, father of Sir Pears Egecombe, had Bodrigan and other parcels of Bodrigan's lands, and Trevanion had part of Bodrigan's lands, as Restronget and Newham, both in Falmouth Haven." In a document in the Augmentation office, bearing date between 1512 and 1524, Lady Broke is called Lady of the Manor of Pendryn. The co-heiress of the second Lord Willoughby de Broke married Pawlet. The first Lord Willoughby was so created by Henry VII. and no doubt had a grant of Sir Henry Bodrugan's property in Pendrym, if it continued in the Bodrugan family till the attainder. Sir Henry Bodrigan was knighted by Edward IV. in 1475. What became of him after flying into Ireland is uncertain; some say that he came over to assist John Earl of Lincoln, and was slain with him at the battle of Stoke; but however that be, this put an end to the greatness of this family. It is said that Sir Henry forfeited an estate of £:10,000 per annum. On this barton is a small round entrenchment, which they call Sir Henry Bodrugan's Castle, but by the barrows it is plain it must be some antient encampment, though so destroyed by often ploughing, that one cannot tell what to make of it. A little on one side of it is a coarse moorish piece of ground, which they call the Woeful Moor, for there they say Sir Henry was defeated by Sir Richard Edgecombe and Trevanion; and beyond it on the slide of the cliff is a place they call Sir Henry Bodrugan's Leap, from whence he took a desperate leap after his defeat on a small place under, where a boat and ship lay ready to take him against all accidents, into which they tell you when he got safe, he turned about, and gave a curse upon Edgecombe and Trevanion, and their posterity; which the neighbourhood do not scruple to say, hath in some part its effect to this day. For so great was the love they bore this Sir Henry for his great hospitality and generous way of living, that his memory is still held in veneration, especially among the elder sort of people. Sir H. B's arms were, Argent, three bends Gules; which, having no relation with the arms of Trenowth, I know not upon what account Mr. Carew calls him Sir Henry Trenouth, since in several deeds, which I have seen of this family, they write Bodrigan without an alias, sealed with these arms, and for their crest a white dexter glove erect, with a ribband round the wrist hanging down with two ends.

The Manor of Bodrigan is of great revenue and very large, extending itself into several parishes; and the advowson of Mevagissey belongs to it, which church was endowed by Sir Otto de Bodrigan as you may see there. Probably it was this Sir Otto, who built the chapel on the point, on his return from his pilgrimage to St. James.

Henry de Bodrigan was Knight of the Shire 35 Edward I.

Otho de Bodrigan was so 17 Edward II. 43 Edward III. and 7 Richard II.

Sir Wm. de Bodrigan was so 3 and 5 Henry V. and 4, 8, and 9 Henry VI.

Otho Bodrigan de Bodrigan was Sheriff 3 Rich. II.

TRADESMEN'S TOKENS.

The merchants at Looe formerly had Tokens coined for their conveniency in giving change against silver, and I have several of them in my possession, which have from time to time been found in old ruins; they are made of brass, about the size of a seven shilling piece, and are tolerably well executed. One of them has "WILLIAM AMBROSE" on one side, and a dolphin in the middle; on the other side "W. A." in the centre, and "IN LOOE 1664" round it. Another has "JOHN CHANDLER," with "J. C." on one side, and "IN LOOE J. C." on the other; there is no date on this token. I have also one with the inscription "BENJAMIN OBEN" round a King's head on one side, and "IN LOOE 1656" round "B. O." on the other; and one of "ELIZABETH HENDRA" round a ship with three masts under sail on one side, and "OF LOWE 1668" round "E. H." on the other side. Between the period of the restoration of Charles II. and the year 1672, cities, towns, and even individuals, were allowed to coin copper money for the convenience of trade. I have also in my possession several pieces of brass coin found among old ruins at Looe, which I understand from the Editor of the Gentleman's Magazine are called Abbey Counters, from the supposition that they were formerly used in abbeys for casting up accounts; they are about the size of a shilling, and very thin; their legends, from the odd forms of the letters, I have never been able to make out; most of them have a mound and cross on one side, and ducal coronets crosswise on the other, within bordures.

SHIPPING OF LOOE.

In the Roll of King Edward the Third's Fleet before Calais, it is said that Looe sent twenty ships and 315 mariners *. By the Act of Parliament 35

---

* Fowey sent forty-seven ships, and 770 men. London only furnished twenty-five ships, and 662 mariners. Plymouth twenty-six ships, 603 mariners. Padstow two ships, 27 mariners.

Geo. III. c. 9, for procuring a supply of men from the several ports of this kingdom for the service of his Majesty's Navy, the port of Looe was assessed at and raised sixteen men. This was, however, done by an allowed bounty paid by Government, and those who entered were not required to be natives or even residents.

SCENERY.

The scenery about Looe is admitted by all who have seen it to be extremely beautiful, and the walks, which are numerous, are consequently delightful ones. The walks on East Looe side are the parade, commonly called Church-end (being at the end of the church), the Hill, Hay-lane, Shutta-lane, Common-wood, St. Martin's-lane, &c. &c. To get into the road of St. Martin's from Looe-hill, you pass up a narrow lane called Cripple's-lane, which brings you to a field called the Lower-windmill, above which is another field called the Higher-windmill; and in this field are the remains of a very antient windmill. There is not the slightest tradition when this windmill was built or at work; probably it

---

Mulbrooke one ship, 12 mariners.—Appendix to General Treatise of the Dominion of the Sea, p. 38.

This shows that Looe and Fowey were then the chief and almost the only ports where shipping were kept in the County of Cornwall.

was erected anterior to any watermill in the neighbourhood. About a quarter of a mile from this windmill, in a field on the right-hand side of the road to St. Martin's, is a large and perfect Barrow, the only one I believe in existence near Looe; though I think another was in a field called the Wool-down, and another in a field called Shuttaball, just above Shutta. At a place called Pulpit, at about half a mile on the Fowey road from West Looe, are the remains of a Barrow, one half of which was carried away for manure a few years since, and the hole made by the body which had been deposited in it exposed to view.

The Parade commands an extensive sea prospect, and to the East the whole stretch of the bold promontory which ends in the Ram-head, and forms Whitsand-bay (so much talked of during the American war, as the intended place of landing for the enemy) on the Looe side; this promontory bearing the shape of an antient battering ram no doubt gave this name to its head, and to the parish of Rame which is on it. Ram-head is somewhat more than nine miles off by sea, and has a small building on its top. The isthmus from the main land to the Ram-head has evidently been fortified by a strong vallum and deep ditch, uniting the two gullies that come up from the sea to the East and West side, part of the vallum near the middle of the isthmus being still apparent.

Mr. Polwhele, in his History of Cornwall, says,

that he was informed that not far from the Ram-head there is a chapel at the base of the cliff, almost covered over (the interior I presume) with unknown characters which bear the marks of great antiquity. I have several times enquired after this chapel, but in vain.

Beyond this promontory of the Rame, you see in clear weather the Bolt-land or promontory stretching itself into the sea. The head of this land is about thirty miles off, and its elevation is about 430 feet. The extreme points of these promontories now and then assume very odd appearances when a haze or fog is near them; sometimes they appear overhanging the sea in a very peculiar manner; at other times, by the same cause, the Bolt-land appears like an island or islands quite separated from the mainland.

SUBMARINE WOOD.

The space between Ram-head and Looe, though now covered with deep water, is supposed to have been formerly covered with wood. Borlase, in his History of Cornwall, intimates this, but on what foundation I know not.

At a beach called Millendreath *, about a mile

---

* Millendreath signifies, in Cornish, a Mill on the Sands. There is no tradition, however, of there ever having been a mill on the sands at this place; there is indeed a mill called Chubb's Mill (being built by a Mr. Chubb of Pellis Court) about a quar-

to the Eastward of Looe, when the sand is much lowered by heavy seas, peat and trunks of trees are exposed, as I have myself seen. This timber is much decayed, and is of a red colour.

Mr. Scawen (I apprehend) in his MS. says, " it is no inconsiderable confirmation, that Cornwall has lost much lands on the Southern coast, that there was a valley between Rame-head and Loo, and that there is to be seen in a clear day, in the bottom of the sea, a league from the shore, a wood of timber lying on its side uncorrupted, as if formerly grown therein when it was dry ground, thrown down by the violence of the waves; of this several persons have informed me (says Mr. Scawen), who have, as they said, often seen the same." I have several times made enquiry of fishermen and others respecting this submarine wood, but have never been able to learn that it was ever seen or indeed ever heard of by them. As there are quantities of very black stones thrown on shore at Playdy beach near Looe, may not this supposed wood be a range of basaltic columns, from whence these stones have been detached. The sea

---

ter of a mile up the valley, and it is very probable that the tide flowed up there formerly.

I find it recorded in the Parish Register of St. Martin's, that in the year 1718 a whale seventy feet in length was driven a shore dead, a little to the eastward of Millendreath. I have heard old people mention it, and that a man mounted on a ladder, in attempting to cut it open, fell into its body, and was nearly suffocated.

has within my own memory encroached considerably on the shores near Looe, and almost every year pieces of the cliffs are washed down by it. In some places near Looe the extreme declivity of the cliffs towards the sea is composed of a mass of clay, and may be called table or flat land, as there are fields on it, such as at Rope-makers field, and at Downderry, near Seaton. The elevation of this table-land from high water mark may be fifty or sixty feet high; and these fields formerly extended in all probability a considerable distance into the sea, and might have had timber growing on them. In a few years perhaps all the table-land will be washed down, as the waves beating against its base in heavy storms bring down large masses of this clay at times. I observed lately one circumstance, which in a geological point of view may be worth mentioning. Under this mass of clay, near a place called Chough-rock, about half a mile from Looe, there is exposed to sight a mass of sand, which is perhaps twenty feet higher than the present high-water mark. How came it there? It could not possibly have been driven in under the clay, but must have been buried up by it; and the sea must previously have been twenty feet higher than it is at present, for how otherwise could this sand have been deposited where it is?

EDYSTONE LIGHTHOUSE
South View.
Printed by C. Hullmandel.

EDDYSTONE LIGHTHOUSE.

Immediately opposite Looe, about fourteen miles off, and visible from the parade and hills, is the Eddystone Lighthouse, built by the late Mr. Smeaton, of Yorkshire. The lanthorn is an octagon of about nine feet diameter. Till within a few years last past it used to be lighted with twenty-four very large candles, sixteen in one round frame and eight in another. Now Argand lamps are used, with highly polished reflectors. The candle light was frequently seen from Looe with the naked eye; now the light is very strong, and in dark nights does not appear above a league distant. At high-water the sea nearly embraces the base of the building. You ascend to the door by a ladder on the outside, almost perpendicular, of, according to my recollection, about fourteen staves long; you then arrive at the stairs within the building, which have (as no space was to be lost) a coal-place under them. The first room you come to is where the men keep their water, &c. the next is a store-room where they keep their provisions, candles, &c. Round this room is engraved, or in relief, " Except the Lord builds the house, they labour in vain that build it;" from this room you ascend to the next, which is the kitchen, by a ladder which goes up into a circular hole in the centre of the room, a large copper cover, like that of a saucepan, is placed on this hole to prevent falling through; you ascend to the next room, which is the bed-room, in the same manner; this room is about twelve feet diameter; you next ascend in like manner into the lanthorn, which has a seat round it; outside the lanthorn is a walk railed in round it. The view from hence is singularly and awfully grand, and perhaps has not its like. On the outside the lanthorn are engraved the cardinal points of the compass, and over the door " 24th August 1759, Laus Deo."

I was at the Eddystone the 4th of August 1788. The men told us that in the preceding winter one of the panes of the extremely thick glass in the lanthorn had been broken during a violent storm, and they imagined by a stone thrown up by the raging billows. The waves in violent storms strike with such force, as to give the building a very sensible tremulous motion, and ascend by meeting this impediment to their course nearly as high as the top of it. The top of the lanthorn is I believe near ninety feet from the rock; from the rock to the bottom of the lanthorn is about seventy feet. When clear weather follows a violent storm, this tremendously grand Jet d'Eau may be seen from Looe hills; the time it takes in falling and the distance it is thrown, will give you some idea how high it has mounted, and with what force it is carried. It is a very grand sight to see. The Eddystone has a peculiarly grand appearance from Looe in the summer

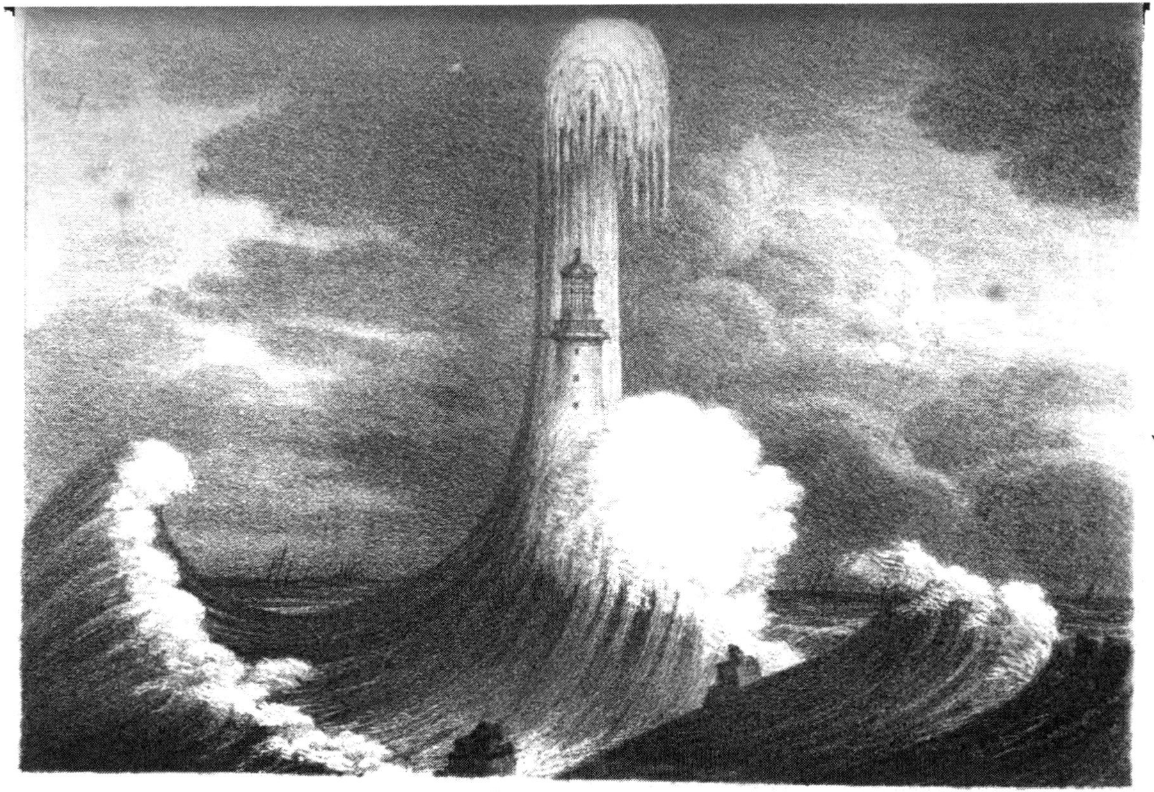

evenings just as the sun is setting, whose rays falling on the glass of the lanthorn are reflected on Looe, and the building then appears, when viewed through a glass, like an immense wax candle lighted up, and affording a most brilliant light. To the naked eye the light appears like a most splendid star rising in the horizon.

The nearest land to the Eddystone is the Ram-head, about nine miles from it. Looe Island and St. Nicholas's in Plymouth Sound are exactly equidistant from it. Having heard that the Eddystone rock contained a quantity of shining talcy matter, I lately procured a small piece therefrom, and which appeared full of shining particle, I believe of talc. I presented this little specimen to the Geological Society at Penzance, and am informed it is limestone. The rock on which the Lighthouse is erected is very properly not allowed to be broken in the slightest degree, for fear of weakening it and the building. The Eddystone Lighthouse was completed August 24, 1759, and on January 15, 1762, Mr. Smeaton had the heartfelt satisfaction of receiving a letter from Dr. John Mudge, of Plymouth, signifying that the building had stood the extraordinary heavy gale of wind which occurred the Monday night and Tuesday morning then preceding. The tide, Dr. Mudge said, rose two feet higher than was ever known in the memory of the oldest man living. The seas came in bodily over the Barbican wall at Plymouth, and one wave with such irresistible violence, that it swept away the parapet below its foundation, and in its return carried off five people then upon it, all of whom were drowned. The new Lammy pier was swept clear away.

Narrative of the Destruction of the old Eddystone Lighthouse[*]:

"On the 22d of August, 1755, the workmen returned on shore, having finished all necessary repairs of that season; between which time and the 2d of December following, the attending boat had been off several times to the Eddystone, and particularly on the 1st of December, and had landed some stores, when the light-keepers made no manner of complaint, and said all was right, except that one or two of the bricks in the kitchen fire-place had been loosened by a late storm. What in reality might occasion the building first catching fire, it has never been possible fully to investigate; but from the most distinct account it appears to have commenced in the very top of the lantern, that is, in the cupola. From whatever cause it originated, it is certain that when the light-keeper then upon the watch (about two o'clock in the morning of the 2d of December) went into the lantern, as usual, to snuff the candles, he found the whole in a smoke, and upon opening the door of the lantern into the balcony, a flame instantly burst from the inside of the cupola; he immediately endeavoured to alarm his companions; but they being in bed and asleep, were

---

[*] From " Smeaton's Account of the Eddystone Lighthouse."

not so ready in coming to his assistance as the occasion required. As there were always some leathern buckets kept in the house, and a tub of water in the lantern, he attempted as speedily as possible to extinguish the fire in the cupola, by throwing water from the balcony with a leather bucket, upon the outside cover of lead. By this time, his comrades approaching, he encouraged them to fetch up water with the leathern buckets from the sea; but as the height would be at a medium full seventy feet, this, added to the natural consternation that must attend such a sudden and totally unexpected event, would occasion this business of bringing up water, at the best, to go on but slowly; meanwhile the flames gathering strength every moment, and the poor man, though making use of every exertion, having the water to throw full four yards higher than his own head, to be of any service, we must by no means be surprized that, under all these difficulties, the fire, instead of being soon extinguished, would increase, and what put a sudden stop to further exertions, was the following most remarkable circumstance: as he was looking up with the utmost attention, to see the direction and success of the water thrown, a quantity of lead, dissolved by the heat of the flames, suddenly rushed like a torrent from the roof, and fell not only on the man's head, face, and shoulders, but over his cloaths: and a part of it made its way through his shirt-collar, and very much burnt his neck and shoulder; from this moment he had a violent internal sensation, and imagined that a quantity of this lead had passed down his throat and got into his body. Under this violence of pain and anxiety, as every attempt had proved ineffectual, and the rage of the flames was increasing, it is not to be wondered at, that the terror and dismay of the three men increased in proportion; so that they all found themselves intimidated, and glad to make their retreat from that immediate scene of horror into one of the rooms below, where they would find themselves precluded from doing any thing; for had they thrown down ever so much water there it could not have extinguished what was burning above them, nor indeed have produced any other effect than that of running down into the room below, and from thence finally into the stair-case, back again into the sea. They seem, therefore, to have had no other resource, or means of retreat, than that of retiring downwards from room to room, as the fire advanced over their heads. How soon the fire was seen from the shore, is not very certain, but early in the morning it was perceived by some of the Cawsand fishermen, and intelligence thereof given to Mr. Edwards of Rame, in that neighbourhood, a gentleman of some fortune, and more humanity. This prompted him immediately to send out a fishing-boat and men to the relief of the people he supposed in distress upon the Eddystone. The boat and men got thither about ten o'clock, after the fire had been burning full eight hours; and in this time the three light-keepers were not only driven from all the rooms, and the stair-case, but to avoid the falling of the timber, and red-hot bolts, &c. upon them, they were found sitting in the hole or cave on the east side of the rock, under the iron ladder, almost in a state of stupefaction, it being then low water.

"At this time the wind was eastward, and did not blow very fresh, but just hard enough to make a landing upon the rock, at the proper landing-place, quite impracticable, or attended with the utmost hazard. It therefore became a difficulty how the men were to be taken off, for the ground swell from the west side produced so great a surf upon the sloping surface, that no boat could attempt to land there. They, however, fell to the following expedient; having a small boat with them, they moored their principal boat by a grappling to the westward, but as near the rock as they durst, and then launching their small boat, they rowed in towards the rock, veering out a rope which they fastened to the large boat, till they got near enough to throw a coil of small rope on the rock, which, having been laid hold of by the men, they one by one fastened it round their waists, and jumping into the sea, they were towed into the small boat, and thence delivered into the large boat: and as they found it was out of their power to do any further service, the boat hastened to Plymouth to get the men relieved. No sooner, however, were they set on shore, than one of them made off, and has never since been heard of, which would, on the first blush, induce one to suppose that there was something culpable in this man; and if it had been a house on the shore, one would have been tempted to suspect he had been guilty of some foul play; but the circumstance of its being a lighthouse, situated so as to afford no retreat in the power of its inhabitants, seems to preclude the possibility of its being done wilfully, as he must know he must perish, or be in extreme danger of so doing at least, along with the rest.

"Such was the fate of Mr. Rudyerd's building; the whole of which, notwithstanding every effort that could be made, was in a few days burned to its foundation; nor could any thing, as is here remarked, but a storm or hard gale at South-west have effectually put out the fire, so as to have saved any material part of the building, which, after a duration of 49 years from its commencement, was doomed to inevitable destruction by an element, of which, as an enemy, the builders never thought, and therefore did not guard against it.

"It remains only to relate the fate of the unfortunate man, who received so peculiar an injury from the melted lead. His name was Henry Hall, of Stonehouse, near Plymouth; and though aged 94 years, being of a good constitution, he was remarkably active, considering his time of life. He had invariably told the surgeon who attended him (Mr. Spry, now Dr. Spry, of Plymouth) that if he would do any thing effectual to his recovery he must relieve his stomach from the lead, which he was sure was within him; and this he told, not only to Dr. Spry, but those about him, though in a very hoarse voice. The reality of the assertion seemed, however, then incredible to Dr. Spry, who could hardly suppose it possible that any human being could exist after receiving melted lead into the stomach, much less that he should be able to bear rowing through the sea from the rock, and also the fatigue and inconvenience from the length of time he was getting on shore, before any remedies could be applied. The man did not shew any symptoms, however, of being either much worse or of amendment till the sixth day after the accident, when he was thought to be better. He constantly took his medicines, and swallowed many things, both liquid and solid, till the tenth and eleventh days; after which he suddenly grew worse; and the twelfth day, being seized with cold sweats and spasms, he soon afterwards expired. On opening the stomach, Dr. Spry found therein a solid piece of lead, of a flat oval form, which weighed seven ounces and five drachms. I have seen (adds Mr. Smeaton) the piece of lead since, and it appeared to me as if a part of the coat of the stomach firmly adhered to the convex side thereof."

When I was at the Eddystone, August 4, 1788, one of the men belonging to it said he would shew me a great curiosity. He went up stairs, and brought down a piece of an old card of the size and shape following, on which was written this inscription:

A form of a
alobe of lead cut
out of a man's belley
swallowed at Eddystone
December ye 4. 1755.

I immediately put the card on a piece of paper, and cut out the exact size and form of it, and copied the inscription literally; and the above is taken (size, shape, and inscription) from that very paper.

PROSPECTS.

On ascending **Looe Hill**, which is an extremely agreeable walk, the prospect becomes more varied and extensive, and Looe Island strikes your attention. The higher you mount, of course the farther off you view at sea. No place in the kingdom, probably, affords a finer sea prospect than Looe. Ships of war and merchant-ships are constantly seen going up or down the Channel, or going into, or coming out from, Plymouth. Fleets, consisting of some hundreds of ships, are at times seen at one view.

In war time squadrons of line of battle ships or frigates are frequently seen within five or six miles; and the grand fleet, in passing up or down Channel, is generally seen, and sometimes not above four or five miles off. As the grand fleet usually, when going out, takes some ships from Plymouth, and in its return leaves some ships there, it probably happens that from no town in the kingdom can the fleet be viewed more entire, nearer, or with more heartfelt pleasure than from Looe.

DISTANCE FROM PLYMOUTH.

Looe is, by water, about four leagues from Plymouth; in a straight line Plymouth cannot be above twelve or thirteen miles off. The sound of the muskets fired by the marines on board the men of war in harbour at sun-set is frequently heard at Looe with great distinctness, particularly so if the wind is Easterly. When the camp was at Maker Heights* (which are seen from Looe, as was the camp, and as the barrack there is) the drums and fifes were fre-

---

* Maker Heights are found, by actual measurement, to be 402 feet above low water mark. Our late most gracious Sovereign, George III. visited these Heights August 20, 1789. I was there at the time. The flag-post where his Majesty stood when the plan of an intended fortification was laid before him by the Duke of Richmond, is visible from Looe.

quently heard at Looe; even the tunes at times could be distinguished, though the sound must have passed over eight or nine miles of water; and indeed I have heard the drums from Plymouth. The roaring of the cannon from the forts and ships at Plymouth is almost every day heard. If ships were to salute the Port Admiral or scale their guns a little farther out at sea than is now customary, the firing would be visible, not only from Looe, but for a long extent of coast both East and West, and would greatly add to the scenery and grandeur of the salute. Sky-rockets let off from Plymouth have a beautiful appearance from Looe, as I have frequently experienced. The flash of the nine o'clock gun is visible in a dark night. Maker Tower, on which signals are made of fleets and ships at sea, is within view of the Parade; and as the signals are published (at least the common ones), when you see any flying you have only to refer to your card and you have them explained. You see a signal for a fleet to the Eastward or Westward, the ships probably not visible from where you stand, take your glass, walk up the hill, and you are gratified with a sight of them.

SIGNAL-POSTS.

During the late war there were three signal-posts, besides that on Maker Tower, visible from Looe: the first at Penhale, about three miles East of Looe;

the second near Maker Tower; and the other on the Bolt, not far from its head. They were erected at the commencement of the war with France. A lieutenant of the Navy and two or three men were stationed at each, small houses being built for their residence. Signals by flags and balls were made to, and answered by, ships at sea, and communicated from one station to the other till they reached the Port Admiral at Plymouth. A look-out was kept by night as well as by day; and the night-signals were made by fires, blue lights, &c.

WALKS.

On West Looe side there are many beautiful walks; that towards Hannafore, or Haunafore (Haven-afore, or Forehaven, probably so corrupted, and most likely took its name before Looe Island was disunited from the main land, and then forming an haven) commands a very extensive sea and land view. The whole of East Looe is seen from hence— the batteries, jutty-head, public quays, the bridge, and the Eastern river — affording a most delightful prospect.

West Looe Down is also a most charming walk, commanding very extensive and delightful views. From hence Caradon Hill, Killmarth Rocks, the Cheesewring Rocks, and the Borough of Liskeard, are visible.

There is also a most delightful walk or ride along the banks of the Western river, in a fine coppice wood, for two miles up. Now and then you are entertained with the notes and a view of the heron, the sea-gull, the curlew, the wood-pecker, and sylvan doves; and the king's-fisher, as if to shew its beautiful plumage, frequently flits from the rock below, and skims along before you. The author of "The Beauties of England and Wales," speaking of the valley through which this river runs, says, "The valley in which is Trelawn mill is one of the most beautiful in the West of England."

I must not forget to mention Looe Bridge as a very agreeable walk in a Summer evening, for a current of fine refreshing air is always passing up or down the river; and the scenery, beautifully reflected in the still water, in the twilight or moonlight, is truly fine.

"Scenes must be beautiful, which daily view'd
Please daily, and whose novelty survives
Long knowledge and the scrutiny of years;
Praise justly due to those that I describe."

I have been told that in calm evenings a horse passing over Looe Bridge is distincly heard at Sandplace, two miles up the river. Probably, however, the tide must be in at the time.

Strangers are generally struck with the idea that the Looes must be uncommonly warm in Summer, being so pent up with hills; but this is a great mistake, for, owing to the flux and reflux of the tides, and the form of the valleys, a fine refreshing air, even in the calmest weather, is constantly passing up or down the river, and consequently must ventilate the towns.

RIDES.

There are many charming rides about Looe (but I must confess the roads are not kept in the best order); that towards Plymouth is very pleasant, being for seven miles on the cliffs, not indeed calculated for a horse given to starting, but by no means dangerous to a steady one. Carriages are out of the question; but there is another road for carriages, safe though rather narrow for about eight miles, when you get on the turnpike leading from Liskeard to Plymouth.

PLAYDY.

The first beach you come to on the cliff road to Plymouth, and about three quarters of a mile from Looe, is called Playdy; why so called I know not. Just before you come to Playdy is a rock called Chough Rock, from choughs constantly building their nests in inaccessible parts of it. And here I may remark that the Cornish daw, with red legs and bill, is very seldom seen about our cliffs.

MILLENDREATH.

The next beach is Millendreath, a Cornish word, signifying the Mill on the Sands; and probably a mill once stood there.

SEATON.

The next and last beach you pass is Seaton, which brings you to Downderry Cliffs and Battern Cliffs, or Cleaves, as usually called. History states there was once a town on the mouth of the river Seaton, and that it was probably a Roman town of some importance. No remains of it are now to be seen; and if a town did stand there, which I much doubt, the sea and sands have usurped its place, for here the defalcations of the coast have been very considerable, if we may regard the tradition of the neighbourhood. There is a place called Seaton in Devonshire. Camden, speaking of it, says, "As for Seaton, I would guess it to be that Moridunum which Antoninus speaketh of, and is placed between Durnovaria and Isca (if the Book be not faulty), and called in Pentegerius' Table by a name cut short, Ridunum, considering both the distance and the signification of the name. For Moridunum, in the British tongue, is the very same as Seaton in English, to wit, a town upon a hill by the sea." Perhaps Seaton near Looe may have been confounded with Seaton in Devonshire, or *vice versa*. Can Downderry Cliffs (which commence at Seaton near Looe) be a corruption of Durnovaria, Durnvery, Downderry? But Isca must mean, I should suppose, Exeter. I know of no place called any thing like Isca, near Looe, unless Pellis-Court, situate near Millendreath, the next rivulet West of Seaton river, about two miles distant, might originally have been called Pell-Isca.

LONG STONE. — WRINKLE.

Just below Battern Cleaves stands a high rock in the sea (not far from the land) called Long Stone; a little to the Eastward of which are a few houses, and a pier called Wrinkle, or Port Wrickle.

CRAFTHOLE.

The first village you come to is Crafthole; and here you get into the turnpike road. Just before you come to Crafthole you pass by

ST. GERMAN'S BEACON.

Near to which, in the side of the cliff, the Earl of St. German's has lately erected a look-out house, commanding an extensive and beautiful sea-view.

The road towards Liskeard is tolerably good and pleasant. About three miles on this road you arrive at

BINDOWN HILL*;
from whence is seen one of the most extensively cultivated prospects in the county, terminated on the North by the Mountains of CARRADON and HINGSTON †; the latter long famous for its store of tin. There is a very old saying respecting this hill:

> Hingston Down well y'wrought
> Is worth London Town dear y'bought.

At present there are a few works of no great consequence on Hingston; but it is astonishing more adventurers are not set on there, as copper is found there as well as tin.

---

* The elevation of Bindown is 658 feet above low water mark. About fifty years since, the furze on this down being set on fire, for improving the pasturage, and it being done after a long drought, the fire got below the surface among the roots, and continued burning for a fortnight or three weeks, as I was told by a person who saw it.

Latitude of Bindown, very accurately ascertained.
    50° 23' 33". Ph. Trans. 1800, p. 644.
Longitude West of Greenwich
    4° 24' 41". In time 17m 38.7s.

And the Latitude and Longitude of the entrance of Looe River, deduced from thence, will be
  Lat. 50° 21' 4". Long. 4° 26' 11". In time 17m 44.7s.

† The elevation of Hingston is 1067 feet, and Carradon 1208. Hensburrow has generally been looked upon as the highest hill in Cornwall; but it is now found to be only 1026 above low water mark; so that Carradon is 182 feet higher, and Hingston 41. Brownwilly, however, is the highest hill in Cornwall, its elevation being 1368 feet. [Extracted from "An Account of the Trigonometrical Survey carried on in the Years 1797, 1798, and 1799, by Order of Marquis Cornwallis, Master-general of the Ordnance." Philosophical Transactions, 1797, p. 471.]

DRAKEWALLS MINE

has at times produced copper and tin, but, generally speaking, may be termed a tin mine. This mine has been in working for one hundred and fifty years, as I ascertain from documents in my own possession, being part owner of the bounds in which it lies, and is, perhaps, the most antient working mine in the county.

HINGSTON HILL

was antiently the place of General Assembly for the Tinners, both of Cornwall and Devon, where they were accustomed to meet to concert the common interest of both parties.

The Danes, about the year 833, having equipped a great naval armament, landed in Cornwall, and, being joined by the Britons, they advanced towards the borders of Devonshire, with a view to penetrate into the territories of Egbert, King of the West Saxons, who gave them battle at Hingston Hill, near Callington (originally, probably, Killingtown, where the battle was fought), where they were totally routed, and almost their whole united army cut in pieces.

FOWEY AND LOSTWITHIEL.

There are also tolerable roads towards Fowey and Lostwithiel. Fowey is about nine miles from Looe, and Lostwithiel twelve. Those who are unacquainted with Cornish miles must, however, be informed that they by no means lack of measure.

WATER EXCURSIONS.

Water Excursions from Looe may be either up the rivers (for there are two of them, as before mentioned) or at sea. Each of the rivers is navigable for about two miles up the country, and brings you to public fruit-gardens and farmers' houses, where milk and cream and syllabubs may be obtained. One of these rivers (the Eastern), as I have before stated, brings you to Sand-place. Just above the houses is an eminence called Tregarland Torr, well worth the trouble of ascending on account of the fine prospect it presents. I have heard it remarked, that, were it not for this eminence, the sea would be visible from some parts of the town of Liskeard.

The road which leads from Sand-place to Duloe Church is called

KIPPISCOMBE LANE,

probably from a consecrated well on the right hand side of the road. The titular saint of this well is supposed to have been St. Cuby, now corrupted into Keby's Well. The spring flows into a circular basin or reservoir of granite, or of some stone like it, two feet four inches at its extreme diameter at top, and about two feet high. It appears to have been neatly carved and ornamented in the lower part with the figure of a griffin, and round the edge with dolphins, now much defaced. The water was formerly carried off by a drain or hole at the bottom, like those usually seen in fonts and piscinas. This basin (which I take to be an old font) was formerly much respected by the neighbours, who conceived some great misfortune would befal the person who should attempt to remove it from where it stood, and that it required immense power to remove it. A daring fellow, however (says a story), once went with a team of oxen for the express purpose of removing it. On his arrival at the spot one of the oxen fell down dead, which so alarmed the fellow that he desisted from the attempt he was about to make. There are several loose stones scattered round this basin or reservoir, perhaps the remains of some building which formerly inclosed it — a small chapel likely. The last time I saw this reservoir it had been taken many feet from where it used to stand; and a piece of the brim of it had been recently struck off.

DRUIDICAL CIRCLE OF STONES.

At a short distance (about North-east) from Duloe Church there is a circle of stones, supposed to have been formed by the Druids. It consists of seven or eight stones, one of which is about nine feet high; four of the others are upright; but the remainder are either broken or concealed by a hedge, which divides the circle, part being in a field and part in an orchard. Its diameter is about twenty-five feet.

SEA EXCURSIONS.

The Sea Excursions may be to the Island, about a mile off, where parties very frequently go to dine and spend the day in the Summer, carrying provisions with them. Lobsters and crabs may be bought of the inhabitants; and a dish of the finest prawns may be taken from the pools, and an appetite caught by the operation. From the top of the Island, in clear weather, you command a sea prospect from the Bolt to the Manacles, beyond Falmouth, a sweep of upwards of twenty leagues, or sixty miles. The Promontory called the Deadman, or Dodman, is situated about half-way from Looe to the Manacles; its elevation 379 feet.

Another excursion by sea may be to the very romantic town of

POLPERRO *,

about three miles West of Looe; and the visitors

---

* Pol, in Cornish, is a Pool, and Pry, Mud. Whether Polperro derives its name from these words, I will not take upon me to say; but I think it is probable it does. It is sometimes called, by way of reproach, Pol-Stink; not unlikely a corruption of Pol-Stagen; Stagen, in Cornish, a Standing Pool; and, as the sea makes a large pool, round which the town is situate, it may have assumed the name from that circumstance. Tonkin, however, says that Polperro is a corruption of Porthpara, *id est*, the Sandy Port.

may almost always be certain of a dish of fish and a leg of mutton for dinner. At the Ship Inn it has been a custom for many years to lay in a leg of mutton for every day of the year. Polperro is a populous place; vessels of 150 tons perhaps are able to come alongside their pier. The town lies in a very deep and narrow vale, in the parishes of Talland and Lansallos, the river, which runs through the town, dividing the parishes. At Polperro some tolerable slate for covering of houses is found; some of it is of a grey colour, and some of it is red. It is rather coarse and thick; but some people prefer it to finer slate, as, from its weight and roughness, it holds on the roof firmer than that of a finer quality. Some of the houses in Polperro are built with the stone raised on the spot on which the houses stand, and are covered in with slate also raised from the same spot; so that in clearing a foundation for the house, wall-stones and covering-stones are met with in sufficient quantity to build and slate it. The road from Looe to Polperro is very hilly. Part of this road passes over a field called Sander's Hill, and there lies upon a bed of red and grey slate, in a decomposed state above; but probably fine slate might be found underneath.

I have been informed that, about a century ago, the people of Polperro had such a dialect among them that even the inhabitants of Looe could scarce understand what they said. Of late years, however, from associating more with strangers, they have nothing particularly striking in their mode of speech, except a few of the old people. A voyage to the Eddystone is a great undertaking, but amply repays those who venture to see it. Parties sometimes go there in an open boat, but it is rather hazardous.

LUGGER'S COVE.

At Whitsand Bay there is a cavern worth seeing called Lugger's Cove, and no doubt an excursion to it by water would be very pleasant. I have never seen this place, but am informed it was scooped out of a solid rock by a Mr. Lugger, who lived near it, during the American war. The depth within is near fifteen feet, and the height near seven feet, and proportionally broad. Benches of stone are formed on each side, sufficient to accommodate about twenty persons. The roof is formed like the Gothic arch. This work is said to have cured Mr. Lugger of the gout, to which he was very much subject.

FISHING.

Persons fond of fishing may find ample amusement at or near Looe. Young pullock and conger eels are taken with a rod and line from the bridge and quays. Flounders (commonly called flukes at Looe) and sometimes turbot are taken with the spear just above the bridge. Farther up the river trout, peal, grey mullet, and salmon fry, are to be met with. Fine bass are often caught in the mouth of the river; and in the salmon season plenty are here taken by drag-nets. Upwards of fourscore have been taken at a draught. The salmon fishery at Looe has commenced within forty years last past. Formerly, it is said, a salmon was scarcely ever met with at Looe; but now every season produces abundance; they are taken not only by drag-nets, but also by nets of a large mesh, put out in dark nights, when the salmon swim against them, thrust their noses through the meshes, and, not being able to extricate themselves, are taken the next morning.

The fish caught on the coast in the neighbourhood of Looe are turbot, sole, flounder, John Dory, plaice, skate*, thornback, red mullet, grey mullet, salmon, cod, ling, conger, hake, mackarel, scads, pilchards, herrings, whiting, bream, chad, pullock, bass, horn or garr-fish, commonly called long noses, &c. &c. &c. Crabs, lobsters, crawfish, prawns,

---

* Skate, scads, and long noses, though in some places esteemed, are here sold for a mere trifle, or cut up to bait crab-pots. The bone of the latter fish, when boiled, is as green as a leek; and I have been told, though I never tried the experiment, that this fish, being cut in pieces, and put into a pan of milk, prevents its creaming. The *acus vulgaris*, or garr-fish, the crocodile, and the parrot, are the only known animals who have their upper jaw moveable. *Ray's Synops. Pisc.*

cockles, muscles *, wrinkles, limpets. Formerly fine large oysters were found above the bridge and in the mill-pool; but of late years few are to be met with, perhaps the increase of mud has destroyed them.

THE PURPURA.

The Purpura (though not the same species which produced the Tyrian Dye) is to be met with in great abundance on the rocks and about the Quays, it is a turbinated testaceous fish of about three-quarters of an inch long, and produces a most charming colour for marking linen, but in small quantity. I remember being shown many years ago another species of Purpura not inclosed in a shell, a very ugly-looking animal, about the size of a hen's egg, found at the rocks called the Limits or Limicks †, a little to the eastward of Looe ‡. Sandys, in his Book of

---

* Muscles were so plenty, about thirty years since, under the quays, &c. as completely to cover the ground and the lower part of the quays and bridge; but of late years they are greatly diminished; some think owing to the vast quantity of lime-stone thrown into the river. Barges are constantly bringing limestone from Plymouth, and it is thrown into the river, from whence flat-bottomed barges carry it up the rivers to the limekilns, which are numerous, there to be burnt for manure.

† It is not improbable that these rocks may be so called from these animals, or from the great quantity of wrinkles there found, Limax (Lat.) signifying a snail, or dew-snail.

‡ Since writing the above I have obtained one of these fish,

Travels, speaking of Tyre, says, "This City did justly boast of her purples, the best of all other, and taken hereabout. A kind of shell-fish having in the midst of his jaws a certain white vein, which contained that precious liquor; a die of sovereign estimation. The invention thereof is ascribed unto Hercules, who walking along the shore with a damsel whom he loved, by chance his dog had seized on one thrown up by the sea, and smeared his lips with the tincture, which she admiring, refused to be his until he had brought her a garment of that colour; who not long after accomplished it. The blood, together with the opened veins, were stilled in a vessel of lead, drawn through a limbeck, with the vapour of a little boiling water. The tongue of a purple is about the length of a finger, so sharp and hard, that he can open therewith the shell of an oyster, which was the cause of their taking. For

---

caught in a shrimping net, and have it now before me in a bason of water. Sometimes it takes the resemblance of a very large dew-snail, and then draws itself up to the resemblance of a tortoise; now and then it thrusts out four antennæ like a snail, and shrinks them back when touched. It has coloured the water with a most beautiful purple, and on my throwing in a small quantity of salt, it has emitted a quantity of this purple liquid.

N. B. I did not know at the time I wrote this note, that Borlase had mentioned this animal, but have since found that he has described it almost in the same words; and what is odd enough he tried the same experiment with salt. I did it with the idea the fish would take it for a flow of the tide, and become more agile; it seems a very dull inactive animal.

the fishermen did bait their weeles therewith, which they suffered to sink into the bottom of the sea, when the purples repairing thereunto, did thrust their tongues between the osiers, and pricking the gaping oysters (kept for that purpose long out of the water), were by the sudden closing of their shells retained; who could neither draw them unto them, nor approach so near as to open them. They gathered together in the first of the spring, and were nowhere to be found at the rising of the dog-starre. The fishermen strove to take them alive, for with their lives they cast up that tincture. The colour did differ according to the coasts which they frequented: on the coasts of Africa resembling a violet, or the sea when enraged; near Tyrus a rose, or rather our scarlet, which name doth seem to be derived from them, for Tyrus was called Sar, in that built upon a rock, which gave a name unto Syria (as the one at this day Sur, and the other Suria) by the Arabians (they pronouncing Scan for San, and Scar for Sar), and the fish was likewise named Sar, or Scar rather in their language," Lib. III. p. 168. Possibly our sur mullet may have derived its name from this word sar, the scarlet or red mullet, and the name given to it by the Phœnicians who traded here for tin.

The Editor of the Gentleman's Magazine for 1809, p. 53, under title " Review of Montague's Natural History of British Shells, &c." says:

" We will only extract one more passage from

this valuable Performance, respecting the Tyrian dye, the Purpura of the antients, which is known to be extracted from a species by no means uncommon with us, the Buccinium lupillus. The part containing the colouring matter is a slender longitudinal vein, just under the skin on the back behind the head, appearing whiter than the rest of the animal; the tenacious matter within this vein is of the consistence of cream, and when put on linen with a hair pencil it becomes at first yellowish, then pale green, changing to a bluish cast, and fixing in a purple red. This stain, as far as our experience goes, is indestructible: neither the nitrous nor vitriolic acid had any power to change the colour; and aqua regia, with or without a solution of tin and marine acid, had not power to produce a change. We, therefore, strongly recommend the use of this fluid for the purpose of marking linen; it is to be procured easily, as every individual of the species, whether male or female, is constantly furnished with it."

NATURAL HISTORY.—SHELLS.—SEA-WEEDS.

Looe Island and the Cliffs about Looe produce vast quantities of SAMPHIRE and SEA-PINKS; and from the sands may be gathered some beautiful SHELLS, the local name for them is castle-beads.

Various sorts of SEA-WEEDS * of singular form and colour are to be met with, and no doubt the Botanist might find much entertainment by exploring the island and cliff productions; and here I cannot help observing, that in the spring, almost every old wall and chimney in East Looe is adorned with a very beautiful and fine smelling yellow flower, called by the inhabitants HEARTSEEDS, probably a corruption of Heart's-ease from its fragrant smell. I never observed any of these flowers at West Looe, or elsewhere out of East Looe, except in gardens. They produce an immense quantity of seed, and wherever the wind drives it, it takes root and grows most luxuriantly †.

Borlase, in his History of Cornwall, has given a description of a truncated SLOW-WORM common at Looe, communicated to him by a Mr. Jago, who formerly lived here, and was Chaplain of Looe chapel. There is also in that work a print and description of a PETEREL, communicated by the same gentleman. The truncated slow-worm is frequently

---

* That kind of Sea-weed from which Kelp is made, grows in vast abundance on the rocks round Looe Island and the Cliffs, and I should think it would be very advantageous to convert it into kelp.

The Alva Lactuca, common laver, is, in its season, very plentiful on the beach before Looe. Fucus Esculentus—Lin. See Stackhouse's Nereis Britannica.

† A friend informs me that he believes it to be the Cheiranthus Cheiri—Lin. He says it has found a place in our gardens, where it has produced a considerable number of varieties, but none which have more delightful scent than the wild ones.

met with about the hill and in the gardens, and I apprehend does not sting. Not long since I could not account for the great number of parts of these animals which I frequently saw in my court, till one day seeing a young cat which I had, playing with something, I found it was one of these slow-worms; the cat after playing with them ate them, and this I have since had several opportunities of observing, and not much to my satisfaction, for sometimes puss would introduce them to the parlour. I once saw my cat with a large adder in its mouth: the cat had so wounded the adder, that it could not close its jaws.

The PETEREL is a Bird very rarely seen but at Sea. On the first of November, 1795, and for several days after, however, great numbers of these birds were seen flying about Looe River. Observing boys throwing stones at the birds which came very near them, and noting that their flight was different from that of Swallows, though they were much like Swallows in plumage, shape, and size, I was led to inquire what birds they were, and by offering a reward to the boys I soon after procured one. Some hundreds were flying about, and I attributed it to the very boisterous weather we had had for some time. The bird is about the size and much like a Swallow, but has an aquiline bill and webbed feet, with three claws on each; the feathers black, except those on the rump, which are white, and the tail not forked. Seamen usually call them Mother Carey's Chicken; others, the Stormy Peterel.

STORMS.

Mentioning Storms brings to my recollection the most awful clap of thunder, which burst over this place on the 21st of February, 1799; it happened about six o'clock in the evening. My window-shutters being closed, I did not see the lightning, but expected from a violent hail shower which then fell, that it would, as is frequently the case, be accompanied by a clap of thunder, having just before seen several flashes of lightning on my return from a walk. On a sudden the thunder burst like the firing of two of the largest cannon, one immediately after the other, and as if quite close to or rather in my house; the fright drove me from my chair into the middle of the room; those in the kitchen came shrieking into the parlour, and thought the kitchen window was burst in. Every one in the two towns described the thunder alike, and several females fainted with the fright; those who saw the lightning say the thunder followed instantaneously, which indicates its nearness. I had no doubt of hearing some grand effect of this ever-to-be-remembered explosion. The next morning I was informed it had broken down the Flag-post at our Four-gun battery on the hill, and had done other damage there. I immediately went to see it, and found the Flag-post broken off about half way down; the post was between twenty and thirty feet long, and had an iron spill on its top. What remained of the post had a spiral furrow on it, of about the width of a man's hand above, and diminishing gradually as it descended, and this furrow was about an inch in depth at the upper part. About five feet from the ground, the electric matter quitted the post, and fell on the side-wall of the battery; this it threw down, and spattered the guns with its rubbish. It seems then to have been attracted by the guns; a small piece of the axle of the left-hand front wheel of the gun next the post was struck off; the next gun had a piece of the axle of the left-hand wheel behind struck off, and there appeared a tinge, as if the electric fire had come out from the gun-carriage just by the axle; but I could not then discover any aperture or other appearance of any kind on the other side. A few days after, however, the passage of the electric fluid became very visible by a tinge on the paint; from this wheel it appeared to have been attracted by the foremost wheel on the same side, and from thence to have descended into the earth, having made a hole or pit therein close by this wheel three-feet deep, and fourteen inches diameter at top, and nearly the same diameter at bottom; it also split the wedge of this gun into two pieces. The lightning was described to me as being quite blue, and rooms not having window-shutters up appeared to be filled with real flame. A woman with a pan of milk before her and the window open, described the lightning as running round the milk-pan, and giving the milk the appearance of brandy or other spirit set on fire. I procured the upper part of the piece of the post which was struck off, and which was thrown at a distance, and also the iron spill; a small splinter at the top of this piece was only struck off, and not running very spirally the iron spill lost its top, which appeared to have been melted off. Extreme darkness continued for about half an hour after the thunder, and then a fine star-light succeeded, and no more lightning was seen for the night. The wind was about South-west.

It may not be improper to add another account of the effects of a storm of thunder and lightning at Looe and its neighbourhood, on the 27th of June, 1756, as communicated to the Rev. Dr. Jeremiah Milles, F.R.S. in two letters, one from the Reverend Mr. Dyer, Minister of Looe; and the other from the Reverend Mr. Milles, Vicar of Duloe in Cornwall,—Read before the Royal Society.

"On Sunday the 27th of June last, it grew on a sudden as dark as a winter evening; soon after the lightning began to flash, and the thunder to roar. The claps were near and extremely loud, and the lightning was more like darting flames of fire, than flashes of enkindled vapour. Happily no damage was done to the town of Looe, which lies very low; but at Bucklauren, a village situated on the top of a hill about two miles from hence, a farm-house was shattered in a most surprising manner. The house fronts the South, the windows of the hall and parlour, and of the chambers over them, which are in the front of the house are sashed; the dairy window is the only one on the West-side of the house; the chimnies are on the North-side, and at the Southwest corner there is a row of old elms on a line with the front, the nearest of which is ten feet distant from the house. The lightning seems to have had a direction from the South-west to the North-east. It first struck the bevelled roof of the South-west corner, near the eaves of the house; made a large breach, and tore up the floor of a garret near the place where it entered, and descended by the West wall, in oblique lines, into the chamber over the parlour; but not having sufficient vent that way, it darted in a line from S.W. to N.E. against the North-wall of the garret, where meeting with resistance, it broke down the floor near the North-wall many feet wide, and, carrying the ceiling of the parlour chamber before it, ran down by the wall of that room in direct lines; where it descended on the West and North walls; it made large and deep furrows in the plaster, and even tore out the stones and the mortar; a large splinter was struck off from the bed-post contiguous to the North-wall, and the bed was set on fire; the chimney-piece was broken into many parts, the window frame was moved out of the wall, every pane of glass was broken, the under sash was torn in pieces, and a large piece of the chimney-board was thrown out of the window against an opposite garden-wall about twenty feet from the

milk the appearance of brandy ... the window
fire. I procured the upper part ... wall and the
post which was struck ... vered, where it
at a distance, and also ... ued in a direct
ter at the top of this ... a great distance
not running very ... ng this dreadful
which appeared to ... was not spent, the
darkness continu... ... discharge. From
thunder, and th... ... t descended by the
more lightning ... ...er it, which is wain-
was about S ... ...e whole breadth of

It may ... ...gs from the wainscot,
of the eff... ...re in the buffet, shi-
Looe an... ...oom, and, ripping off a
1756, ...oor, burst it open, and
Mill... ...n the window, the frame
Mr. ... ...he wall, and the glass
the ... ...he bottle-room there was
wa... ...on wainscoting, which
... ...e hall, about eight inches
s... ...nrough this crevice the
l... ... which serves at present
... ...g with some pewter in its
... ...e shelf about the rooms,
... ...r that stood in the corner,
... ...e a trembling and desultory
... ...ps into the chimney, and
... ...ood there into the middle
... a large brass pot out of its
... ...r a table, and then darted

… in the windows, carrying away a pane of glass … out of the upper sash to the distance of many feet. The mistress of the house and her son were sitting at this window. They were the only persons in the house, and providentially received no hurt. Some part of the lightning found a way between the door and door-case of the hall. The door is pannelled, and the lightning in passing through penetrated into a close mortice, and split off a large splinter from the outside of the door, close to the tenon. In its course it left a smoky tinge on the wall and timber, like that of fired gunpowder; a sulphureous smell remained in the house for many hours. Another (or probably a part of the same) flash of lightning struck the dairy window, melted the lead, and burnt the glass where it penetrated, and set the window-frame on fire; from thence it darted in a line from S.W. to N.E. downward, made a large hole in a plastered partition near the floor into the barn, shattered a large paving rag-stone in pieces, and, turning up the ground, I suppose sunk into the earth. The elms were affected with the lightning, particularly that nearest the house, from the top of which to the root appeared large furrows in the moss which grew on the bark, in some places in an irregular spiral, but for the most part in a perpendicular line, and from the root of it the ground was torn up in furrows, as if done with a plough-share, about six feet long, the furrows gradually lessening, according to their distance from the tree. All this was done instantaneously. How amazingly swift, subtle, and powerful is the force of lightning!

    I am, Rev. Sir,
        Your most obedient Servant,
            JAMES DYER."

A Letter from the Rev. Mr. MILLES on the same subject:

"About four of the clock on Sunday afternoon, the same day that the lightning struck the farm-house at Bucklawren, it fell upon another house, called Pelyne, in the parish of Lanreuth, about six miles distant. The house fronts the East. The chimney, which is at the North end, is cracked, and opened about two or three inches wide from the top to the roof, where it entered the slating through a small hole on the Eastern side, forced its way through the upper chamber, where it melted an old copper skillet, a pair of sheep-shears, and some old brass buckles and candlesticks that lay on the wall; consumed the laths adjoining, and then made its way through a small crevice in the upper part of the window. Another and more severe part of the same lightning descended the chimney, struck two women who were sitting on each side of it, without any further hurt, overturned a long table that was placed before the window in the ground room upon two men who were sitting on the inside with their backs towards the window. One of the men was miserably burnt in his right arm. The lightning seems to have struck him a little above the elbow, making a small orifice about the bigness of a pea. The burn from thence to the shoulder is near an inch deep. His right thigh was likewise burnt on the inside, and the outside of his right leg, from a little below his knee, quite over the ancle, to his toes. Both knees were burnt across slightly, and his left thigh. His shirt sleeve and the upper part of his waistcoat were reduced to tinder; the buckles in his shoes were melted in different parts and in different directions. He has not been able to use his arm since, and is under the care of a surgeon, who has reduced the wound to a hand's breadth, which was in the beginning advancing fast towards a mortification. The other man was but slightly wounded. The lightning afterwards found its way through the window in three different places, and melted the glass, leaving a smutty tinge like that of fired gunpowder. A boy about ten years old, son to the under-tenant, was also struck down, as he was standing at the door, but not hurt. The father and his daughter felt no ill effects, but saw the lightning roll on the floor, and thought the room was on fire."

From the foregoing statements it may be thought by some that the Looes are particularly obnoxious to thunder-storms; but I do not think that this is the case, not more so than any other part of the county. Nor do I think that we have more rain than elsewhere; indeed I rather think we have less rain than even Liskeard has, which is only eight miles from us. The high hills in the vicinity of Liskeard probably attract the passing clouds, and produce partial showers which do not reach us; and most certainly we have not so much rain as the Plymouth Calendar states to fall there; nor are our prognosticks of the weather similar. The Plymouth Calendar states that there

> The South wind always brings wet weather;
> The North wind, wet and cold together.
> The West wind always brings us rain;
> The East wind blows it back again.
> If the sun in red should set,
> The next day surely will be wet;
> If the sun should set in grey,
> The next will be a rainy day.

On the 27th of May, 1792, about half past twelve o'clock at night, I felt the shock of an earthquake at Looe. It was accompanied by a noise like distant thunder. I was awake at the time this earthquake happened, and hearing the distant thunder, as I first thought it, I was struck with the idea how such distant thunder should shake my bed candlestick by my bedside, and thereon concluded it to be an earthquake. On coming down stairs next morning, I said to my servant that I believed there was an earthquake last night. The answer was, that many people in town were speaking of it. I afterwards found it was felt at Liskeard, and at various places in the neighbourhood.

ORE.

Though no metallic Ore of any kind has been discovered near Looe, yet if confidence may be given to the Virgula Divina, a load of some kind of metal passes under the houses near the Conduit in East Looe. This I was informed of by the late Miss Elizabeth Debell, of East Looe, who stated that her cousin Wm. Cookworthy (the late celebrated Chemist, of Plymouth), made several trials with the rod outside her Quay door, at the back of her house near the Conduit, and who was persuaded from his trials that such was the fact. Mr. Cookworthy always put great confidence in the divining rod.

ROADS.

Looe, by its vicinity to Plymouth, is a much more considerable thoroughfare than is generally imagined, travellers on horseback preferring this road to that inland, on account of its cutting off a pretty considerable angle, and on account of the fine sea prospect. I think it would answer very well if a carriage were to run from Torpoint to Lostwithiel or Fowey through Looe, and so back again, once a week. There is no carriage kept at Looe except a tilted cart, which goes once a week to Torpoint.

On the 16th of September, 1814, an actual measurement of the road from Looe to Crafthole was made by the Custom-house officers, and the result was as follows:

	M.	Q.	P.
From the bottom of Castle Street in East Looe to the four gun battery on the hill	0	1	0
— to Sander's Lane	0	2	0
— to Kellow Lane End	1	0	0
— to Seaton Bridge	3	2	0
— to upper turning on Battern Cleaves	5	0	0
— to lane leading down to Wrinkle	7	0	0
To Wrinkle Pier, being the extreme Eastern point of the Port of Looe	7	1	26
— to Crafthole Turnpike-gate	7	3	0

FAIRS.

East Looe by Charter has four Fairs yearly [*]:— 1. on the feast of St. Michael, and the vigil and morrow of the same feast; 2. on the Purification of the Blessed Virgin Mary, and the vigil and morrow; 3. on the first of May, and to continue by the space of two days next ensuing; 4. on the first of August, and to continue for two days next ensuing. These fairs were formerly of some consequence, but are now dwindled into nothing. There is indeed a pretty good fair holden at West Looe on the sixth of May. Regular chartered fairs owe their destruction to the great number of these parish fairs, com-

---

[*] East Looe, in the reign of Edward I. as appears by the claim of Henry de Bodrigan, then lord of the manor, possessed a market and fair, a ducking-stool and a pillory.

monly called Shews of Cattle, now holden in almost every parish by the prerogative of the neighbouring farmers. How far such fairs may be legal or beneficial to the State may be well worthy the consideration of those superintending the policy of the country. The regular market-day at East Looe is Saturday. Though the market is small, the market-place is one of the largest in the county, and no doubt was formerly fully occupied. There is no market at West Looe, though they are entitled to hold one by charter every Wednesday; and two fairs, one on the feast of St. Mark and for three days after, and the other on the fifteenth day of October and for two days after. This latter fair has been long discontinued.

PROPOSED CANAL.

A few years since it was in agitation to get a Canal formed from Looe to Liskeard, and an actual survey was made by Messieurs Bentley and Bolton, of Birmingham, but, owing to the difficulty of effecting such a work, it was given over. The length of the line surveyed for the intended canal, from the end of Market Street, Liskeard, to a place called Steps, in Morval parish, was found to be only six miles and three quarters; but many locks would have been required from Lodge Barton to the town of Liskeard. Great advantages would certainly have arisen to Liskeard and the neighbourhood had such a work been formed. Lime and sand for manure, and merchandize goods imported at Looe, would have furnished the boats going up the canal, and the various productions of the country the boats coming down. Much waste land in the parishes of St. Pinnock, St. Neot, and St. Cleer, and neighbouring parishes, would have found the good effects thereof. Though a canal is not practicable, I should however think, if a turnpike was made from Sand-place to the turnpike leading from Lostwithiel to Liskeard, it would be found of considerable advantage, and might be effected at a trifling comparative expence to that of a canal.

SEA-BATHING.

From the situation of the two Looes, and the conveniency of sea-bathing, one should have imagined that they would be more frequented in Summer than they usually are. It may be thought, perhaps, that proper accommodation cannot be met with; but it may be answered that few watering-places at their outset are furnished with better. Tolerably decent lodgings may generally be obtained; and there can be no doubt but accommodations would keep pace with the demand for them. Several new houses have lately been built at Looe. When the bathing-machine was in existence, it could be used many hours in the day. It was let into the water and drawn out by means of a capstan; and, owing to the convenience of the beach, the bather did not enter it till it was in its proper place for bathing, and then walked into it immediately from the beach.

POST.

The Post comes in from Polperro every morning about ten o'clock; goes on to Liskeard, and returns every evening. The regulation for conveyance of letters from Looe to Polperro is a very curious one. If a letter is put into Looe office for Polperro after the post is gone from Looe to Liskeard, it lies in Looe office all that day and all the next night. It is then sent to Liskeard; brought back again to Looe in the evening, and then carried on to Polperro; which takes up about two days and one night for a distance of three miles, and is actually carried near twenty miles.

POPULATION.

On the 10th of March, 1801, the Overseers of the Poor of East Looe and West Looe, by virtue of the Act 41 Geo. III. proceeded to take an account of the Population of these Boroughs; their returns were as follow:

East Looe.

Houses inhabited 117; occupied by 143 families. Uninhabited houses 9. Males 207; females 260; total 467.

At the next Census, May 27, 1811:— Inhabited houses 128; occupied by 168 families. Uninhabited houses 14. Males 254; females 354; total 608. Males increased 47; females ditto 94; total increase 141.

At the Census May 28, 1821:— Inhabited houses 128; occupied by 169 families. Uninhabited houses 14. Males 337; females 433; total 770. Males increased 83; females ditto 79; total increase 162.

West Looe.

March 10, 1801:— Houses inhabited 79; occupied by 85 families. Uninhabited houses 3. Males 164; females 212; total 376.

At the next Census, May 27, 1811:— Houses inhabited 92; occupied by 112 families. Uninhabited houses 1. Males 191; females 242; total 433; increase 57.

At the Census May 28, 1821:— Males 236; females 303; total 539; increase 106.

TIDES.

It is high water at Looe, at new and full moon, about half after five o'clock in the evening. The water reaches the bridge at half-tide. When very high tides happen (which is generally the case about the equinoxes, particularly the vernal one) the principal street in East Looe is inundated, and, as most of the houses are sunk down a step below the street, they get filled with salt water, unless sliding boards are put to the doors to prevent this mishap; and indeed this precaution will not do for some houses, for the water forces itself through the floors. How our ancestors came to form their houses with a step down instead of a step up is singular enough. I can only account for it that the buildings were erected in Summer, and that the inhabitants did not advert to Winter storms. And this brings to my mind the worthy old character Sir Roger de Coverley, who, making his will in a very cold Winter's day, ordered therein that his executors should give to each of his bearers a frieze great coat, to keep them warm while attending his funeral, not adverting that he might possibly die in the dog-days, when a frieze great coat would not be wanted to keep out the cold.

I have heard it remarked that the highest tides are at the new not the full moon; but I cannot say I ever made the observation. When high tides occur, so as to inundate the street, the waves, as they come into the river, occasion the water to rush up the street with great violence, at times rising two or three feet in height, and then retreating again till another wave comes in. This run of the water is locally called The Seech — they say, the Seech is coming, or the Seech is going back; and it has been thought by some persons that this word is a corruption of Surge. I find, in Sandys' Travels, that in Egypt officers called Sieches are appointed to give a warning to the people when the Nile begins to rise. And I also find that the Lake of Geneva, at times, overflows some of its shores, without any known cause for its so doing, and that this overflowing is there called The Seech. De Saussure thought that sudden local variations in the pressure of the atmosphere may account for the Seiches in the Lake of Geneva, and for analogous appearances elsewhere.

BALLAST.—FENCES AGAINST THE SEA.

The men of war at Plymouth, in times of peace, used to be ballasted with shingle taken from Looe Beach, at so much *per* ton, by permission of the Corporation. Immense quantities of this shingle having been taken away, the beach before East Looe became greatly reduced; and, as the town is built on sand and shingle, had this practice been continued, the place might have suffered materially by this cause.

An entry in one of the Town Books, dated about the year 1593, states, "that the inhabitants of this Borough were very much charged with the making, keeping, and maintaining of divers friths and fences against the sea, without the which the whole town were very likely to be overwhelmed, and in short time swallowed and sunk of the same." Thus thought our ancestors, and so ought the present inhabitants to think; for, should the Church-end-wall and Looe-quay-head be washed down, I think it highly probable that great part of East Looe would be washed down, for it would be impossible for the houses to withstand the force of the immense waves which at times are thrown in; and besides, as the houses are all built on sand, the waves would soon displace their foundations, and nothing could prevent their total ruin. The inhabitants, therefore, should be particularly attentive to keep Church-end-wall and Looe-quay-head in perfect repair.

On the night of the 19th of January, 1817, East Looe was in a perilous situation from the hurricane which then blew from the South-west; and it being the highest tide of the spring, the water rose very high and deluged many of the streets. The waves in the morning, just before day-break, were truly tremendous, and broke in over the wall at Church-end, the upper part of which wall they threw down, and also a court wall inside it. Had the gale continued to the next tide, most probably the chapel and several houses near it would have been destroyed. A rock about twenty feet high was washed out of the cliff under Looe Hill, and still stands, and may stand for ages, as a memorial of this great storm. In falling, it pitched on its bottom on the rocks below; is of a pyramidal form; and its weight must be several hundred tons *.

SITUATION.

There is some resemblance between the Looes and Weymouth and Melcombe Regis; but the Looes are upon a less scale, and have high land behind them. A river separates the two Looes, and a bridge connects them. A jutty-head runs out from the river just in the same manner and situation as that at Weymouth. Looe Island is situated to Looe as Portland to Weymouth; and the Ram Head runs out like St. Alban's: but I think the view towards the sea is preferable even to that of Weymouth.

---

* On the 28th of December, 1821, about two o'clock in the morning came on a very violent gale of wind from the Southeast, and continued, with heavy rain, till noon. My barometer fell to 28° 1¼', which was lower than I ever saw it before. We had a high tide in the morning, and my front parlour got full of water by its coming through the walls, or soaking up through the sand. The sea ran high, and the high rock above mentioned was thrown down, and in falling broken in two pieces.

WEST HUNDRED.

The Boroughs of East Looe and West Looe, as I stated in the beginning of this book, are situated in the hundred called West. As the derivation of the name of this hundred is not generally known, I shall add what Hals, in his "Parochial History of Cornwall," says of it, under the title "St. Cleather Vicarage."—" In this parish or part of Davidstow is Foys-fenton, signifying the Walled Spring of Water, or Well, the original fountain or source of the Foys River; which well in old records is also called West Fenton (*i. e.* the West Well), to distinguish it from Mark Well in Larrick, otherwise East Well; from which places the two cantreds of East-well-shire and West-well-shire are denominated. And to this purport it is evident, from Mr. Carew, that, *anno* 3 Henry IV. Reginald de Ferrer held in East Fenton and West Fenton several knights' fees of land of the honor of Tremeton, which are now East and West Hundreds." Before I met with this derivation of the name of Fowey River, I had a notion it might have been so called from the magnificent mound mentioned in the beginning of this book, which, as before stated, reaches to Lerryn, on the Fowey River; and that, as this mound might have been a Roman way, the Britons might have named the river, from this circumstance, Foe-way

River, or the river near the way or road of their foes, the Romans or other enemies.

The Hundred of West contains four towns, *viz.* Liskeard, East Looe, West Looe, and Polperro; and nineteen parishes, *viz.*

	Statute Acres.
Boconnock	1772
Broadoak	2935
Cardinham	7750
St. Cleer	9118
Duloe	5051
St. Kaine	769
Lanreath	4353
Lansallos	2774
Llanteglos by Fowey	2773
Liskeard	7126
St. Martin's	2719
Morval	2925
St. Neot	12739
Pelynt	4170
St. Pennock	2674
Talland	2208
St. Veep	2394
Warleggan	1807
St. Winnow	5501
Total	81558

GENTLEMEN'S SEATS.

The Boroughs of East and West Looe are, if I may use the expression, hedged in on the land side with Gentlemen's Seats. A compass extended three miles from Looe, and swept from the sea West to the sea East, would include the following seats, some of them at present, and the rest of them formerly, occupied by genteel families; viz. Talland, Killigarth, Trelawny, Tregarrick, Kilminorth, Port Looe, Polvellan, Trenant Park, Treworgey, Westnorth, Morval, Bray, Keveril. I have placed them just as they occur in the sweep of the compass, beginning from the West.

TALLAND.

The manor of Talland antiently belonged to a family called De Tallan. Nichol de Tallan was one of the witnesses to Treverbyn's Charter to West Looe, previous to the reign of Henry the Sixth. The heiress of this family married Murth about the middle of the sixteenth century. Arms of Tallan: Argent, a stag Gules, couchant on turf proper. This manor belonged, for many generations, to the family of Murth, or Morth, who possessed and resided on the Barton in Carew's time. It is now the property of John Morth Woolcombe, Esq. of Ashbury, in

Devon, by inheritance from the family of Murth. What remains of the old mansion is occupied as a farm-house. It is situated in a parish of the same name, Talland. — Tal-lan signifies in Cornish the High Church, and such is its situation. Tradition says that one of the Murth family had a French servant, who, upon a war breaking out with France, returned home, and shortly after landed near his old master's house, took him prisoner, together with his guests, at a Christmas supper, and forced him to redeem his liberty by a sacrifice of the greatest part of his fortune. I remember seeing in the old house (part of which was pulled down fifteen or twenty years since) a secret door-way behind a chest of drawers, which was said to have been placed there to prevent another mishap of the above or similar kind.

On the 10th of January, 1786, the Trecothick outward-bound West Indiaman, the day after she had sailed from Plymouth, being overtaken by a violent storm, and it being hazy weather, mistaking a point of land just under this house for Ram Head, ran ashore, and in a few hours was so completely dashed to pieces that a horse, as I was told, might have carried the largest piece of the wreck. Most of the people were drowned.

About a century since the Rev. Richard Dodge was vicar of this parish of Talland, and was, by traditionary accounts, a very singular man. He had the reputation of being deeply skilled in the black art, and could raise ghosts, or send them into the Red Sea, at the nod of his head. The common people, not only in his own parish but throughout the neighbourhood, stood in the greatest awe of him, and to meet him on the highway at midnight produced the utmost horror; he was then driving about the evil spirits; many of them were seen, in all sorts of shapes, flying and running before him, and he pursuing them, with his whip, in a most daring manner. Not unfrequently he would be seen in the church-yard at dead of night, to the great terror of passers-by. He was a worthy man, and much respected; but had his eccentricities.

He died at Talland, and was there buried, as the following inscription on his tomb-stone states:

"Here lieth the body of the Rev. Mr. RICHARD DODGE, late of Talland, Vicar, who departed this life the 13th day of January 1746, in the 93d year of his age."

KILLIGARTH.

The manor of Killigarth was, at an early period, the property and seat of a family of that name. John de Kylgat was one of those who had estates of 20*l. per annum*, or upwards, in the reign of Edward the First. The heiress of Killygarth brought this estate to the Beres in the reign of Henry the Sixth (and then, perhaps, the name of Killygarth became extinct); and the heiress of Bere to the grandfather of Sir William Beville, who was Carew's contemporary [*], and the last heir-male of an antient and respectable family. A coheiress of the Bevilles brought Killigarth to Sir Bernard Granville, who sold it to the Hallotts. Thomas Kendall, Esq. who married a coheiress of the last-mentioned family, left an only daughter, Mrs. Mary Kendall, who dying unmarried, in the year 1710, was buried in Westminster Abbey, by her own desire, near the

---

[*] Carew says, "The mention of this Knight calleth to my remembrance a sometimes uncooth servant of his, whose monstrous conditions partly resembled that of Polyphemus, described by Homer and Virgil, and lively imitated by Ariosto, in his Orco; or rather that Egyptian Polyphagus in whome (by Suetonius' report) the Emperour Nero took such pleasure. This fellow was taken up by Sir William under a hedge, in the deepest of Winter, wel neere starved with cold and hunger. He was of stature meane, of constitution leane, of face freckled, of composition well proportioned, of diet naturally spare, and cleanely enough; yet, at his master's bidding, he would devoure nettles, thistles, the pith of artichokes, raw and living birds, and fishes with their scales, and feathers, burning coles and candles, and whatsoever else, however unsavorie, if it might be swallowed; neither this a little but in such quantitie as it often had a second wonder how his belly should contain so much. Moreover, he would take a hot yron out of the fire with his bare hand; never changed his apparell but by constraint, and used to lie in strawe, with his head downe, and his heeles upwards. Spare he was of speech, and instead of halfe his words, used this term—Size—as, I will size him, for strike him — he is a good size, for man, &c. Over sleeping, or some other accident, made him lose a day in his account of the weeke, so as he would not beleeve but that Sunday was Saturday, Saturday Friday, &c. To Sir William he bore

monument of the Countess of Ranelagh, mother of her intimate friend, Lady Catherine Jones, as appears by the inscription on her own monument. This lady bequeathed Killygarth to the Rev. Nicholas Kendall, Archdeacon of Totness, grandfather of the Rev. Nicholas Kendall, of Pelyn, the late proprietor. So say Messieurs Lysons; but I have an extract from an unpublished manuscript which differs from it in some degree; thus: " John Bevil, of this place, Esq. was Sheriff of Cornwall in the

---

such faithfulnesse that he would follow his horse like a spanyell, without regard of way or wearinesse, waite at his chamber-doore the night-time, suffering none to come neare him, and performe whatsoever hee commanded, were it never so unlawful or dangerous. On a time his master, expecting strangers, sent him with a panier to his cater at the sea-side to fetch some fish. In his way he passed by a river, whereinto the tide then flowed, and certain fishermen were drawing their nets; which after John Size had a while beheld, he casts to have a share amongst them for his master. So into the water he leaps, and there, for the space of a flight shoot, wadeth and walloweth (for swimme he could not), sometimes up and sometimes downe, carrying his panier still before him, to his own extreme hazard of drowning, and the beholders' great pittying; until at last, all wet and wearied, out he scrambleth, and home he hieth, with a bitter complaint to his master of his ill fortune, that he could not catch some fish, as well as the rest, where so much was going. In this sort he continued for divers yeeres, untill (upon I wot not what veake or unkindnesse) away he gets, and abroad he rogues: which remitter brought him the end to his fore deferred and not avoyded destiny; for as under a hedge he was found pyning, so under a hedge he found his miserable death, through penury."

fourth and fifth of Philip and Mary. John Bevil (I suppose his son) was also Sheriff of Cornwall 16 Elizabeth, as was his son, William Bevil, Esq. (afterwards Sir William) 31 Elizabeth. The said Sir William was likewise Knight of the Shire 35 Elizabeth. Sir William's lady was re-married to Sir ... Manours; and, upon her decease, this, with the rest of Sir William's estate, came to Philip Bevil, Esq. of Brinn, whose only daughter and heir, Elizabeth Bevil, being married to Sir Bernard Granville, of Stow, brought it into that family, where it did not long continue, for their son, the famous Sir Bevil Granville, sold this lordship to ... Hollick, of Looe, merchant, whose daughter and coheir was married to Thomas Kendall, Esq. of Chiswick, in Middlesex, but son of ..... Kendall. This Mr. Kendall lived sometimes here, and, dying, left one sole daughter and heir, who dying unmarried, left this place, by will, to the Rev. Mr. Nicholas Kendall, Archdeacon of Totness, who chose this place for his residence, and resigned Pelyn to his eldest son, William Kendall, Esq. Mr. Thomas Kendall had a younger brother, Colonel James Kendall, who was Governor of Barbadoes, and was one of the Lords of the Admiralty under Queen Anne, and a Member of Parliament in several Parliaments. He died suddenly, unmarried, July 10, 1708, at his house in London, very rich."

In the Extent of Cornish Acres, 12 Edward I. this manor was valued in 9.

Killygarth, says Mr. Carew, being interpreted in English, signifieth "He hath lost his griping or reaching." Mr. Tonkin says that it signifieth " the Higher Grove," and that Mr. Carew's is a very ridiculous interpretation. The name, however, I think, is more likely to have been derived from the circumstances of the place, Killy signifying a Grove or Wood, and Garth is a British word, commonly denoting a steep elevated ride, or precipitous mountain, which tallies precisely with the place.

The Bere arms were, Argent, a bear saliant Sable; the Bevil's, Argent, a bull passant Gules, armed and tipped Or; the Killigarth's I have not been able to discover.

TRELAWNY.

The seat of the Rev. Sir Harry Trelawny, Clerk, and Baronet. This place at an early period belonged to the Bodrugans. Sir Henry de Bodrugan gave it as a marriage portion with his daughter to Henry Champernowne. The heiress of this branch of the Champernowns married Polglass; and the heiress of Polglass, Herle. Sir John Herle the younger, who died without issue, settled the reversion of Trelawny on Sir William (afterwards Lord) Bonville, the last of an antient Devonshire family. It was a remarkable circumstance attending this family, that the havock of civil war annihilated three generations within the space of two months. At the battle of Wakefield Lord Bonville witnessed the death of his son, Sir William Bonville, and of his grandson, William Lord Harington, who enjoyed that title as having married the heiress of Lord Harington of Harington. This was on the last day of December 1460. In the month of February following the aged grandfather was taken prisoner at the second battle of St. Alban's; and although his life had been promised, he was beheaded by order of the Queen, who bore resentment against him as having been one of those who had the King's person in custody after the battle of Northampton. Elizabeth Lady Harrington, after the accession of Edward IV. had a large dower assigned her out of Lord Bonville's estates in Cornwall. Her only daughter by Bonville brought Trelawny and other estates to Thomas Grey, Marquis of Dorset; on the attainder of whose grandson, Henry Duke of Suffolk, they were seized by the Crown.

Queen Elizabeth, in the 42d year of her reign, sold the manor of Trelawny (and the lands of Hendersich and Portallo, in Talland parish) to Sir Jonathan Trelawny. — Trelawny is a good old house; the hall is one of the largest and best in Cornwall; it is hung round with pictures of the family. The late King and Queen's pictures are also there, in full size, painted, I apprehend, by Sir Joshua Reynolds. In the drawing-room is a fine portrait, by Sir Godfrey Kneller, of Sir Jonathan

Trelawny, Bishop of Winchester, who was born here. Sir Jonathan was one of the seven Bishops sent to the Tower by King James II. In a genealogical achievement over the chimney there are no less than 37 coats of arms inserted.

Trelawny is a charming place, beautifully laid out by nature and art, finely wooded, and commands extensive and delightful views. It is in the parish of Pelynt. In the church of this parish is the following curious epitaph on Edward Trelawny, Esq.:

EDWARD TRELAWNY   Ana:
We wander, alter, dy.
O what a bubble, vapour, puff of breath,
A nut of worms, a lump of pallid earth,
Is mud-wald man: before we mount on high,
We cope with change, we wander, alter, dy.
Causidicum claudit tumulus (miraris) honestum —
Gentibus hoc cunctis dixeris esse novum.
Here lyes an honest lawyer, wot you what
A thing for all the world to wonder at.
June the 7, 1630.

The old and famous family of Trelawny took its name from the Barton of Trelawn-y, in the parish of Altarnun, in Cornwall. The name signifies either the Oak Grove Town, or the Wool Town by the Water, or the Open Town or Place, or Open Prospect or Clean Town.

The arms of the Trelawnys are, Argent, a chevron Sable, and sometimes charged with three oak-leaves proper, perhaps in allusion to the Oak Grove Town. It is said that Sir John Trelawny was so eminent in the wars of France that Henry the Fifth, Sept. 27, in his seventh year, at Gisors, in Normandy, granted him 20*l.* yearly for life, as a just recompence for his signal services. And Henry the Sixth was pleased to confirm it to him again, in the first year of that King's reign; and granted him, as it is said, an augmentation to his arms — three oaken or laurel leaves, the symbols of conquest (and perhaps with an allusion to the name). He was certainly the first of this family who bore that addition. Under the picture of Henry V. which stood formerly over the gate at Launceston, was this rhyme:

He that will do aught for mee,
Let him love well Sir John Trelawnee.

There was an antient saying in Cornwall; "That a Godolphin was never known to want wit, a Trelawny courage, or a Granville loyalty."

TREGARRICK

is also in the parish of Pelynt*, and was the chief seat in Cornwall of the Winslades, whose family

---

* "In Domesday — Plunent, from Plu, a Parish, and Nent, Nynn, Nunn, the Parish of St. Nunn. This, says Polwhele, is a harsh derivation. We have Pellyn, a place near Lostwithiel, with the addition of the letter (*t*), so frequent in Cornish; Pel-

were Hereditary Esquires of the White Spur. Spelman says that these Esquires were created by the King, being invested with a silver collar of S S and a pair of silver spurs; whence, in the West of England, they were called White Spurs. Weever adds, that the rank was hereditary to the elder son only. The manor of Tregarrick was forfeited by the attainder of John Winslade, Esq. who suffered death for being one of the ringleaders of the Cornish Rebellion in 1549. It was granted by King Ed-

---

lyn is lengthened at once into Pelynt, and contracted again into Plynt; and Pelen, a Spire, furnishes us with a much easier etymon." The parish is generally called Plint; and this may be a corruption of Pillynt, from Pill, a Bulwark, and Lhyn, a Grove. Pellyn or Pelhyn signifies the Head of the Grove; Pillhyn, the Bulwark and Grove; and may refer to the antient earthwork, entrenchment, and mound, spoken of in p. 64, which are situated in or near a grove.

The manor of Plunent was one of the 288 manors given by the Conqueror to the Earl of Moreton. Pelynt was of old the lands and church of the family surnamed De Cancellis, or Chanceaux, of Devon, of whom we read (in the Pleas of the Crown and the Inquisition of King John, in the twelfth year of his reign, Roll 33 in Northampton) that Nicholas de Chanceaux "tenet manerium de Upton in comitatu predict. quod est antiq. domin. coronæ regis per servitium inveniendi unum hominem armatum A. D. 1211." His son, Sir Giles de Cancellis, or Chanceaux, lord of the manor of Lifton, in Devon, and Plenint, in Cornwall, gave the manor of Plenint and the advowson of this church of Plint to the Abbey of Newhaven, in Devon, for the good of his soul, and lies therein interred; whence I conclude, says Hals, that these Chanceauxs endowed this church.

ward VI. to Sir Reginald Mohun; and purchased of him, in the succeeding reign, by John Trelawny, Esq. and Mrs. Margaret Buller. This manor, which was long held in moieties by the Trelawnys and Bullers, is now the sole property of the Rev. Sir Harry Trelawny, Bart. Tregarrick was the first seat of the Bullers when they came into Cornwall, in consequence of marrying the heiress of Trethurfe. The old mansion is now occupied as a farm-house.

Tre-ger-ick signifies the Town on the River — Tre-gerrick, Tre-gerry, the Green or Fruitful Place, or the Dwelling of Love.

KILMINORTH.

The manor of Kilminorth or Kilmenorth was parcel of the possession of Sir Robert Tresilian, Chief Justice of the King's Bench; on whose attainder it was granted to John Hawley, who married Emma, his daughter and heir. Hawley's only daughter and heir brought it to the Copplestones. I have seen a deed, dated January 25, 1621, by which Henry Pollard, then late of Killmynot, Esq. releases to William Martin, of Broadhempston, Devon, Gent. the fee of Killmynot, and other lands in the parish of Tallant, alias Talante. This estate, which is not now esteemed a manor, is the property of the Rev. Sir Harry Trelawny, Bart. by purchase from Mr. Cosserat. The Barton-house is occupied by a farmer.

Sir Charles Wager, Knt. in the early part of the la t century, made this place his residence. He is said by some authors to have been a native of West Looe; but I have not, in searching the Register of the parish of Talland (in which parish West Looe is), been able to find any name at all like that of Wager therein; and there is no tradition of where he was born, or from whence or from what family he came. I have heard that Sir Charles Wager was highly esteemed and respected in this neighbourhood*. There is a field in Kilminorth, not far from the house, called The Warren, surrounded by

---

* A Biographer, speaking of Sir Charles Wager, says, "This excellent officer and truly estimable man was one of those brave and enterprizing seamen who, by dint of their own merit, unassisted by powerful connections or influence, have acquired immortal reputation, and attained the highest ranks in their profession. His first appointment was that of Captain of the Fuzee fire-ship in 1692; soon after that, he was removed into an armed ship of forty-four guns, and sent to convoy a fleet of merchantmen bound to New England. During the latter part of the reign of King William, and the early part of that of Queen Anne, he commanded different line-of-battle ships, under Sir George Rooke, Sir Cloudesley Shovel, and Admiral Byng, and participated in the dangers and glory of those great men.

"In the Spring of the year 1707 he was sent, as commodore of a squadron, to the West Indies, and hoisted his broad pendant on board the Expedition, of seventy guns. His first care, on his arrival in the West Indies, was to provide for the security of the British Settlements; where he introduced such prudent regulations, and was so attentive, on all occasions, to the protection of commerce, that both the Colonies themselves and their trade

a circular stone wall about eight feet high. Its

---

flourished more during his continuance on that station than they had ever done since the Revolution.

"Early in the year 1708 the Commodore received advice that the celebrated French Chef d'Escadre, Du Casse, was daily expected in the West Indies, with a squadron of great force, destined, as it was generally supposed, for an attack upon the Island of Jamaica. This apprehension, however, was soon removed, for certain intelligence arrived that Du Casse's real destination was to the Havannah, to convey from thence the galleons bound to Spain, whose whole marine was at that time in such a wretched condition as to be utterly inadequate to the protection of so vast a treasure.

"The Commodore immediately formed a project for attacking the galleons, before they had joined their protectors, as M. Du Casse's force was too great for him to expect any success afterwards. He knew perfectly the routes of the galleons, that they were to sail from Porto Bello to Carthagena, and from thence to the Havannah; and he resolved to try if it was not possible to intercept them in their passage from Porto Bello to Carthagena. With this view he sent Capt. Pudner, in the Severn, to watch the Enemy's motions in Porto Bello; from whom he received intelligence, on the 23d of May, that the galleons had sailed from thence on the 19th. The Commodore immediately sailed in quest of them, and cruised till the 27th, when not meeting with them, he began to fear that they had intelligence of his being on the coast, and were gone for the Havannah. On the 28th of May, about noon, the galleons, in all seventeen in number, were discovered from the mast-head[*], and the Spaniards, at the same

---

[*] The spy-glass through which Sir Charles Wager discovered these galleons was given by him to one of my ancestors, and I now have it in my possession. It is a curious old thing, and at present would not be deemed a bad glass. I have also several letters from Sir Charles to my ancestors.

name, probably, may be a corruption of War-ring.

---

time, had sight of the British squadron, but despising the small force the Commodore had with him, they did not alter their course. The British squadron consisted of the following ships:

Expedition	- - 70 guns -	{ Commodore Wager. Captain Long.
Kingston	- - - 60 - - - - - -	Bridges.
Portland	- - - 60 - - - - - -	Windsor.
Severn	- - - 48 - - - - - -	Pudner.

Vulture Fire-ship.

"The Commodore immediately gave chace to the Spaniards, which continued until evening, when the Enemy, finding they could not weather the Baru, an island in their passage to Carthagena, resolved to contest the matter, and drew out, as well as they could, in line of battle, under easy sail. At sun-set the engagement commenced between the two Commanders in Chief, and continued for an hour and a half, when the Spanish Admiral's ship blew up,; a vast quantity of the flaming wreck fell on board the Expedition, but was happily extinguished without doing much damage. After this accident the Spaniards began to separate, and the night being very dark favoured their escape; but the Commodore discovering one of them, which was the Rear-admiral, he made sail after her, and coming up with her about ten o'clock at night, fired so effectual a broadside as disabled the Enemy. The Spaniard, however, continued to defend his ship with great gallantry till two in the morning, when the Kingston and Portland coming up, he struck his colours, and called out for quarter.

"At day-light four sail were seen directly to windward, which the Commodore made the signal for the Kingston and Portland to chase, his own ship being too much disabled, besides having no less than 300 prisoners on board.

"The Commodore, having repaired his own damages, and refitted the prize as well as circumstances would permit, resolved

and it originally might have been an encampment.

to proceed, without loss of time, to Jamaica; but being greatly straightened for provisions and water, and the wind contrary, he yielded to the urgent entreaties of his prisoners, and put them on shore at the island of Baru. The Spanish Rear-admiral, as long as he lived, retained a grateful sense of this act of humanity.—On the 31st the Commodore was joined by the Kingston and Portland, whose Captains informed him that the ships they had pursued was the Spanish Vice-admiral, who, running among the shoals of Salmadinas, off Carthagena, they were obliged to tack and stand off, although they had got so near as to fire several broad-sides into her. This gave the Commodore great dissatisfaction, and he determined to bring the Captains to a Court Martial; but in the mean time he sent them to take or destroy a galleon of forty guns, which he understood, by a Swedish ship that had been trading at Baru, had taken shelter in that island. The galleon was coming out of harbour just as the Kingston and Portland appeared; but, on the sight of the English ships, the Spaniards run their vessel on shore and burnt her. After this, the Commodore returned to Jamaica, and arrived in safety at Port Royal on the 13th of July.

"The Captains of the Kingston and Portland were tried by a Court Martial, on a charge of neglect of duty, in not pursuing the Spanish Vice-admiral, when the Pilots offered to carry the ships within the shoals; and being found guilty of part of the XIIth and XIVth Articles of War, were sentenced to be dismissed from the commands of their respective ships.

"According to the account given to the Commodore by his prisoners, the loss sustained by the Enemy must have been immense. The Admiral's ship, which blew up, mounted sixty-four brass guns; had a complement of near seven hundred men, seventeen of whom only were saved; and had on board about seven millions of gold and silver.—The ship which was captured mounted forty-four guns, and had on board thirteen chests of

It has or had two entrances, one opposite to the

pieces of eight, and a very considerable treasure in silver. The galleon destroyed had a rich cargo of merchandize on board; but we do not find any estimate made of her value. — It is related as an anecdote of Commodore Wager, that in private conversation he used to say, 'a man who would not fight for a galleon, would fight for nothing;' and this, probably, was said in allusion to the misconduct of his Captains, who permitted the Spanish Vice-admiral to escape, on board whose ship were six millions in gold and silver.

"In the distribution of the captured property the Commodore exhibited a most honourable proof of integrity and disinterestedness. Previous to this year there was no established regulation for dividing the property taken from an Enemy among the Captors; but each individual plundered and appropriated to his own use as much as could be found out of the hold. There were indeed some ill-defined regulations, which custom had in a certain degree erected into law; but these were as often broken through as observed, and even where they were most strictly maintained were, to the major part of the crew, inequitable and unjust. To remedy this defect, and to animate the seamen to more spirited exertions, by holding out to them a liberal recompence, an Act of Parliament was passed for settling the future distribution of captured property. This arrived at Jamaica a short time before the Commodore's return with the galleons; and though he had, according to what was then the usual custom of the service, permitted the people to plunder at the time of taking the prize, he now appointed regular agents for the captors, in compliance with the law; and, to satisfy the sailors with the fairness of his intentions, he ordered Captain Long to deliver up near £30,000. worth of silver and effects which he had seized between decks for the Commodore's use and his own. This honourable instance of self-denial made a strong impression on the minds of the seamen under him, and becoming, as

other, and is at a short distance from the Giant's

---

all good and generous actions ought to be, universally known, rendered him one of the most popular characters in the service.

"Soon after this encounter with the galleons he received a commission appointing him Rear-admiral of the Blue; and was ordered to return home.

"Immediately on his arrival in England he was promoted to be Rear-admiral of the Red; and the Queen conferred on him the honour of knighthood.

"With these flattering but justly-deserved marks of Royal approbation, and the esteem and love of all ranks of his Countrymen, Sir Charles retired into private life, and enjoyed a relaxation from the fatigues of service during the remainder of Queen Anne's reign. On the accession of George I. he was appointed Commander in Chief on the Mediterranean station; and at the same time made Comptroller of the Navy. His Mediterranean command produced nothing interesting, it being a period of profound peace; and on his return from thence he remained unemployed, as a flag-officer, till the year 1722, when some disputes with Portugal caused a fleet to be equipped, to the command of which Sir Charles Wager was appointed. Matters not proceeding to extremities with the Court of Lisbon, the British fleet was dismantled, without even putting to sea, and Sir Charles was not again called into service till the year 1726. On this occasion he commanded the fleet in the Baltic; but the naval campaign, like most in that quarter, proved a pacific one, and afforded Sir Charles no opportunity of gathering laurels.

"The following year he hoisted his flag as Vice-admiral of the Red, and sailed with a squadron of six ships of the line and two frigates to the relief and protection of Gibraltar, which was then openly threatened by the Spaniards. On his arrival, the Admiral found the Conde de las Torres, the Spanish General, was encamped within a league of the place, having under him an army of fifteen thousand men. No hostilities, however, had com-

Hedge, spoken of in p. 64. There is an old story,

menced; the Spanish boats and small vessels were permitted to pass by the English squadron without any molestation; but on the 10th of February, the intentions of the Enemy became more apparent, by the Spanish General openly commencing the erection of a battery, pointing directly against the fortifications of the British Garrison. This produced a correspondence between Sir Charles and the Spanish General, which not ending to the satisfaction of the former, the Admiral ordered three of his ships to anchor in a station where they could enfilade the Enemy's entrenchments. This was followed by hostilities, and a variety of those enterprizes and transactions which necessarily ensue between assailants and defenders took place, but none of sufficient importance to demand explanation. On the 23d of June the Spaniards agreed to a suspension of arms, which early in the ensuing year was followed by a treaty of peace. After this period, Sir Charles commanded successively in the Mediterranean station, the Channel fleet, and a squadron of observation in the Downs. On the death of Lord Viscount Torrington in 1733, he was appointed First Lord of the Admiralty, and never went to sea afterwards.—In 1734 he was advanced to be Admiral of the White, under the apprehension that Great Britain might be ultimately involved in a war, which at that time had spread over the face of the Continent, and in which case it was determined that Sir Charles Wager should command the Grand Fleet. The nation, however, continued at peace, and Sir Charles was not called into service. He continued to hold his high office at the Board of Admiralty, with much reputation and inflexible integrity, till the 19th of March 1741, when he quitted it, and was appointed in the month of December following to the lucrative post of Treasurer of the Navy. This appointment he did not long enjoy, dying on the 24th of May 1743, in the 79th year of his age. Private gratitude has erected a sumptuous monument to his memory, in Westminster Abbey, bearing the following

that some enemies made the owner of this estate

inscription, which contains a very just and faithful delineation of his character.

"To the Memory of
Sir CHARLES WAGER, Kn[t]
Admiral of the White, First Commissioner of the Admiralty,
And Privy Counsellor;
A man of great natural talents,
Improved by industry, and long experience;
Who bore the highest commands,
And passed through the greatest employments,
With credit to himself and honour to his Country.
He was in private life
Humane, temperate, just, and bountiful;
In public station,
Valiant, prudent, wise, and honest;
Easy of access to all;
Steady and resolute in his conduct;
So remarkably happy in his presence of mind,
That no danger ever discomposed him:
Esteemed and favoured by his King,
Beloved and honoured by his Country,
He died the 24th of May, 1743, aged 79.
This Monument was erected
By FRANCIS GASHRY, Esq.
In gratitude to his Great Patron, A. D. 1747."

Among the Records of the Corporation of West Looe are the following entries:

1699, 3 May.—At the Court Leet then held, Carolus Wager, Ar. tunc jurat. fuit liber Burgens Burgi pr[d].

N. B. This is the first mention of Mr. Wager that I have met with.

prisoner, and threatened to kill him unless he gave them all his possessions. His answer was, "You shall have all my lands but Kill-me-not," meaning Killminorth, and so saved the estate by this pun.— Beacon Park, in this Barton, is well worth being visited, as it commands very extensive and beautiful views in all directions; from it are seen Roach Rock and Tower, and the Mountains of Hainsborough, Rowtor, Brownwilly, Cheeswring, Kilmar, Carradon, Hingston, &c. &c. ; likewise part of Dartmoor, and an extensive sea view.

PORTLOOE

is in the parish of Talland, and was the residence of the late Edward Buller, Esq. (youngest brother of the late Judge Buller), who became entitled to it by his marriage with Miss Hoskin, whose father resided there.

1724, 26 July.—Ad hanc curiam Carolus Wager, Mil. debite elect. et jurat. Capital Burgens Burgi pr[d].

1741, 12 May.—The Right Hon'ble Sir Charles Wager, Kn[t]. and Benj[n]. Keene, Esq. were elected Members of Parliament for West Looe.

1742, 27 Dec.—Right Hon'ble Sir Charles Wager (having vacated his seat by accepting the office of Treasurer of the Navy) was re-elected M. P. for West Looe.

1743, 10 Dec.—John Frederick, Esq. was elected M. P. for West Looe, in the room of Sir Charles Wager lately deceased.

POLVELLAN,

also in the parish of Talland, and within the precincts of the Borough of West Looe, was built by John Lemon, Esq. (brother to Sir William Lemon, Bart. who has been fifty years M. P. for Cornwall), and was first occupied by him in the year 1789, and has been herein before spoken of.

TRENANT PARK.

The manor of Great Trenant was, at an early period, in the Hievis family, from whom it descended, with Tremoderet, to the Coleshills, Arundells, and Whittingtons. In 1620 it was in moieties between the St. Aubins, in right of a coheiress of Whittingtons, and the Giffard family. At a late period the whole became vested in the family of Treise, from whom, after the decease of Sir Christopher Treise without issue, it passed to the Morsheads. John Morshead, Esq. of Trenant Park, was created a Baronet in 1783. In 1806 he sold this estate to John Buller, Esq.; upon whose death (May 3, 1807) without issue, it vested in his brother and heir-at-law, Vice-admiral Sir Edward Buller, Bart. who was created a Baronet in 1808.

Trenant Park is in the parish of Duloe, and is as beautiful a spot as any in the county. The estate lies between the two rivers before mentioned, which unite at its South-eastern point (commonly called Trenant Point), at about a quarter of a mile from Looe Bridge. The land is high, and diversified in the most beautiful manner by nature, and skirted all round with woods. The prospects are extensive and delightful, and vary at every step. The land here and round about is thrown up into hemispherical mounts of elegant sweeps and considerable elevations from their bases.

Trenant in Cornish signifies, it seems, the Valley Town, or a Dwelling near the River. Trenant Park was formerly the seat of the Medhops, two of whom, father and son, were Rectors of St. Martin's by Looe[*]. The Medhops are supposed to have been descended from the Mydhops of Essex, some of whose ancestors gave lands in frank almoine to the Abbey of Furneaux there, 1290; *viz.* Roger de Mydhop, son and heir of Henry de Mydhop, who gave for his arms, Ermine, a lion rampant Azure, crowned Or. The same arms are on a tomb-stone on one of the above Rectors in the church-yard of St. Martin's.

Sir Edward Buller has been at great expence in machinery for forcing water to Trenant House from the bottom of the vale beneath. A deep well near the house is frequently drained of its contents by, in all probability, a natural syphon.

---

[*] See before, pp. 22, 23.

TREWORGEY.

Hals, in his "Parochial History of Cornwall," says, "Tre-wor-gye, *i. e.* the Village or Farm Town;" but I rather think it means Trewarguy, *alias* Treworgey, which in Cornish signifies the Town above or upon the Water or River, and such is its situation.

"*Conveniunt rebus nomina sæpe suis.*"

The names, as oftentimes we see,
With things themselves full well agree.

This place Hals supposed to be the same which in Domesday Roll was taxed by the name of Treworgan, being still (when Hals wrote) the Voke Land of an antient Barton * and Manor which claims the Royalty or Liberty of fishing over the River and Haven of Looe, by virtue of a Grant thereof from the antient Earls and Dukes of Corn-

---

* Barton. This is a corruption of the Saxon word Beretun, a Farm or Grange. Bere in that tongue signified Barley, by some called Beere or Bere; from whence came Bern or Barn; quasi Bere-ern, a Place for Barley, and Beer, which we drink.— Tun signified a House or Dwelling-place inclosed. Perhaps "Town of Trees," a common expression in some parts of Cornwall, may from hence mean the Inclosed Trees, or Trees in an Inclosure.

"Oppidum autem Britanni vocant, quum sylvas impeditas vallo atque fossâ munierunt, quò, incursionis hostium vitandæ causâ, convenire consueverunt." *Cæsar's Comm. lib. V.* § 17.

"l. in right of their Honour, Manor, Burrough, and Castle of Liskeard, situate upon the same river. Which place (Treworgey) was the mansion of the antient, worshipful, and genteel family of the Kendalls for many ages; and, in particular, here lived Richard Kendall, Sheriff of Cornwall 8 Richard II. 1385, as his posterity have ever since, till John Kendall, Esq. having no issue, temp. William III. sold this barton and manor to William Williams, of Bodinnick, merchant, now (when Hals wrote) in possession thereof. The arms of Kendall are, Argent, a chevron between three dolphins Sable. Ken-dale signifies to see or behold the Dale or Valley; otherwise, Kendall or Cendall is Fine Linen; and Cendale may be a corruption of Pendale, *i. e.* the Head of the Valley. The estate, now let to farm, belongs to ——— Eliot, Esq. of London, who claims the right of fishery over the river Looe.

WESTNORTH,

formerly the seat of the Anstis's, from whom came Anstis, Garter King of Arms *. Hals says, that West-North, or rather North-West, was the Voke Land of a dismembered manor formerly belonging to the Kendalls of Treworgye, and was by one of

---

* " Knock with a purse of gold at Anstis' gate,
      And beg to be descended from the Great."
This satire is in Young's " Love of Fame," sect. I. line 155. See his portrait in Nichols's " Illustrations of the Literary History of the Eighteenth Century," vol. IV. p. 139.

them, temp. Edward IV. given with his daughter in marriage with Kellyowe, whose only daughter and heir was married to ——— Bastard, a barrister at law, temp. Henry VIII. which brought this then undivided manor into that family, who seated themselves therein for several generations, till Sir William Bastard sold it to John Anstis, Gent. Registrar of the Archdeaconry of Cornwall, (when Hals wrote) in possession thereof. Bastard's arms are painted, as Hals says, in several of the glass windows of this house, together with divers matches or quarterings, whose arms are, Or, a chevron Azure.

West-North is in the parish of Duloe. In a vault in the church of this parish are deposited the remains of several of the Anstis family. John Anstis, whose "Register of the Most Noble Order of the Garter," in two volumes, folio, and other works, are well known to all lovers of Heraldry, was born at St. Neot, Cornwall, in September 1669. He was made Garter King of Arms 13th Anne; died the 4th of March, 1744; and was interred in this vault. Besides the books which he published, it is said he left in manuscript a History of Launceston, a Treatise on the Antiquities of Cornwall, and many other works and collections; but what are become of them nobody seems to know. His son John, who in 1725 was joined to his father in the office of Garter King of Arms, and had likewise the additional offices of Genealogist and Register of the Order of the Bath, died December 5, 1754, and was also buried in the family-vault. The heraldic regalia of the father and son were, at the time of her death, in the possession of Mrs. Fookes, who resided at West-North. This place now belongs to Thomas Bewes, Esq. but is occupied by a farmer.

MORVAL.

The seat of John Buller, Esq. The house is situated in a valley, which is well wooded and laid out to the best advantage; it is in the parish of Morval, and about a stone's throw from the church.

Mor, in the Cornish language, signified either Lake or Sea-water, and Val, a Valley. So that this parish may be so called from the circumstances of the church standing in a valley into which the sea-water flows. Or else from Morvael, a British Saint.

The Barton of Morville or Morvale, gave name to an old family, hence called De Morville, and as tradition saith, Hugh de Morville, Knight, one of the murderers of Becket, was of this house. There is, however, a place called Morvael in Cumberland, and Hugh de Morville is said to have been born there.

Kirk-Orwald, Cumberland.—Hugh de Morville, who obtained these possessions by marriage, procured a licence in the 2d of King John, to inclose his woods at Kirk-Orwald, to fortify his manor-house, and to have there an annual fair, and weekly market. Hugh de Morville was one of the murderers of Archbishop Becket; and the weapon with which that ambitious prelate was slain at the altar, was long deposited in this fortress. The legends of superstition team with the peculiar judgments which befel his assassins; yet no sudden deaths awaited them, nor were they marked as the Monks have feigned, with tails issuing from behind. "William de Tracey," says Pennant, "lived almost to the reign of King John, and Hugh de Morville till about the sixth of that Monarch, nor did his remorse seem to have been very deep, if it is true that he preserved the sword with which he did the murder." From the Morvilles, the castle passed to a younger branch of the Multon family.

The grave of Ewain, son of Urien, is in the space inclosed by four carved ridges beneath the soil of the church of Morvael (Cumberland). The principal ground on which this statement can be contested, is the difficulty of identifying the church of Morvael with that of Penrith, but as we know Morvael was a British Saint, it seems probable that Penrith Church, when originally built, was dedicated to St. Morvael, though on the advancement of Christianity, it found a new patron in St. Andrew.

The hypothesis in the text derives additional support from an Elegy on Ewain, in the Welch language, which mentions him as the chief of the splendid Llewins; words that can only be referred to Castle Llewin, constantly asserted by tradition to have been possessed by King Ewain.

Sir Hugh de Morville bestowed the Rectory of Burgh or Burgh-on-Sands, in Cumberland, on the Abbey of Holm Cultrum, as a penitential atonement for the murder of Archbishop Becket.

The manor of Morval (Cornwall) passed with one of the coheiresses of Glynn*, in the reign of Henry

---

* The manor of Morval was, for many generations, the property and residence of the family of Glynn. In the year 1471 John Glynn, Esq. was barbarously murdered at Higher Wringworthy, in this parish, by several ruffians, employed by Thomas Clemens, whom he had superseded in the office of Under-steward of the Duchy. In the preceding year he had been assaulted and grievously wounded in the face by the retainers of Clemens, as he was holding the King's Court at Liskeard, and thrown into Liskeard prison, where he signed a compulsory obligation not to prosecute; some months preceding the murder, the retainers of Clemens went to Morvall, and plundered the house and premises of goods and chattels to the value of £.200 and upwards, as then estimated: all this appears from the petition of Jane Glynn, the widow, to Parliament, which sets forth that she could have no redress for their horrible outrages in the County of Cornwall, by reason of the general dread of the malice of Clemens and his lawless gang: she prayed, therefore, that her appeal might be tried in London by a Cornish jury; and that, in default of Clemens appearing to take his trial, he might be dealt with as convicted and attainted: her petition was granted.

The words of Jane Glynn's Petition to Parliament, are:—
" The said Thomas Flete, &c. &c. then and there, at four of the clok in the mornyng, hym felonsly and horribly slewe and murdred, and clove his head in four partics, and gave hym ten dede woondes in his body; and when he was dede, they kutt off oon of his legges, and oone of his armes, and his hede from his body to make hym sure; and over that, then and there his purs and £.22 of money nombered, a signet of gulde, a grete signet of

VIII. (and in which family it had been for many generations) to the Coodes, and with the heiress of Coode to a younger branch of the Bullers, who, on

sylver in the same purs contayned, a double cloke of muster-deviles, a sword, and a dagger to the value of six marks, of the goodes and catelx of the said John Glyn, felonsly from hym they robbed, toke, and bare awey." Rot. Parl. vol VI. p. 36.

The following enumeration of the particulars, as contained in the schedule, annexed to Jane Glyn's Petition, may perhaps be thought interesting, as giving some idea of the furniture and stock of a gentleman's mansion in the reign of Edw. IV.:

" Fourteen oxen; 10 kien; a bull; 8 hors; 60 bolokis; 400 shepe; 10 swyne; 6 flikkes of bacon; 300 weight of woll; 3 brasynpannes, everych conteynyng 60 gallons; 16 payre of blankets; 12 payre of shetes; 4 matres; 3 fether beddes; 10 coverletys; 12 pilowes of feders; 4 long gounes; 6 short gownes; 4 women gounes; 2 draught beddes; a hanging for a chamber; 3 bankerders; 12 quyssions of tapsterwork; 4 cuppes of sylver; 3 dozen of peauter vessell; 2 basons conterfet of latyn; 2 other basons of latyn; 2 dozen of sylver spoones; a saltsaler of sylver; 2 basons of peauter; 2 saltsalers of peauter; 3 pipes of Gascoyn wine; a hoggeshede of swete wyne; 2 pipes of sider; 4 hoggshedes of bere; 400 galons of ale; 3 foldyng tabules; 2 feyre long London tables; 4 peyre of trestell; a pipefull of salt beef; a hundred of milwell and lyng drye; a quartern of mersau'te lynge; a hundred-weight of talowe; 40 pounds of candell; 200 hopes; ten barrell; five large pypes; 8 kevis; ten pottes of brasse; 14 pannes of brasse; 4 pettys of yron; 4 andyeris; 2 knedyng fates; 100 galons of oyle; 6 galons of grese; 300 pounds of hoppes; 200 bushell of malt; 40 bushell of barly; 60 bushell of otys; 4 harwyis; 10 oxen·tices; 2 plowes; 10 yokk; 12 London stolys; 4 pruse coffers, and 3 London coffers, within the same, conteyned 4 standing cuppes covered, whereof oon gilt; dyvers evidences and muniments concernyng the possession of the said John Glyn." Rot. Parl. vol. VI. pp. 37, 38.

the death of James Buller, Esq. (one of the representatives of the County) in 1720, succeeded to the Shillingham estate. James Buller, Esq. of Shillingham and Morval, who died in 1765, left Morval to his eldest son (by a second marriage) John, the father of John Buller, Esq. the present proprietor. The late Sir Francis Buller, sometime one of the Justices of the King's Bench, and afterwards of the Common Pleas, highly distinguished by his abilities as a Judge, was another of the sons of the said James by the second marriage, and is said to have been born at Morval.

BRAY,

the seat of the Mayow family. In Cornish, Bray, Bre, Brea, signifies the Hill; and this place is situated on the side of Bindown Hill. Bray commands very beautiful prospects. The manor of Bray, then held under the Vyvyans, as of their manor of Treviderow, was, in the reign of Charles the First, in the Heles, who were succeeded by the Mayows, of which family was Dr. John Mayow, an eminent physician in the reign of King Charles II. who contributed some papers, on respiration and other subjects, to the Philosophical Transactions. Bray is now the property and occasional residence of Philip Wynill Mayow, Esq.

Another account, which I have met with, states that Philip Mayow, of Looe, whose epitaph I have given p. 21, purchased, in the sixth of Elizabeth, anno 1564, the manor of Bree, or Bray, in the parish of Morval, of Christopher Copplestone, of Warleigh, Esq. These accounts therefore vary; and which is right I cannot ascertain.

POLGOVER, some time a seat of the Mayows (and near Bray), and LYDCOTT (about a mile from thence), a seat of the family of Hill, are now farm-houses, belonging, the former to Mr. Mayow, and the latter to Mr. Braddon.

KEVEREL.

This seat, which is in the parish of St. Martin's, near Looe, at a remote period was the residence of a family called Keverell. The heiress married Langdon. Arms of Keverell: Sable, two lions, one in chief passant, the other in base, preparing to spring, Or.— Langdon originally bore the name of Lizard; that of Langdon was adopted from Langdon in Jacobstow, eight generations before 1620. This antient family, which became extinct in 1676, had married heiresses of Grimscot, Hender, Bukeden or Trethewey, Bicton, and Keverell. *Lysons, Mag. Brit.*

Carew conjectures this place to have taken its name from Cheverule, a French word, signifying a wild Goat, as the high cliffs thereabout afford them a commodious inhabitance. But Mr. Hals says, Keverall, or Keveroll, imports to regain or recover;— whether to be construed with reference to recovering the lost health or wealth of the inhabitants who first settled there, or otherwise, let them, if they can, resolve. He further says, this barton, for many descents, was the seat of the Langdons (whose name imports Mischief or Treachery Hill or Fortress), gentlemen heretofore of large wealth and estate. But this place, by purchase, is become the possession of John Buller, Esq. who married the relict of Langdon. Langdon's arms were, Argent, a chevron between three boars' heads erased Sable. In St. Martin's church, within which parish this estate lies, there is an aile called the Keverel Aile, on the seats of which these arms are carved. Keverel is now occupied by a farmer, but belongs to John Buller, Esq. of Morval.

I have now swept my compass from the sea West to the sea East; and have given a brief description of the gentlemen's seats it has inclosed.

TREMADART

is a little beyond the three miles sweep of the compass from Looe. It was a seat of one of the branches of the Arundell family, and lies in the parish of Duloe. Hals, speaking of this place, says, "Tremadah signifies the Ecstacy or Transport Town, *alias* Tremo-dart, that is, the Dart or Javelin Affliction (as Cornish-English for Hobel is a Dart). Hals understood that this barton and manor was the dwelling of the Colshills, *i. e.* Neck Shield; so called from their wearing, in time of battle, a shield or coat armour, with a ribbon about their neck, originally denominated from Colshill parish, in Arden hundred, in Warwickshire. And, in particular, here lived John Colshill, Sheriff of Cornwall in 16 Richard II. 1393. John Colshill was Sheriff of Cornwall 21 Richard II. John Colshill was Sheriff of Cornwall 17 Henry VI. John Colshill, Knt. was Sheriff of Cornwall 7 Edward IV.; whose issue male dying, the inheritance fell amongst two daughters, married to Seyntaubin and Arundell (a younger branch of the Arundells of Trerice), who married Kellond, his Father Drew, and gave for his arms as the Arundells of Trerice. The lords of this manor and barton of Tremadah, Hals supposes, were the founders and endowers of the vicarage and rectory church of Duloe.

The manor of Tremoderet, now called Tremadart, belonged, at an early period, to the family of Hewis, or Heivis. Emmeline, or Emma, the heiress of this family, brought it to Sir Robert Tresilian, Chief Justice of the King's Bench, who was executed at Tyburn in 1388, for having been the adviser of arbitrary measures, which his misguided Sovereign had not the power to enforce. In the year 1391 Sir John Coleshill, second son of Emmeline, procured a grant to him, his wife, and their heirs, of this and some other manors, which had been forfeited by the Chief Justice's attainder. Sir John

Coleshill, their son, being then about twenty-three years of age, was slain at the battle of Agincourt, leaving an infant son, who died without issue, being then Sir John Coleshill, Knight. His only sister, Joanna, was thrice married — to Sir Renfrey Arundell, a younger son of the Lanhorne family, Sir John Nanfan, and Sir William Hawton. By the former she had two sons, Sir Renfry and John, who was made Bishop of Lichfield and Coventry in 1497, and in 1501 translated to Exeter. On the death of Sir Edmund Arundell, grandson to Sir Renfrey, without issue, Tremadart and several other estates in Cornwall devolved to the two sisters of Sir Renfrey Arundell the younger (married to Stradling and Whittington) and their half-sister (the daughter of the heiress of Coleshill, by her second husband, Sir John Nanfan) married to Bolles, or their representatives. A descendant of Whittington (a Gloucestershire family) left six daughters coheiresses, married to Poole, Berkeley, Bodenham, Throgmorton, St. Aubyn, and Nanfan. The latter having no issue, her share in the inheritance of the Coleshills was divided among her sisters. John Arundell, Esq. of Trerice, having purchased Bodenham's share, left it to his second son, Thomas, younger brother of John Arundell, the brave defender of Pendennis Castle. This Thomas settled at Tremoderet, and purchased not only the smaller shares which had belonged to the Pooles and Berkeleys, but the two thirds of the estate which had been purchased of the families of Danvers (heirs of Stradling) and Bolles by the Bevilles, and had descended to the Granvilles. Thomas Arundell died in 1648, being possessed of the whole of the estate, except St. Aubyn's inheritance and that of Throgmorton, which had been purchased by the St. Aubyns. In 1708 John Arundell, Esq. (the last of this branch of the family) bought what belonged to the St. Aubyns, and in 1711 sold the whole to Sir John Anstis, Garter King of Arms, from whom the present proprietor, Thomas Bewes, Esq. of Tothill, near Plymouth, is descended in the female line. The mansion-house is now occupied by the tenant of the demesne farm.

William of Worcester, who wrote an Itinerary of Cornwall in the reign of Edward IV. speaks of a dilapidated castle, called Bolleit, near Sir John Coleshill's mansion of Tremoderet. This, probably, was Botelet, in the adjoining parish of Lanreath, which was a manor of the Bottereaux family.

Mr. Thomas, of Treworgy, has now in building a handsome house on West Looe side of the river; the views from it are very beautiful, and it will greatly add to the scenery.

Such a number of gentlemen's seats within three miles of the Looes (though now most of them are occupied by farmers) sufficiently declare what a pleasant part of the county this is.

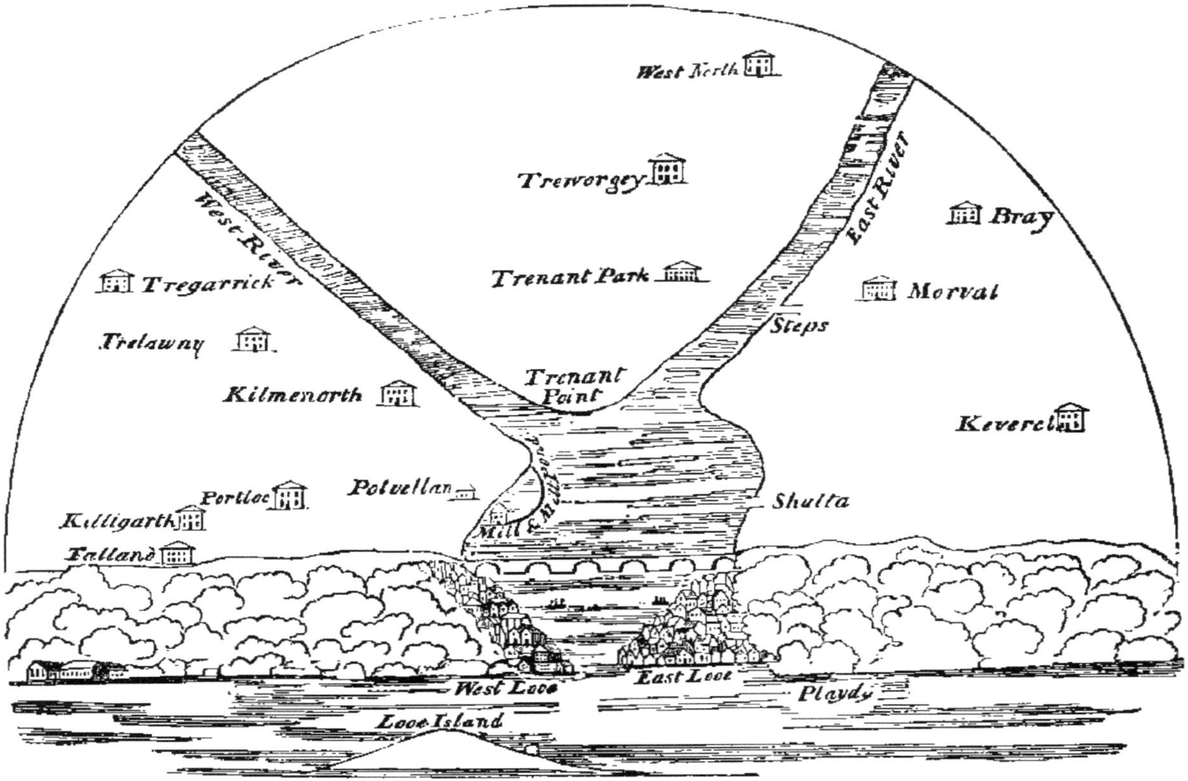
West North
Treworgey
West River
East River
Bray
Tregarrick
Trenant Park
Morval
Trelawny
Steps
Trenant Point
Kilmenorth
Keverel
Polvellan
Shulta
Portloe
Killigarth
Mill & Millpond
Talland
West Looe
East Looe
Playdy
Looe Island

WATERLOO VILLA.

A neat house and pleasure-grounds, so called, have, within a few years past, started up just over the town of East Looe. The house was begun by the late Major Nicholas, of East Looe; but he dying before it was finished, it has been completed by his representative, Nicholas Harris Nicolas, Esq. of the Inner Temple. Its situation is very beautiful, and adds much to the scenery from every point of view.

The late Major Nicholas was a native of East Looe, and was Major of the Royal Cornwall Fencible Dragoons, and Captain of the 44th Regiment of Foot. He was at the taking of Bunker's Hill, and one of the first who entered the battery which proved so destructive to our troops. The late Lieutenants Charles Bawden and John Dyer, natives of Looe, were also there.

Major Nicholas died, very suddenly, on the 2d of November, 1816. His wife, Mrs. Phillis Nicholas (formerly Blake, niece of Mr. Toup), died Feb. 8, 1799. There are two handsome marble monuments erected in St. Martin's church to their memory.

There is also a small marble monument in the same church to the momory of

General WILLIAM MACARMICK,
late Lieutenant-governor of Cape Breton,
in North America,
who died 20th August, 1815, aged 73.

NATURAL AND ARTIFICIAL CURIOSITIES WITHIN A RIDE OF LOOE.

DOSMERY POOL,

about twelve miles off. Mr. Carew says,
" Dosmery Poole, amid the moores
　　On top stands of a hill,
　More than a mile about, no streams
　　It empt, nor any fill."

It is a lake of fresh water, about a mile in circumference, the only one in Cornwall (unless the Loe Pool, near Helstone, may be deemed such), and probably takes its name from Douce-Mer, Sweet or Fresh Water Sea. It is about eight or ten feet deep in some parts. The notion entertained by some, of there being a whirlpool in its middle, I can contradict, having, some years ago, passed all over it in a boat then kept there.

ST. NEOT'S CHURCH.

In going from Looe to Dosmery Pool you pass by St. Neot's Church, well worth seeing, on account of the curiously-painted glass in the windows. Neot was an Abbot distinguished for his birth, learning, regularity, and zeal for promoting the interest of the true religion. Some say he was nearly related to King Alfred; and others, that he was descended from the blood royal of East Anglia. He died in 896, in Cornwall, where he left his name to the town of Neotstow, or St. Neot's, at which place he was buried; and when Earl Alric's seat in Huntingdonshire was turned into a monastery upon his account, his body was removed thither, and the town, before called Ainulphsbury, was from him named St. Neot's; from whence his bones were a third time removed to Croyland Minster, in 1213. The Rev. Benjamin Forster, of Boconnoc, in this county (Cornwall), a few years since published an Account of St. Neot and the Church; and Prints of all the Windows (seventeen in number) were intended to have been published; but I believe only a few of them were printed.

A few years since Mr. Whitaker (who has since written the History of St. Neot) had the receptacle in the wall of St. Neot's Church, in which the bones of St. Neot are said to have been deposited, opened, but nothing was found therein except nutshells, carried there, probably, by rats or mice. This receptacle, or stone casket, is inside the Church, near the East end of the Northern aile (or rather nave), and measures eighteen inches by fourteen; the end is only visible, jutting out of the wall two or three inches, four or five feet from the floor; and I have no doubt was a piscina for holy water. Just over this casket is a wooden tablet, with the following inscription:

> Hic (olim noti) jacuere relicta Neoti,
> Nunc præter cineres, nil superesse vides;
> Tempus in hac fossâ carnē cōsumpsit et ossa,
> Nomen perpetuum, Sancte Neote, tuum.

Consuming Time Neotus' flesh and bones to dust translated;
A sacred tomb this dust inclos'd, which now is ruinated.
Tho' flesh and bones, and dust and tomb, thro' tract of time be rotten,
Yet Neot's fame remains with us, which ne'er shall be forgotten:
Whose father was a Saxon King, St. Dunstan was his teacher,
In famous Oxford he was eke the first professed preacher,
That then in schools by quaintest terms the sacred themes expoūded;
Which schools by his advice, the good King Alfred well had founded.
But in those days the furious Danes the Saxons' peace molested,
And Neot forced was to leave that place, so much infested
With hostile spoils: then Ainsbury his place of refuge was,
Within the shire of Huntingdon; where since it came to pass,
That for his sake the place from him doth take its cōmon name.
The vulgar call it now St. Need's, their market town of fame.
There Alfric built a monastry, to Neot 'twas behested;
And Rosey, wife to the erle of Clare, with means the same invested,
For maintenance in after times: where long he did not stay,
But thence, enforc'd by furious Danes, he forward took his way
To Guerriers Stoke, for his repose; this place so called of yore,
But now best known by Neot's name, more famous than before.
For why? a College here of Clarks he had, whose fame increased,
When as his corpse was clad in clay, and he from hence deceased.
Some say his bones were carried home; St. Need's will have it so,
Which claims the grace of Neot's tomb; but hereto we say, No!

> Neotus floruit anō Dom. 896.

WRING CHEESE, OR CHEESE WRING. — DUNGERTH'S MONUMENT. — THE HURLERS.

Not far from Dosmery Pool may be seen a curious heap of rocks, called Wring Cheese or Cheese Wring; and, at a short distance therefrom, an artificial curiosity called The Hurlers, and another called The Other-half-stone.

Camden, in his Britannia, speaking of St. Neot's parish, says, "Near unto this, as I have heard, within the parish of St. Cleer, there are to be seen, in a place called Pennant, that is, the Head of the Vale, two monuments of stone; of which the one in the upper part is wrought hollow, in manner of a chair; the other, named Other-halfe-stone, hath an inscription of barbarous characters, now in a manner worn out," which he thinks should be read thus: DONIERT ROGAVIT PRO ANIMA. As for this Doniert, Camden thinks he was that Prince of Cornwall whom the Chroniclers name Dungerth, and record that he was drowned in the year of our salvation 872. Camden also says, "Hard by there is a number of good big rockes heaped up together; and under them one stone of a lesser size, fashioned naturally in form of a cheese, so as it seemeth to be pressed like a cheese; whereupon it is named Wring Cheese. Many other stones besides, in some sort four-square, are to be seen upon the plain adjoining; of which seven or eight are pitched upright of equal distances asunder. The neighbouring inhabitants term them Hurlers, as being by a devout and godly errour persuaded, they had been men sometimes transformed into stones, for profaning the Lord's day with hurling the ball. Others would have it to be a trophy (as it were) or a monument in memorial of some battle. And some think verily they were set as mere stones or landmarks; as having read in those authors that wrote on limits, that stones were gathered together of both parties, and the same erected for bounders. In this coast the river Loo maketh way and runneth into the sea, and in his very mouth giveth name to two little towns joined with a bridge together."

On the 6th August, 1802, I went with a party of friends to see these natural and artificial curiosities, mentioned by Camden. I first got the party to Red-gate *, in St. Cleer parish, about four miles from Liskeard, in order to find out Doniert or Dungerth's monument, which I understood was somewhere near to it. I made enquiry at the house at Red-gate after this monument, but could get no account of it for some time, though I questioned in a variety of ways; at last, however, we got information where it was situated. It is about a quarter of

---

* Probably this place took its name not from a gate painted red being there placed, as is generally imagined, but from its being situated just above Fowey river; Rhie-gat signifies River's course. The Fowey river at this place is not above half a mile from the source of Looe river.

a mile off from Red-gate, eastward, in a field next the high road. We got into this field, and seeing an erect stone went towards it, and found it to be the monument we sought. One moorstone stands erect, and the other with the inscription on it, lies in a pit close by. The figures of these stones in Borlase's History are most like them of any I have seen *. I made out and copied the inscription very perfectly, by rubbing a soft stone which left its mark, in the letters.

---

* The following account of these stones is copied from Mr. Polwhele's Cornwall, vol. II. p. 195.

"In the parish of St. Clere, about 200 paces to the eastward of Redgate, are two monumental stones which seem parts of two different crosses. They have no such relation to each other as to warrant the conclusion, that they ever contributed to form one monument. One is inscribed; the other, without an inscription, called ' *the other half stone,*' seems to have been the shaft of a cross, and originally stood upright, but has latterly been thrown down, from an idle curiosity to ascertain whether any concealed treasures were beneath its base. On one of its sides are some ornamental asterisks, but no letters of any kind. Its present length is about eight feet; yet it seems to have been one longer, as the upper part is broken, and displays part of a mortice. The inscribed stone, nearly square, appears to have been a plinth of a monumental cross, having the words ' Doniert rogavit pro anima' inscribed upon it, in similar characters to those used about the ninth century. *Doniert* is supposed to mean *Dungerth*, who was king of Cornwall, and accidentally drowned about the year 872." Of the meaning and intention of this Monument, see Borlase, pp. 361, 362; and Hals, p. 48.

```
  DONI
  ERT: RO
  GAUIT
  PRO AN
  ICOA
```

This stone by recollection is about two feet wide at top, and about five or six feet in length. And the other stone, which still stands erect and ornamented with cross lines, &c. is about the same in height.

The West front is quite plain; the top has the remains of a kind of mortice, left hand corner broken off.—The East front is dotted over, but has no letters.

I find in Hals, that the pit in which the stone with the inscription lies, was formed in the latter-end of the reign of King Charles II. in consequence of his, Hals's, going there at that period with some gentlemen to view, as he says, the, at that time thought barbarous, inscription; for some tinners in the contiguous country, taking notice of these gentlemen visiting this place, apprehended they came there in quest of some hidden treasure; whereupon, as Hals says, some of them wiser than the rest, lay their heads together, and resolved in council to be before-hand, and accordingly went with pickaxes and shovels, and opened the earth round about the monument, to the depth of about six feet; when they discovered a spacious vault walled about, and arched over with stones, having on the sides thereof two stone seats, not unlike those in churches for auricular confession. The sight of all which struck them with consternation, or a kind of horror, that they incontinently gave over search, and with the utmost hurry and dread, throwing earth and turf to fill up the pit they made, they departed, having neither of them the courage to enter or even to inspect into the further circumstances of the place; which account, Hals says, he had from the mouths of some of the very fellows themselves. Some short while after, the loose earth, by reason of some heavy rains which fell, sunk away, into the vault, which occasioning also a sort of terræ-motus and concession of the earth adjoining, the said monument was at length so undermined thereby, that it fell to the ground, where it still remains. Would some gentlemen of ability and curiosity, says Hals, and so say I, be at the charge of again opening and cleansing this under-ground Chapel, or whatever else it may be denominated, it might probably afford matter of pleasing amusement, if not grand speculation to the learned searchers into matters of antiquity.

This monument formerly went by the name of "The other half stone." Some translate the inscription, " Pray for the soul of Dungerth," others " Doniert asked for his soul;" and there seems to be great controversy for what purpose this monument was erected. High stones might originally, in the early ages of Christianity, have been erected near roads in desolate situations, and at short distances from each other, to direct travellers in their journies; and crosses might have been placed on them as a memento for thanksgiving, when the traveller had effected this part of his journey in safety. Now if the inscription on the above monument is meant for " Pray for the soul of Dungerth," may we not suppose that it was meant as a request to those who should happen to be praying for themselves, to offer up a prayer also for Dungerth, who probably caused that monument to be erected, or who was buried near the same, perhaps in the chapel before mentioned to have been discovered by the tinners. Or if the inscription is to be read, " Doniert asked for his soul," which seems the proper translation; may we not suppose that Doniert (who by all accounts was a very pious prince) erected this stone, and prayed or asked for mercy thereat. Perhaps originally these stones might have been called Ave stones, from the Latin word " Ave," all hail! God speed you; God save you, &c. a very appropriate expression in a desolate situation to a wanderer or traveller. And the reference to another Ave stone might signify the one which is a little to the eastward of it, bearing a cross, and by its appearance formerly a legend underneath. This word Ave (pronounced in the same manner it is in Ave-Mary-Lane, London) might be corrupted into Half; so that Ave stone and Half stone might mean one and the same thing. And in Cornwall the F is very frequently pronounced as a V, and the V as an F, at this present time *. If this does not meet approbation, I will add another conjecture. As the circle of stones, called the Hurlers, are at a short distance from this monument and the cross before mentioned, might not the monument and the cross be called the " one heave stone," and the other, " the other or outer heave stone," places from whence the ball during the game of hurling was thrown. The traditionary story of the stones called the hurlers, being once men turned into stone for profaning the Sabbath, will give some slight sanction to this conjecture; and in addition, even at this time the high-cross is vulgarly believed to have been the man who ran off with the ball.

With respect to the stones called the Hurlers being once men, I will say with Hals, " Did but

---

* I take some credit to myself for this conjecture as to the original meaning of " the other half stone." And I have, long since writing this, accidentally discovered what strongly confirms my opinion. The authors of the Beauties of England and Wales, speaking of inscribed stones at Ebchester, in Durham, say, there is one having the single word " Have" for Ave, on it. This stone is supposed by Horsley to be Sepulchral. Have Melitina Sanctissima. The custom of thus saluting, as it were, the dead, or taking their last farewel of them, is very well known, and it may seem almost needless to produce any instances of it. Thus Æneas bids eternal adieu to Pallas :

Salve æternum mihi, maxime Palla,
Æternumque vale.—Æneid, XI. 97.
Thus also a passage in Catullus,—Ave atque vale.

the ball which these Hurlers used when flesh and blood, appear directly over them immoveably pendant in the air, one might be apt to credit some little of the tale;" but as this is not the case, I must add my belief of their being erected by the Druids for some purpose or other, probably a Court of Justice; long subsequent to which erection, however, they may have served as the gaol for hurl players. And indeed a finer spot for such a game could not be fixed on perhaps any where. But I believe the Hurlers took their names from some other source than that of the game of hurling the ball being used there.

After sufficiently viewing Dungerth's monument, we directed our course towards Cheese-wring, and soon came to the Hurlers, but first we rode up to the High Cross before mentioned, which at a distance looked somewhat like a man. Under its cross it has an oblong square, as if the border of an inscription, but at present there is not the least vestige of a letter on it. Soon after we came to the Hurlers, which we found to be moorstones of about five or six feet high, forming two circles one without the other (not as represented in Hals' Parochial History, but like that in Borlase), the circle nearest Cheese-wring less than that of the other. Some of the stones are fallen down, and remain where they fell, and others have probably been carried off for gate posts and other purposes. The areas of the circles are not level, there being many pits in them, as if the earth had sunk over large graves. I confess I was not much struck with the appearance of these famous stones, not having faith to believe they once were men. Near this place we fell in with a man going to Cheese-wring, and were glad to follow him as a guide. Among other questions, I asked him, as we passed along, whether he could tell me the name of the tenement on which Dungerth's monument was; he answered Pennant. I also asked him whether he knew where the source of the Looe river was; he said in a field next below Dungerth's monument. I was sorry to hear this, as we could not conveniently return to see it, but I learned from him it was a mere spring of water uninclosed.

When we reached Cheese-wring, we discovered a man and woman on the top of the mount (on the declivity of which Cheese-wring stands), who, we afterwards found, were cutting turfs for fuel. Our guide first led us to the house of the late Daniel Gumb (a stone-cutter), cut by him out of a solid rock of granite (the rocks all around this place are granite, or moorstone as commonly called in Cornwall, and of the finest quality). This artificial cavern may be about twelve feet deep and not quite so broad; the roof consists of one flat stone of many tons weight, supported by the natural rock on one side, and by pillars of small stones on the other. How Gumb formed this last support is not easily conceived. We entered with hesitation lest the covering should be our grave-stone. On the right-hand side the door is " D. Gumb," with a date engraved 1735 (or 3). On the upper part of the covering stone, channels are cut to carry off the rain, or probably to cause it to fall into a bucket for his use; there is also engraved on it some geometrical device formed by Gumb, as our guide told us, who also said that Gumb was accounted a pretty sensible man. I have no hesitation in saying, he must have been a pretty eccentric character to have fixed on this place for his habitation; but here he dwelt for several years with his wife and children, several of whom were born and died here. His calling was that of a stone-cutter, and he fixed himself on a spot where materials could be met with to employ a thousand men for a thousand years.

After quitting this house, we ascended a few paces to the pile of rocks called Cheese-wring, the resemblance of which is well expressed by the print in Borlase's Nat. Hist. We were all struck with astonishment at this wonderful work of nature; we surveyed it over and over again, went round it several times, and viewed it from every part. It is about thirty-two feet high. The uppermost stone I have no doubt has Druidical basons formed in it. One of them shows itself by the edge of the stone having fallen away. After spending some time in viewing this tremendously awful pile of rocks, we ascended to the summit of the mount on the side of which it stands. This summit is surrounded by an artificial

CHEESE-WRING.

rampart of loose stones, not piled up; possibly they might have formed a wall, or have been carried there for building one; for if they were placed as they now are with an intention so to remain, they could not have been very defensive to this mount. Possibly the name of Cheese-wring may be derived from this ring of stones, and not from the vulgar idea of the Cheese-wring rocks being like a cheese-press.

The area within the rampart may be about half an acre of ground, and has rocks scattered all over it; but in some places verdure even in this rude region makes its appearance. We found a man and a woman within the area cutting turfs between the rocks for fuel. Among other questions, I asked the man to whom the spot belonged; his answer was, " he believed to nobody."

Several curious piles of rocks, some forming cromlechs, and others of various forms and positions, are here also to be seen, and several of them have Druidical basons on them. The rocks having these basons, are the most lofty or most remarkable for shape or situation. On some rocks there are two or three basons; and where there are more basons than one, they generally communicate by a channel. The basons here are of different sizes, though all of them are of the same shape, which is circular. Some of them are about a foot and a half in diameter, and six or eight inches deep, others not so large or deep. Never having seen any Druidical basons before, and having had my doubts till this time, whether they might not be natural productions caused by rain, lightning, &c. I was led to examine other rocks, whether they had (though equally exposed to the weather) similar formations, but could not find a bason on any rock that was not singular either for its shape or situation. I therefore concluded that these basons were the work of art, and not of nature; and I think they were not intended for the purpose of receiving the rain for common uses, for if so, why were they not made on rocks of easy access. It is possible, however, that rain being held in a natural hollow of a rock, may decompose that part of the rock on which it rests, and being whirled about by the wind from time to time, may form these basons which we attribute to art, and if this is the case, they must continue increasing in size and depth. Have such basons ever been seen but on granite rocks: if not, probably water dissolves the feltspar and disunites the quartz and mica; and the winds driving round the water with particles of quartz at the bottom of the bason, must consequently fret away the rock and enlarge the bason. A rock of white marble lies on the seabeach near Looe, completely covered with hollows like what are termed Druidical basons; these hollows in this rock I have no doubt have been formed by the sea; it lies near an insulated high rock under Sanders lane, and is every tide covered with the sea, and is very frequently covered with sand. A person fancying the basons on this rock of marble to be an artificial work, might also fancy that it once was placed on top of the elevated rock near it; the contrast of the white marble on top of the elevated rock, which is of a very dark colour, would give a singular appearance. When this high rock is shown to strangers, they are generally told, with a serious face, that when it hears a cock crowing at Hay (which is a farm just above it) it turns round three times!

SHARPY TORRY.

After leaving the area before mentioned we mounted our horses, and went towards another very considerable rocky eminence, about half a mile north-east; the road to which over the Down is full of rocks and stones, so as to prevent a horse from going other than step and step at times. On our way we passed a small circle of stones, the remains I rather think of an antient Barrow, whose earth had been washed away by the rains. We shortly after passed another pretty large circle of stones, just about the diameter to appearance of the lesser circle of the Hurlers; at length we arrived at the pile of rocks, called by our guide Sharpy-torry (Sharp-torr from its conical shape), we alighted from our horses and ascended. On the north or north-west side of it there appears a hollow, more like a large chimney than any other thing I can compare it to; the outside of which seems to have given way, and the steep hill below is strewed with an immense quantity of rocks and large stones, as if carried down or poured out from this hollow. Whether this was caused by the operation of fire or water bursting from this hollow or crater, if I may use the expression, I will not take upon me to say, but that one or other of these agents burst from this mount appears to be extremely probable, for the rocks and stones seem exactly as if they had been tumbled or thrown out of this crater by a current of some kind. We could not, however, discover lava, therefore it is probable water might have burst out, unless the lava has been decomposed. The views from this place are truly sublime. The spot is nearly the centre of the broadest part of the County; from it we saw both seas, north and south, and consequently the intervening land; and I believe it is the only eminence (except perhaps Brownwilly) in the eastern part of Cornwall, from whence both seas may be seen. We also saw in the north sea a very high land, which we concluded must be Lundy island; but the horizon to the north being rather hazy, I will not take upon me to say positively that it was that island, though it is probable to have been so. The prospect was equally extensive East and West, and as I took a pocket spying-glass with me, we viewed therewith the vast extent we commanded. We discovered Launceston Castle with the naked eye; through the glass it became very visible, we were much struck with the beautiful and highly-cultivated lands to the East of us, terminated in part by the high land of Dartmoor. To the Westward, nothing was to be seen but a vast continuance of moor land, without a hedge, without a tree, for a stretch of many miles. The cultivated land commenced just below our feet to the Eastward, and the uncultivated from where we stood Westward; the contrast on turning from West to East, or *vice versâ*, was astonishing. Our station seemed to be amidst the wreck of mountains of granite, rocks piled on rocks were strewed around in awful grandeur. The extreme point of our Western view, dimmed by distance, showed us that elevated rock called Roach rock, and we also saw Dosmerry pool about four or five miles off; our South view commanded Plymouth Sound, and a long extent of coast and sea; the Northward in one part was terminated by the sea. The views brought to my mind the beautiful lines in Ovid:

"Tum freta diffundi, rapidisque tumescere ventis
Jussit, et ambitæ circumdare littora terræ.
Addidit et fontes, immensaque stagna lacusque.
Jussit et extendi campos, subsidere valles,
Fronde tegi silvas, lapidosos surgere montes."

"Then he ordered the seas to be poured abroad, and to swell with furious winds, and to draw a shore quite round the inclosed earth. He likewise added springs, and immense pools and lakes. He ordered likewise plains to be extended, and valleys to sink; the woods to be covered with green leaves, and the rocky mountains to rise."

From this elevated spot (Sharp Tor) Hingston Hill appeared considerably beneath us. After spending some time on Sharp Tor, we reluctantly descended and went towards another range of rocks, called Killmarth Hill (which signifies the Holy hill or land, or perhaps Holy Grove), about three-quarters of a mile off. This range of rocks looks from Sharp Tor, like an immense wall of artificial masonry, with here and there turrets ascending, and it brought to my mind Sir George Staunton's account of the Chinese wall. When we arrived at its base, we alighted from our horses, and ascended. This natural wall-looking range is composed of granite rocks of, I should suppose some of them, a thousand tons weight. We traversed along the ridge, with some difficulty, towards the first turret, and from that to the next and so on, but the highest which at a distance looked somewhat like Wringcheese was yet to be explored; at length we arrived at it, and found it, if possible, more curious than Cheese-wring itself. It consists of immense rocks piled one on the other, to the height of twenty or thirty feet, and it leans so much, that a perpendicular dropped from its top would, I may venture to say, reach the bottom fifteen or more feet from its base; and from where we stood on the ridge, its support at the base appeared so slight as if a man could shove the whole mass over the precipice. Some of the uppermost stones of this pile are I should think from fifteen to twenty feet over, and the base of the whole fabric appeared so slight, that I imagined the handle of my whip would have exceeded its thickness. Upon descending to take another view of this astonishing structure, we found that the rocks were considerably thicker on one side than the other; so that the thick parts formed a counterpoise to the overhanging parts; but this not being apparent from the spot on which we first stood, was the cause of our great astonishment. However, though our astonishment was somewhat lessened, yet much remained at this stupendous pile. This is the most Western turret.

From this place one of the party and myself, the others not chusing to accompany us, went to explore the Easternmost turret. Upon our arrival at its base we found much difficulty in ascending it; the rocks jutted out, one over the other, in such a manner that, had we slipped but a few inches, we must have dropped over a considerable precipice. I arrived first at the base, and attempted to ascend, but fear pulled me back. Upon my friend's arrival we thought we would exert ourselves to get up, as we conjectured there might be a Druidical basin at top. My friend got up the first rock by creeping at full length under the overhanging rock; and I was under the necessity of several times desiring him, in the most energetic manner, to keep as close in as possible; for if the body had gone a few inches further out, it must have slid over the sloping rock which overhung the precipice. It took him a few minutes to drag himself in in this manner. In this creeping state he thought he should have broken his watch to pieces, as he was obliged, as before stated, to crawl at full length, there being no possibility, on account of the overhanging rock, of going on hands and knees. Upon trying to get out his watch, I earnestly entreated him to desist, for fear of losing his centre of gravity, for on the left hand was the precipice, and raising his right side ever so little might have been attended with most serious consequences. He took my advice, and by another exertion got far enough in to raise himself on his hands and knees, and then on his legs. I then followed him in the same manner. We then examined the rocks above us, in order to observe the best mode of ascending them. I first made the ascent, and in the uppermost rock discovered the largest Druidical basin we had met with, and observed it had a lip or channel facing the South. The horrid precipices on each side prevented my getting on the top of this rock, as I felt a slight vertigo. I then got down on a lower rock, and my friend ascended the uppermost one, and not finding himself dizzy, got into the basin itself (where I hope he will never go again), and waved his hat to our companions below. I desired him to measure the circumference of this basin, which he did with his whip, and found it to be about three feet and a half in diameter. We did not take its depth, but I think it must have been about a foot; it was of a circular form. The next thing to be considered was, how we should get down again; which at last, however, we effected nearly in the same manner (only reversing our movements) as we got up; and I believe nothing will ever induce me to pay a second visit to the top of this rock.

We had a very fine day for our excursion; the sun being clouded, it was not over warm; and there was but little wind: had there been more wind, we should not have been able to ascend some of the places we did, particularly the last. The air was somewhat hazy over the North and South seas, which was the only thing we had to regret.

A finer situation for Druidical * residence, rites, and ceremonies, I think, could not be fixed on any

---

* DRUID, DRUIDES, OR DRUIDÆ. — Some derive this word from the Hebrew Derussim, or Drussim; which they translate Contemplatores. Pliny, Salmasius, Vigenereus, and others, derive the name from $δρῦς$, an Oak, on account of their inhabiting, or at least frequenting and teaching in forests, or because they sacrificed under the oak. Menage derives the word from the old British "Drus," which signifies "Dæmon," or "Magician;" Borel, from the old British "Dru," or "Deru;" whence he takes $δρῦς$ to be derived. Goropius Becanus, lib. I. takes "Druis" to be an old Celtic or German word, formed from "trowis" or "truis," signifying a "Doctor of the Truth and Faith." Father Peyron, in his book of the Original of the Celtic Language, will have both Greek and Latin to come from Celtic; and if so, the Greek word $δρῦς$ must come from the Celtic "deru." The groves where they worshipped were called Llwyn; thence, probably, is derived the word "Llan," signifying now, in Welsh, a Church. These groves

where; every thing around is awfully magnificent; probably in antient days these masses of rocks were surrounded with trees. Our guide indeed informed us that on digging the soil, trunks of large trees have been there discovered; and Kil-mar, Kill-mark, Kil-marth signify, in Cornish, the Great, the Horse, or the Wonderful Grove.

Since writing the above, I have been again to see these curiosities (but did not visit the top of the

---

were inclosures of spreading oak, ever surrounding their sacred places; and in these were, "1st. Gorseddan," or Hillocks, where they sat, and from whence they pronounced their decrees, and delivered their orations to the people; "2nd. Carnedde," or Heaps of Stones, on which they had a peculiar mode of worship; "3rd. Cromleche," or Altars, on which they performed the solemnities of sacrifice.

There were several orders of them: — 1st. Druids; the chief of these was a sort of Pontifex Maximus, or High Priest; these had the care and direction of matters respecting religion.—2nd. Bards; who were an inferior order to the Druids, and whose business it was to celebrate the praises of their Heroes, in songs composed and sung to their harps. — 3rd. Eubates; who applied themselves chiefly to the study of Philosophy, and the contemplation of the wonderful works of Nature.

There were Women as well as Men Druids; for it was a female Druid who foretold to Dioclesian, when a private soldier, that he would be Emperor of Rome. They taught physicks, or natural philosophy; were versed in astronomy and the computation of time; were skilled in arithmetick and mechanicks; and appear to have been the grand source from whence the ages in which they lived derived all the knowledge which they possessed.

Among the numerous places sacred to Druidical worship many

Easternmost turret), and went by the way of St. Cleer Church-town, near which is a curious old well, with a moor-stone cross by it, worth seeing; the stone itself is in form of a cross, and it has a cross in relief cut on its cross. About a mile from

---

hieroglyphical characters have been discovered, which doubtless were intended for something relative to their opinions of the Deity to whom they paid their adoration. But, in addition to this, they taught their pupils a number of verses, which were only a sort of memorials or annals in use amongst them. Some persons remained twenty years under their instruction, which they did not deem it lawful to commit to writing. They used indeed the Greek alphabet, but not the language, as appears by a note, chap. XIII. lib. VI. of Cæsar's Commentaries *de Bell. Gall.* This custom, according to Julius Cæsar, seems to have been adopted for two reasons: first, not to expose their doctrines to the common people; and, secondly, lest their scholars, trusting to letters, should be less anxious to remember their precepts, because such assistance commonly diminishes application and weakens the memory.

The original manner of writing amongst the antient Britons was by cutting the letters with a knife upon sticks, which were commonly squared, and sometimes formed with three sides. Their religious ceremonies were but few, and similar to those of the antient Hebrews. The unity of the Supreme Being was the foundation of their religion; and Origen, in his Commentaries of Ezekiel, inquiring into the reasons of the rapid progress of Christianity in Britain, says, "this island had long been pre-disposed to it by the doctrine of the Druids, which had ever taught the unity of God the Creator."

Extracted from the Monthly Magazine and Literary Panorama for November 1819.

216 CROMLECH.

St. Cleer Church (on the way to Cheese Wring) stands a most magnificent

CROMLECH,

on a barrow in a field near the high road, on the tenement called Trethevye. A friend who was with me took a rough measurement of the upper or covering stone, and calculated it to be about five tons weight. The stones which form this Cromlech are supposed to have been brought some miles from where they stand, as there are none of the same kind near it. That this is a work of art there cannot be a doubt. One can hardly, however, suppose it possible that such immense stones could have been brought from a distance, and erected in the manner they are. What machinery was used baffles all conjecture. The upper or covering stone has a hole in it; for what purpose I have no idea, unless to support a flag-pole. One of the party remarked it might have been made for a chain to drag it by; but I rather thought it too near the edge for that purpose. Mr. Britton, in his "Beauties of England and Wales," has given a vignette of this Cromlech, which is well executed, and like the original.— Speaking of this Cromlech, Mr. B. says, he believes it has not been described by any writer[*], though it

---

[*] This author is mistaken. Norden not only speaks of it as follows, but has given a tolerably good plate of it. He says,

is more curious and of greater magnitude than that of Mona, or any other he was acquainted with. He says " it standeth about one mile and a half East of St. Cleer, on an eminence commanding an extensive tract of country, particularly to the East, South, and South-west; and is provincially denominated Trevethey Stone. On the North the high ground of the Moors exalts its swelling outline above it. It is all of granite, and consists of six upright stones, and one large slab covering them in an inclined position. This impost measures sixteen feet in length and ten broad, and is at a medium about fourteen inches thick. It rests on five of the uprights only; and at its upper end is perforated by a small circular hole. No tradition exists as to the time of its erection; but its name at once designates its being a work of the Britons, and sepulchral; the term Trevedi (Trevethi) signifying, in the British language, the place of the Graves."

"Trethevic, called in Latin Casa Gigantis, a little house raysed of mightie stones, standing on a little hill within a field, the forme hereunder expressed. This monument standeth in the parish of St. Cleer. The cover being all one stone is from A to B 16 foote in length; the breadth from C to D is 10 foote; the thickness from G to H is 2 foote. E is an artificial hole 8 inches diameter, made thorowe the roofe very rounde, which served, as it seemeth, to put out a staffe, whereof the house itself was not capable. F was the door or entrance."

CLICKITOR ROCKS,

about a mile on the right of the road from Looe to Liskeard, are worth seeing. It has lately been discovered that many of these rocks are serpentine, and some of them contain asbestos. Perhaps the name, Clickitor, or Clivacker, may be a corruption of the Saxon word Cliviger, which signified a Rocky District; and probably Kellick, the stone with which fishermen moor their boats, may be of Saxon origin. The Erica Vagans, or Didyma, so abundant on the serpentine formation near the Lizard, is said to be found here.

ST. KAYNE'S WELL.

About four miles from Looe is the famous Well of St. Kayne, described by Carew as follows: "Next I will relate you another of the Cornish wonders, *viz.* St. Kayne's Well; but lest you make a wonder first at the Saint before you take notice of the Well, you must understand that this was not Kayne the Manqueller, but one of a gentler spirit and milder sex—to wit, a woman*. He who caused

---

* St. Kayne was a holy virgin of the British Blood Royal, daughter of Braganus, Prince of Brecknockshire; she lived about the year 490. Her festival was celebrated on the 30th of September. She is said to have gone a pilgrimage to St. Michael's Mount in Cornwall, and to have made no short visit there; for she staid long enough, by the sanctity of her life and

the Spring to be pictured added this rhyme for an exposition :

> In name, in shape, in quality,
>   This Well is very quaint :
> The name to lot of Kayne befell,
>   No over holy Saint.
> In shape, 4 trees of divers kinds,
>   Withy, Oak, Elm, and Ash,
> Make with their roots an arched roofe,
>   Whose floore this Spring doth wash.
> The quality, that man or wife
>   Whose chance or choice attaines
> First of this sacred Stream to drink
>   Thereby the mastry gains.

---

the miracles she was thought to have performed, to ingratiate herself with the inhabitants; for, some years after this, St. Cadoc, making a pilgrimage to the same place, found here, to his great surprise, St. Kayne, his aunt by his mother's side: at which rejoicing, he endeavoured to persuade her to go back with him to her native country, Brecknockshire (the intercourse between Cornwall and Wales being then frequent and familiar); but the people of the country interfering would not endure her removal; at last, having had an express command from above, the Saint, obedient to the Heavenly monition, retired to her own country.

Keynsham, a parish in Somersetshire, on the South bank of the river Avon, and about midway between the cities of Bristol and Bath, is said to have derived its name from Keyna, daughter of Braganus, Prince of the Province of Wales, now called Brecknockshire, who lived towards the end of the fifth century. This lady, we are informed by Capgrave (a writer of the fourteenth century), was, in her youth, much famed for her beauty, and sought in marriage by many distinguished personages, all of whom, however, she rejected, and devoted her life to virginity.

Mr. Norden (in his Topographical and Historical Description of Cornwall) speaking of this Well, says, "It is a Spring rising under a Tree of a most straunge condition, for, beyinge but one bodie, it beareth the braunches of four kindes, Oke, Ashe, Elm, and Withye. This Kayne is sayde to be a Woman Saynte, of whom it taketh name; but it better resembleth Kayne the Devill, who had the shape of a Man, the name of an Apostle, the quallytie of a Traytor, and the handes of a Bryber."

Hence she acquired the name of Keyn-wyryf, or Keyna the Virgin. Travelling from her native home to seek some solitary spot, where she might indulge her religious contemplations undisturbed, she passed beyond the Severn, and requested permission from the Chief of this part of the country to reside at Keynsham, then a desert wood. The Prince said he would readily comply with her request; but added that it was impossible for any human being to live in that neighbourhood, as it swarmed with serpents of the most venomous species. Keyna, who had great confidence in the efficacy of her prayers, answered the Prince, that she would soon rid the country of that poisonous brood. Accordingly, the place was granted to her, and by her prayers all the snakes and vipers were converted into stones. And to this day (continues Capgrave's translator) the stones in that country resemble the windings of serpents, through all the fields and villages, as if they had been so formed by the hand of the engraver.

This is one of the instances in which natural phænomena are referred, by superstitious monks and impostors, to miraculous causes. The stones alluded to are examples of that curious but well-known *lusus Naturæ* the Cornua Ammonis, or Snake Stone, which abounds in the quarries of this parish.

Those trees spoken of by Carew and Norden were blown down in the great November storm of 1703, and it is said that the present trees were planted by Mr. Rashleigh, father of the late Philip Rashleigh, Esq. of Menabilly, some years after that event. The present trees are five in number, Oak, Elm, and Ash, they grow over the Well in a very odd manner, and are well worth seeing. The Well itself is arched with stone; the trees grow over the arch, or rather on it, and appear all united at the stock or root; on standing between the trees over the Well you can touch the trunks of all of them with your hand, without moving from the centre. According to my recollection there are two Oaks, two Ashes, and one remarkably fine grown Elm, very lofty, and, about five feet from the ground, seven feet in circumference. One or two of the trees droop over the Well like a weeping willow; and they all together form a very beautiful tuft. I sent a Sketch of the Trees and Well to the Editor of the Gentleman's Magazine, and it is engraved in that work for 1799, vol. LXIX. p. 193.

The following humourous Verses * on this Well made their appearance, a few years since, in several periodical publications. I understand they were written by Mr. Southey, the present Poet Laureat.

---

* Another Ballad on the same subject may be seen in the Gentleman's Magazine for June 1822, vol. XCII. p. 546.

ST. KAYNE'S WELL.

A Well there is, in the West Country,
   And a clearer one never was seen;
There is not a wife in the West Country
   But has heard of the Well of St. Keyne.

An Oak and an Elm tree stand behind,
   And beside does an Ash tree grow;
And a Willow from the bank above
   Droops to the water below.

A trav'ler came to the Well of St. Keyne;
   Pleasant it was to his eye,
For from cock-crow he had been travelling,
   And there was not a cloud in the sky.

He drank of the water so cool and clear,
   For thirsty and hot was he;
And he sat down upon the bank
   Under the Willow tree.

There came a man from the neighbouring town,
   At the Well to fill his pail;
On the Well side he rested it,
   And bade the stranger hail.

" Now, art thou a Bachelor, stranger ?" quoth he;
   " For if thou hast a wife,
The happiest draught thou hast drank to day
   That ever thou didst in thy life.

" Or has your good woman, if one you have,
   In Cornwall ever been?
For an if she have, I 'll venture my life
   She has drank of the Well of St. Keyne."

" I have left a good woman, who never was here,"
   The stranger he made reply.
" But that my draught should be better for that,
   I pray you answer me why."

"St. Keyne," quoth the countryman, "many a time
  Drank of this Crystal Well;
And before the Angel summoned her,
  She laid on the Well a spell: —

"If the husband of this gifted Well
  Shall drink before his wife,
A happy man thenceforth is he,
  For he shall be master for life.

"But if the wife should drink of it first,
  God help the husband then."
The stranger stoopt to the Well of St. Keyne,
  And he drank of the water again.

"You drank of the Well, I warrant, betime,"
  He to the countryman said;
But the countryman smiled as the stranger spoke,
  And sheepishly shook his head.

"I hasten'd as soon as the wedding was done,
  And left my wife in the porch;
But i'faith she had been wiser than me,
  For she took a bottle to church."

The water of this Well is at times covered over with a very beautiful, slender, fern-like vegetable, which feels, when dry, like velvet. Whether it grows on the sides or at the bottom of the Well, I do not recollect.

SUPPLY OF WATER.

In speaking of water I may here state that the two Looes have very fine water. At East Looe there is a Conduit at the Western end of the town, which generally supplies the place, though sometimes, in long drought, it runs but a small stream, when St. Martin's Well, within the precincts of the borough, or the Spring at Shuta, may be resorted to, each affording a supply of very fine water. There is also a Well within the borough, called Lady Well, near Barbican Rocks; but this Well does not supply much water in Summer. These two Wells (St. Martin's and Our Lady's) I have no doubt were consecrated and dedicated to the Saints whose names they bear. East Looe, from its increased population, requires to be supplied with more water: Shutta Spring and St. Martin's Well are rather too far off: the conveying the water from either of these Springs, in pipes or otherwise, owing to local situation and circumstances of the intervening ground, would be attended with a great expense. Perhaps the best and easiest mode of getting a supply would be by driving an adit into the hill from whence the Spring issues which supplies the Conduit. The present Cistern of the Conduit contains about twenty hogsheads. In the front of the Conduit is a leaden tablet with the following inscription:

> Repaired at the Charge
> of Sir JOHN TRELAWNY, Bart.
> Cost Thirty Pounds.
> In the Mayoralty of
> JOHN CHUBB, Jun.
> 1727.

West Looe Shoot affords fine water, and plentiful, even after the longest droughts; but it is rather too far from East Looe.

APPENDIX.

LIMITS OF THE PORT OF LOOE,

TAKEN FROM THE RETURN OF THE COMMISSIONERS.

WE whose names are subscribed, being four of the Commissioners in the Commission hereunto annexed mentioned, for the doing and executing the several matters and things in the said commission contained relating to the Town of Looe, a Member of the port of Plymouth, in the said commission mentioned, in pursuance of and obedience unto the said commission, do humbly certify the Right Hon. the Barons of his Majesty's Court of Exchequer at Westminster; that by virtue of the said commission to us and others therein named and directed, we did, on the sixth day of February one thousand six hundred and seventy-six, and at several days and times afterwards, and before the return of the said commission, personally repair unto the town of Looe, a member of the port of Plymouth aforesaid, in the said commission mentioned, and did search, view, and survey the open places there and thereabouts. And by virtue of the said commission we do hereby set down, appoint, and settle the extents, bounds, and limits of the said member to be as followeth: *viz.*

From Knaland Point, in the parish of Lan-sallas, in a supposed direct or right line eastward, to a town or village commonly called Wrickle, about five miles Eastward from Looe, together with all bays, harbours, havens, creeks, rivers, pills, strands, streams, barrs, roads, channels, or places within the said limits contained. And by virtue of the said commission we have assigned and appointed, and by these presents do assign and appoint, the several places hereafter-mentioned to be places, keys, or wharfs respectively, for the landing and discharging, lading or shipping of any goods, wares, or merchandize within the said Town of Looe, a member as aforesaid, or within the limits or districts thereof (that is to say), that open place, key, or wharf, commonly called the higher key, which is built into the river, containing in length from the front or head thereof Eastward, to Mr. Richard Pope's wall, fifty foot or thereabout, and in breadth at the front or head from North to South, and in all other places twenty-seven foot or thereabout; also the Middle key or Crane key, being likewise built into the river, and containing in length, from the front or head Eastward to Mr. Philip Pope's wall, forty-eight feet or thereabout, and in breadth at the head or front, and in each other place, forty-two foot or thereabout; also the Lower key, at the South end of the town, which is also built into the river, and containing in length, from the front or head Eastward to the street, forty-five feet or thereabout, and in breadth at the head or front, and at each other place, thirty-one foot or thereabout; which said places so assigned and appointed are, in our judgments and discretions, most convenient and fit for the uses and services aforesaid. And we do by these presents set down, appoint, and settle the extents, bounds, and limits of the said places, keys, or wharfs to be as aforesaid. And we do hereby and by virtue of the said commission utterly prohibit, disannul, make void, determine, and declare all other places within the said town of Looe, a member as aforesaid, or within the limits or districts thereof, from the privilege, right, and benefit of a place, key, or wharf, for the landing or discharging, lading or shipping of any goods or merchandize as aforesaid (except as in the said commission is excepted). In witness whereof, we have hereunto set our hands and seals, in Looe aforesaid.

    Phillip Pope, Mayor.
    Charles Osborne, Surveyor-general
     of the Customs.
    John Martin, Searcher.
    John Natt.
    Et Carolus Osborne, Ar.
    Lodovic Shirley, Ar.
    Et Samuel Neale, Gen.
    Tres Commmissiona' in com'is'on pr^d.
     nomi'at.

MEMBERS OF PARLIAMENT FOR EAST LOOE.

EDWARD III.

A. D. A. R.
1340   14   J. Hurston.—East Looe and Fowey sent one and the same merchant, then called a ship owner, to a council at Westminster (not to Parliament), and perhaps this was the person sent.

ELIZABETH.

1570   13   J. Wolley, E. Cordell.
1572   14   Thomas Stone and Thomas West.
1584   27   A. Rous, R. Spencer, gent.
  85   28   A. Hartwell, A. Trelawny.
  88   30   Sir R. German, knt., A. Everarde.
  92   35   W. Hampden, esq. G. Dounhall, gent.
  97   39   Ambrose Bellatt and Robert Gawdy, esq.
1601   43   Robert Yardeley and John Hannam, esq.

JAMES I.

1603   1   Sir Robert Phillips and Sir John Parker knts.
1620   18   Sir John Walter and Sir Jerome Horsey, knts.
  23   21   Sir John Walter, knt. and Paul Speccott, esq.

APPENDIX. 229

CHARLES I.

A. D.	A. R.		
1625		23 Jan.	Jacob Bagg.
		24 Jan.	John Chudleigh.
		23 April	Jacob Bagg.
		28 April	John Trevor.
1627		4 March	Wm. Murray.
		5 March	Paul Speccott.
1640	15 C. 1		Wm. Scawen and Wm. Code, esqrs.
41	16		Francis Bagge and Thomas ....

OLIVER CROMWELL.

1654   3 July
Keepers of England—Anthonie Rous elected for East Looe and West Looe.
Same year 12 July Robert Bennett elected for East Looe and West Looe.

The writ and Sheriff's precept thereon required the election of one Burgess only for the two Boroughs; but the corporations do not seem to have approved of this, as I have before-mentioned. See page 6.

RICHARD CROMWELL.

1   John Buller and John Kendall, esqrs.

CHARLES II.

| 1660 | 12 | Geo. Shelley and Nathan. Moyle, esqrs. |
| 62 | 13 | Hen. Seymour and Rob. Atkyns, esqrs. |

A. D.　A. R.
1668　　　Charles Trelawny and Henry Trelawny, esqrs.
　74　25　Walter Langdon.
　78　29　Charles Osborne.
　80　 .　Sir Jonathan Trelawny, bart. and Henry Seymour.
　82　33　Sir Jonathan Trelawny, bart. and John Kendall, esq.

WILLIAM AND MARY.

　89　 2　Charles Trelawny and Henry Trelawny, esqrs.

WILLIAM III.

1695　 7　Charles Trelawny and Henry Trelawny, esqrs.
　98　　　Charles Trelawny and Henry Trelawny, esqrs.
1700　12　Francis Godolphin and Sir Henry Seymour.
　 1　13　Ditto　　　　　　Ditto.
　　　　　George Courtney, esq.

ANNE.

1702　 1　Francis Godolphin and Sir Henry Seymour.
　 5　 4　Sir Henry Seymour and George Clarke, esq.

APPENDIX. 231

A. D. A. R.
1708   7   Sir Henry Seymour and Harry Trelawny, esq.
  11   9   Sir Henry Seymour and Thom. Smith.
  13 12   Charles Hedges and Henry Jennings, esqrs.

GEORGE I.

1714   1   John Smith, esq. and Sir Jacob Bateman.
  18   5   Horatio Walpole.
  22   8   John Smith and Horace Walpole.
  22   9   William Lowndes.
  23   George Cholmondeley.
  23   Sir Henry Haughton.
  27 13   George Cholmondeley, re-elected.

GEORGE II.

  27   1   Sir John Trelawny and Charles Longueville.
  34   8   Samuel Holden.
  34   Edw. Trelawny and George Longueville.
1740 14   Henry Legge.
  41   James Buller and John Gushry.
  47   Ditto   ditto.
  54   Ditto   ditto.

GEORGE III.

1761   1   Francis Gushry and John Buller, esqrs.
  62   2   Lord Palmerston.

APPENDIX.

A. D.	A. R.	
1765	6	John Buller, esq.
		Lord Palmerston.
66	7	Lord Palmerston.
68	8	John Buller and Richard Hussey, esqrs.
1770	11	Richard Leigh.
72	12	John Purling.
74	14	John Buller, esq. and Sir Charles Whitworth.
75	15	Thomas Graves, esq.
Same year		William Graves, esq.
1780	20	John Buller and Wm. Graves, esqrs.
83	24	John James Hamilton, esq.
84	24	John Buller, esq.
	24	John Buller and Wm. Graves, esqrs.
1786	26	Alexander Irwine, esq.
Same year		Richard Grosvenor, esq.
1788	28	Lord Belgrave.
89	29	Ditto.
1790	30	John Proby Earl of Carysfort.
Same year		William Wesley Pole and Robert Wood, esqrs.
1795	35	Charles Arbuthnot, esq.
96	36	John Buller and Wm. Graves, esqrs.
98	38	Frederic Wm. Buller, esq.
99	39	John Smith, esq.
Same year		Sir John Mitford.
1802		James Buller, esq.
Same year		John Buller and Edward Buller, esqrs.
1806	47	Ditto ditto.

APPENDIX.

A.D.	A.R.	
1807	47	Edward Buller and David Vanderheyden, esqrs.
12	52	Sir Edward Buller, bart. and David Vanderheyden, esqr.
16	55	Thomas Potter Macqueen, esq.
18	60	Vice Admiral Sir Edw. Buller, bart. and Thomas Potter Macqueen, esq.

GEORGE IV.

| 1820 | 1 | Thomas Potter Macqueen and George Watson Taylor, esqrs. |

MAYORS OF EAST LOOE.

1699	Thomas Bond.	1711	
1700	Thomas Blight.	12	
1	John Dyer.	13	
2	John Chubb.	14	John Dyer.
3	Thomas Bond.	15	
4	John Oben.	16	John Chubb.
5	John Dyer.	17	
6	John Hawkey.	18	
7	John Chubb.	19	
8	John Oben.	20	
9		21	Warwick Oben.
1710		22	Ditto.

1723 Sampson Rider.
24
25 John Chubb.
26 John Chubb, jun.
27
28
29
30 John Chubb, jun.
31 Thomas Bond.
32
33
34
35
36 Thomas Bond.
37
38
39
40
41
42
43 John Chubb.
44 Paul Nicholas.
45 Charles Trelawny, esq.
46 John Buller, esq. N. Dyer, deputy.
47 Waldron Dyer.
48 Nicholas Dyer.
49 George Dyer.

1750 John Chubb, died in office, N. Dyer succeeded.
51 Charles Trelawny, esq.
52 James Buller, esq.
53 James Dyer.
54 John Buller, esq.
55 Waldron Dyer.
56 Nicholas Dyer.
57 John Serle.
58 John Hoskings.
59 Waldron Dyer.
1760 Rev. Wm. Buller.
61 John Serle.
62 Francis Buller, John Serle, deputy.
63 John Hoskings.
64 Waldron Dyer.
65 James Dyer.
66 Thomas Bond.
67 Rev. Wm. Buller.
68 John Serle.
69 John Hoskings, James Dyer, jun. deputy.
1770 James Nicholas.
71 Waldron Dyer.

APPENDIX. 235

1772 John Buller, esq.
James Nicholas, deputy.
73 James Dyer, jun.
74 Rev. Wm. Buller,
James Nicholas, deputy.
75 Paul Nicholas.
76 Wm. Graves, esq.
James Dyer, deputy.
77 Thomas Ball.
78 John Whitter,
James Nicholas, deputy.
79 Waldron Dyer.
1780 Rev. Wm. Buller,
John Whitter, deputy.
81 James Nicholas.
82 Paul Harris Nicholas.
83 Thomas Ball.
84 William Keast.
85 Char. Morice Pole, esq. John Whitter, deputy.
86 Wm. Graves, esq. John Whitter, deputy.

1787 James Nicholas.
88 John Soady.
89 Thomas Bond.
1790 John Whitter.
91 James Nicholas.
92 Edw. Buller, esq.
93 John Soady.
94 Thomas Bond.
95 John Whitter.
96 John Soady.
97 John Whitter.
98 Thomas Bond.
99 John Soady.
1800 John Whitter.
1 John Soady.
2 Hender Whitter.
3 George Coytmor.
4 James Nicholas.
5 Thomas Bond.
6 Charles Bawden.
7 John Soady.
8 Thomas Campbell.
9 James Nicholas.
10 John Harris Nicholas.
11 James Nicholas.
12 Thomas Campbell.
13 John Keast.
14 William Soady.
15 James Nicholas.

1816 John Harris Nicholas.
17 Thomas Campbell.
1818 John Keast.
19 William Soady.
20 James Nicholas.

RECORDERS OF EAST LOOE.

By Queen Eliz. Charter, 1587, Sir Wm. Mohun, knt. first Recorder.

By James II. Charter, 1685, John Earl of Bath.

1620 Sir Reginald Mohun, knt. and bart.
1677 Sir Jonathan Trelawny, bart. was Recorder.
1724 Sir John Trelawny, bart.
1754 John Buller, esq. in room of Edward Trelawny, esq. said to be lately deceased.
1786 Rev. William Buller, clerk, in room of his brother John Buller, esq. deceased.
1797 William Graves, esq. in room of Dr. William Buller, Bishop of Exeter, deceased.
1802 Edward Buller, esq. in room of Wm. Graves, esq. deceased.
1802 John Buller, esq. in room of his brother Edward Buller, resigned.
1807 Edward Buller, esq. in room of his brother John Buller, deceased.

TOWN CLERKS OF EAST LOOE.

1620 Joseph Bastard.
1668 Edward Tomlinson.
1722 John Oben.
1739 Wallis Fisher.
1742 William Dungar, died 6 July, 1789.
1789 Thomas Bond.

MEMBERS OF PARLIAMENT FOR WEST LOOE.

EDWARD VI.

A. D.   A. R.
1552   6   J. Ashley and W. Morice.

MARY.

1553   1   A. Nevel, R. Clere, W. Bendlus, R. Mounson.

PHILIP AND MARY.

1554   1,2   C. Heygsham, A. Gilbert, esqrs.
  5   2,3   W. St. Aubyn, J. St. Clere, esqrs.
  7   4,5   O. Becket, J. Carminowe, gents.

ELIZABETH.

1558   1   J. Carminowe, esq.
1562   5   J. Fouler, J. Young, esqrs.

APPENDIX.

A. D.	A. R.	
1570	13	C. Thrackmorton, J. Fynneux, esqrs.
1	14	W. Hammond, J. Audeley, esqrs.
1585	28	R. Champernoune, J. Hammond, esqrs.
8	31	M. Patteson, R. Saunderson, esqrs.
1592	35	J. Shelbery, H. Beeston, esqrs.
96	39	R. Hitcham, esq. Sir H. Lennard, knt.
1600	43	J. Hare, R. Verney, esqrs.

JAMES I.

1603	1	W. Wade, ...
20	18	H. Finch, C. Harris, esqrs.

CHARLES I.

1625	1	J. Walstemholme, E. Thomas, esqrs.
		J. Walstemholme, J. Rudhall, esqrs.
27	3	E. Thomas, J. Parker, esqrs.
39	15	A. Mildmay, G. Potter, esqrs.
40	16	T. Arundell*, H. Killigrew*, J. Arundell, esqrs.

OLIVER CROMWELL. See East Looe.

RICHARD CROMWELL.

1 W. Whitelock, William Petty, esqrs.

---

* Disabled 1643 for adhering to the King's party.

CHARLES II.

A. D.	A. R.	
1660	12	J. Buller, J. Kendall, esqrs.
1	13	J. Nicholas*, J. Trelawny, esqrs.
1679	31	J. Trelawny, J. Trelawny, jun. esqrs.
		T. Kendall, H. Courtenay, esqrs.
1680	32	J. Trelawny, J. Trelawny, jun. esqrs.

JAMES II.

1685	1	H. Trelawny, J. Kendall, esqrs.

WILLIAM AND MARY.

1689	1	Percy Kirk, James Kendall, esqrs.
90	2	Edw. Seymour, John Trelawny, esqrs.

WILLIAM III.

1695	7	James Kendall, John Mounsteven.
98	10	Ditto ditto.
1701	13	Lord Ranelagh, James Kendall.

ANNE.

1702	1	Charles Seymour, Henry Pooley.
5	4	Sir Charles Hedges, Francis Palms.
8	7	John Conyers, Sir Charles Hedges.
10	9	John Trelawny, Sir Charles Hedges.
13	12	Sir Charles Wager, John Trelawny, esq.

---

* In his place, Sir Henry Vernon, bart.

GEORGE I.

A.D.	A.R.	
1714	1	Thomas Maynard, Geo. Delaval, esqrs.
22	9	John Trelawny, Edw. Trelawny, esqrs.

GEORGE II.

1728	2	J. Willes, E. Trelawny, esqrs.
33	7	J. Willes, T. Walker, esqrs.
35	9	J. Willis, E. Trelawny, esqrs.
1740	14	Sir Charles Wager, B. Keene, esq.
42	16	B. Keene, J. Frederick, esqrs.
47	21	J. Frederick, W. Noel, esqrs.
53	27	Ditto ditto.
56	30	J. Frederick, Wm. Trelawny, esqrs.

GEORGE III.

1761	2	Wm. Trelawny, Francis Buller, esqrs.
65	4	Francis Buller, esq. re-elected on being appointed Groom Porter of all his Majesty's houses in England and elsewhere.
67	8	James Townsend, esq. vice Sir Wm. Trelawny, bart. appointed Governor of Jamaica.
68	9	James Townsend, Wm. Graves, esqrs.
1774	14	William James, Charles Ogilvie, esqrs.
	5	John Rogers, vice Charles Ogilvie.
1780	16	Sir Wm. James, bart. John Buller, esq.

A. R.

John Somers Cocks, vice John Buller, esq. resigned.

John Buller, esq. vice Sir Wm. James, deceased.

John Lemon, John Scott, esqrs.

John Adams, esq. vice John Lemon, esq. resigned.

32 Sir John Wm. De la Pole, bart. J. Pardoe, esq.

John Buller, Sitwell Sitwell, esqrs.

John Hookham Frere, esq. vice John Buller, esq. resigned.

James Buller, Thomas Smith, esqrs.

Quintin Dick, esq. vice Thomas Smith, esq. resigned.

Ralph Allen Daniel, esq. vice James Buller, esq. resigned.

James Buller, Ralph Allen Daniel, esqrs.

James Buller, esq. re-elected on being appointed a Commissioner of the Admiralty.

James Buller, Ralph Allen Daniel, esqrs.

Sir Joseph Sidney Yorke, in room of James Buller, esq. appointed one of the Clerks in Ordinary to His Majesty's Privy Council.

Charles Buller, Antony Buller, esqrs.

A. D. A. R.
1816 Two elections same day. { Charles Hulse, esq. in room of Antony Buller, esq. appointed one of His Majesty's Justices in Bengal.
Henry Wm. Fitzgerald De Roos, in room of Charles Buller, esq. resigned.

1818 Sir Charles Hulse, bart. Henry Goulburn, esq.

GEORGE IV.

1820 Sir Charles Hulse, bart. Henry Goulburn, esq.

MAYORS FOR WEST LOOE.

1759 Samuel Bawden.
1760 Sam. Bawden, jun.
   1 C. Trelawny, esq.
   2 No election, owing to equal votes.
   3 June 27, John Buller, esq. (by mandamus).
   3 No election, owing to equal votes.
   4 John Buller, esq.
1765 June 24, Robert Hearle, (by mandamus).
   5 Sir Wm. Trelawny.
   6 Joseph Bawden.
   7 Edward Stephens.
   8 Rich. Puddicombe, elected 30 Sept.
   9 Step. Puddicombe.
1770 Robert Hearle.
   1 Jonathan Bawden.

1772 No Mayor elected, owing to equal votes.
3 Thomas Soady.
4 Rd. Puddicombe.
5 Step. Puddicombe.
6 Jonathan Bawden.
7 Thomas Soady.
8 Rd. Puddicombe.
9 Step. Puddicombe.
1780 Jonathan Bawden.
1 Rd. Puddicombe.
2 Nathaniel Hearle.
3 Step. Puddicombe.
4 Rd. Puddicombe.
5 Rob. Johns, died in office, and Nathaniel Hearle elected for the remainder of the year.
6 Step. Puddicombe.
7 Rd. Puddicombe.
8 Nathaniel Hearle.
9 Step. Puddicombe.
1790 Nathaniel Hearle.
1 Step. Puddicombe,
2 Nathaniel Hearle.
3 Anthony Jeeves.
4 Step. Puddicombe.
5 Nathaniel Hearle.
1796 Step. Puddicombe.
7 Anthony Jeeves.
8 Nathaniel Hearle.
9 Step. Puddicombe.
1800 Nathaniel Hearle.
1 Anthony Jeeves.
2 Step. Puddicombe.
3 Nathaniel Hearle.
4 Anthony Jeeves.
5 Nathaniel Hearle.
6 Anthony Jeeves.
7 Nathaniel Hearle.
8 27 July, Anthony Jeeves, in place of Mr. Nath Hearle, who died 19 July.
8 Nathaniel Hearle, son of the former.
9 Isaac Willcocks.
1810 Nathaniel Hearle.
11 Isaac Willcocks.
12 Nathaniel Hearle.
13 Isaac Willcocks.
14 Nathaniel Hearle.
15 Isaac Willcocks.
16 Nathaniel Hearle.
17 Isaac Willcocks.
18 Nathaniel Hearle.
19 Isaac Willcocks.
20 Nathaniel Hearle.

HIGH STEWARDS OF WEST LOOE.

1652, 26 Oct. Mr. Thomas Clements was elected and sworn Steward.
1660. John Trelawny, Esq.—called Recorder.
1665. Henry Seymour, Esq.—called Recorder.
1759. William Trelawny, Esq.
1765. John Dunning, Esq. in room of Sir William Trelawny.
1783, 3 Dec. James Templer, Esq. in room of John Lord Ashburton, deceased.
1814, 2 Mar. John Lemon, Esq.
1814, 2 Nov. Charles Buller, Esq.
1816, 12 June. John Buller, Esq.

TOWN-CLERKS OF WEST LOOE.

1660. Edward Tomlinson,—appointed by John Trelawny, Esq.
1665. Ditto—appointed by Henry Seymour, Esq.
1722. John Oben.
1739. Wallis Fisher.
——— Reymondo Putt.
1742. William Dangar—died July 6, 1789.
1789. Thomas Bond.

FLEETS OF THE ENEMY. — SIGNALS.

In the year 1779 the Combined Fleets of France and Spain, amounting to sixty-six sail of the line, twenty-eight frigates and corvettes, and having 15,000 troops on board, appeared off Plymouth Harbour, and, consequently, were visible from Looe. They lay-to on the 15th, 16th, 17th, and 18th of August, and then stood down Channel, without performing a single action worthy of record, except taking the Ardent, of sixty-four, Capt. Boteler, who gallantly fought three seventy-fours and two frigates (off the Bolt-head) before he struck, in sight of the Combined Fleet. In the mean time the Cork Convoy of 100 sail passed within three leagues of the Van division of the Enemy without molestation, and ran into Plymouth Sound, Hamoaze, and Catwater, without the loss of a ship. The Combined Fleets, notwithstanding their great superiority, were offered battle for two days by the gallant Admiral Hardy, who lay-to off the Lizard for them on the 23d and 24th of August, with only thirty-seven sail of the line. The object of the Enemy was to make a combined attack upon the Citadel, Arsenal, and Dock-yard of Plymouth; but they were panic-struck at the idea of being blocked up in the Sound by Admiral Hardy, whilst they were landing their troops. The signals for the Enemy's being off the Coast were at Maker Tower — a bloody flag at the pole, and two blue flags at the outriggers, three guns fired at the Batteries, and repeated by the Citadel — which was done during the four days the Enemy were off the Sound. Whether the Enemy intend at present (written in 1805) to try to bring out the Brest Fleet, and push up the Channel, we know not; but the same signals as those used at the period we have mentioned have lately been directed, in General Garrison Orders at Plymouth, to be observed, should the Enemy make their appearance. The beacons are to be lighted, and the troops of all descriptions are to form on their respective parades, where they are to wait for further orders, fully accoutred for service, with sixty rounds of ball-cartridges.

Ex Bundel Return Bri'um Parl. de Anno R'ni Regine Elizabethe decimo-quarto.

Hec Indentura f'ca apud Estlowe in Com. Cornub. xxiij° die Aprilis, an'o regni D'ne n're Elizabethe Dei gra. Anglie, Franc' et Hib'n'e R'ne, Fidei Defensoris, &c. xiiij^{to}, inter Will'm Mohun, Ar', Vic' Cornub', ex una p'te, et Will'm Pope, Major, Ville et Burgi de Eastlow pr^d, et Burgiens' ejusdem Ville, ex altera p'te. Testat' q^d pr$^{d'}$ Major et Co'itas Burgi pr'd' ex eor' assensu et eor' consensu eligerunt Thomam Stone et Thomam Weste, Armigeros, duos discretos et magis idoneos Burgiens's Burgi pr'd' libr' et indifferent' elect' plena et sufficient' potestate p' Co'itate Burgi pr'd' ac ip'is h'entis ad faciend' et consentiend' hijs q' de Co'i Consilio Regni Anglie in P'liament' ex nu'c' p' tenend' contingerint ordinari p'petu'.

In cujus rei testimoniu' p'sent' p'tin' pr'd' sigilla alternat' sunt appensa.

Dat' die anno et loco supradict'.

[The original is in the Chapel of the Rolls.]

Ex Bundle Bri'um Parliamen' pro Comitatu Cornwall de anno D'ni 1653, being the fifth year of Oliver Cromwell.

Oliver, Lord Protector of the Com'on Wealth of England, Scotland, and Ireland, and the Dominions thereto . . . [obliterated in the record] . . of the County of Cornwall, greetinge. In pursuance of the Government of the Com'on Wealth of England, Scotland, and Ireland, as itt . . . the sixteenth day of December, in the year of our Lord one thousand six hundred fiftie and three, and for the weightie and urgent affairs . . . the state and defence of the said Com'on Wealth, Wee, by the advice and assent of our Counsel, have ordained a Parliament . . . tie of Westminster, upon the third day of September next comeing, and there to consult and advise with the Knights, Citizens, and Burgesses . . . . Wealth. We do command you firmelie enjoyninge that Proclamac'on being made of the day and place aforesaid (in every market towne within . . . cause to be freelie and indifferently chosen by them who shall be p'sent att such Elec'on eight of the most fitt and discrete p'sons to serve as Knights . . . . for that County of Cornwall; and for the Boroughs of Dunishevett, otherwise Launceston, one Burgesse, for the Borough of Truro one Burgesse, for the Boroughe of Penryn one Burgesse, and for the Borough of Eastlow and Westlowe one Burgess, of the more discreete and sufficient. And the names . . . . said Knights and Burgesses, so to be chosen, whether they be p'sent or absent, you cause to be inserted in certain Indentures, thereupon to be made between you and them who shall be p'sent at such choice. And that you cause them to come att the day and place aforesaid, soe that the said Knights severally may have full and sufficient power, for themselves and the people of that Countie, and the said several Burgesses, for themselves and the people of the Boroughes aforesaid, to do and consent unto those things which then and there by com'on counsel of the said Com'on Wealth in Parliament (by God's blessinge) shall be ordained upon the weightie affairs aforesaid; soe that, for defect of such like power, or by reason of improvident choice of the Knights & Burgesses aforesaid, the said affairs may not remayne undone in any wise. And We will that neither you nor any other Sheriffe of the said Com'on Wealth be in any wise chosen; and the said choice, distinctly and openlie so to be made, you certifie to Us, in o^r Chancery, under yor

seale and the seales of them who shall be present at such choice, sending unto Us the other p'te of the saide Indenture, annexed together with this our Writt. And in yor proceedings and execuc'on hereof We will that you pursue and observe the several direc'ons lymitted, appointed, and p'scribed by the Government aforesaid. Witness Ourself, at Westminster, the first day of June, in the year of our Lord one thousand six hundred and fifty-four.

LENTHALL.

The execution of this Writt appears in certain Indentures to this Writt annexed.

J. PRAED, Sheriff.

[The original is in the Tower of London.]

———

This Indenture, made the third day of July, in the yeare of our Lord one thousand six hundred and fiftie-fower, between James Praed, Highe Sheriffe of the County of Cornwall, Esq. of the one p'tie, and Thomas Fraunces, Maior of the Borough of Portbigham, . . . Robert Fraunces, Anthonie Grubb, George Epps, Thomas Frawne, Thomas Boaden, Robert Harle, Nicholas Popham, Capital Burgesses, and John . . . . Ambros, Capital Burgesses of East Looe, of the other p'tie, wth the consent of the number of fortye and two free Burgesses of the said Inhabitants of the said . . . . . . Looe, witnesseth, that, by virtue of a Warrant unto Thomas Clemens and Thomas Fraunces, Maiors of the said Burroughs of East and West Looe, . . . to them directed for the electinge and choosinge of one Burgesse, of good understandinge, knowlege, and discretion, for causes concerninge the publique good of the Com'on Wealth, to be at his Highness's Parliam^t, to be holden at Westminster the third day of September next, wee the said Burgesses and Inhabitants there have made choice and elect[ion] of Anthonie Rowse, Esq. to be Burgesse of the said Burroughes of East and West Looe, to attend at the said Parliament, according to the tenour of the said [warrant unto] them the said Thomas Clemens and Thomas Fraunces directed in that behalf, who, for themselves and all the people of the said Burroughes, hathe full power to do and consent to those things wch in the said Parliament shall then and there, by common counsel and consent, happen to be ordained. Provided, [and] it is hereby declared, that they shall not have power to alter the Government as it is now settled in one single P'son and a Parliam^t. In witness whereof wee . . . . the p'ties above named to these p'sents interchangeably have put our hands and seales the day above written.

  JOHN HOSKINS. ROBERT FRANCIS.
  WILLIAM AMBROSE. ANTHONY GRUBB.
  ROBERT HEARLE. THOMAS BOADEN.
  NICHOLAS POPHAM. GEORGE EPSE.
  THOMAS FRANCIS, Mayor. THOMAS FRANCIS.

[The original is in the Tower of London.]

This Indenture, made the twelfe day of Julie, in the yeare of our Lord one thousand six hundred fifty and foure, between James Praed, Esq. High Sheriffe of the County of Cornwall, of the one part, and Thomas Clements, Gent. Thomas Dobbins, Walter Vine, William Pope, Edward Dobbins, et John Le Poor, Marchants, Peter Code, John Trefree, John Williams, Matthewe Rodd, William Dobbins, and William Couch, Burgesses and Inhabitants of the Boroughs of East Loo and West Loo, or Portbigham, of the other part, witnesseth, that, by virtue of a Warrant unto Thomas Clements, Mayor of the said Borough of East Loo, and Thomas Francis, Mayor of the said Borough of West Loo, or Portbigham, from the said High Sheriffe to them directed, for the electinge and choosinge of one Burgesse, of good understandinge, knowlege, and discretion, for causes concerninge the publique good of this Com'on Wealth, to be at his Highness Parliament, to be holden at Westminster the third day of September next, wee the said Burgesses and Inhabitants there have made choice and election of Robert Bennett, Esq. to be the Burgesse of the said Burroughes of East Loo, and West Loo, or Portbigham, to attend at the said Parliament, according to the tenour of the said Warrant unto them the said Thomas Clements and Thomas Francis directed in that behalfe; who, for himselfe and all, the people of the said Burroughes, hath full power to doe and consent unto those things wch in the aforesaid Parliament shall then and there, by com'on counsel and consent, happen to be ordained: Provided, and it is hereby declared, that he shall not have power to alter the Government as it is now settled in one single P'son and a Parliament. In witness whereof, wee the parties above named to these presents interchangeably set our hands and seales the day and year first above written.

>   PETER COODE.
>   JOHN TREFRY.
>   JOHN WILLIAMS.
> Sealed, signed, and deli-   MATTHEW RODD.
> vered in the presence of   WILLIAM DOBBING.
> JOHN FITZWILLIAM.   WILLIAM COUCH.
> WILLIAM COLLINGES.   WALTER VINE.
> JAMES DOWLINGE.   WILLIAM POPE.
> THOMAS RAWLINGE.   EDWARD DOBBING.
>   THOM. CLEMENTS, Mayor.
>   THOMAS DOBBINS, Justice.
>   JOHN SPOONER.

[The original is in the Tower of London.]

Ex Bundel Bri'um Parliamen' de Anno 1658.
. . . . . of the Com'on Wealth . . . . Scotland and Ireland, and the . . . Dominions and Territories thereunto belonging, to the Sheriff of Cornwall . . . ing . . . Councell for . . certain greate and weighty affaires concerning . . . the state and defence of the said . . . . ordaine our Pa . . . nt to be held at

our City of Westminster the seaven and twentieth day of January next comeing, and there . . ith the greate M . . . of the said Com'on Wealth; therefore We command you . . . . enjoyning that Proclamation being . . . aforesaid . . County to be held after the receipte of this our Writt you cau . . . be freely and indifferently chosen by . . . Knights with their swords girt of the most fite and discreet . . . sons of the County aforesaid, and of every Citt . . Cittizens, and of every Burrough two Burgesses of the most discreet and sufficient . . . according to the form of the Statute the . . . And the names of the same Knights, Citizens, and Burgesses, so to be chosen, whether they be present or absent, you cause to be . . . . certaine Indentures whereupon to be made between you and them who shall be present at such choice; and that you cause them to come at the . . . soe that the said Knights, for themselves and the Commonalty of the said County, and the said Cittizens and Burgesses for . . . . of the Cities and . . Burroughes aforesaid severally may have full and sufficient power to doe and consent unto those things . . . Councel of the said Com'on Wealth (by God's blessing) shall happen to be ord . . . . on the affaires aforesaid, so that, for defect, . . . ever or . . . . . by cause of improvident choice of the Knights, Cittizens, or Burgesses aforesaid, . . . affaires may not remaine undone in any wise. And We will that . . . . nor any other Sheriffe of the said Com'on Wealth be in any wise chosen . . . . in your full Countie made, you certify to Us in our Chancery, at the day and place aforesaid, distinctly and openly, without delay, under your seal and the seals of them who shall be present at such choice . . . . the other parte of the Indentures aforesaid to these Presents . . . with this Writ. Witness Ourself, at Westminster, the . . . . December, in the year of our Lord one thousand six hundred and fifty-eight.

  On the dors,   LENTHALL.
NICHOLAS COSS, Sheriffe.
  [The original is in the Tower of London.]

  This Indenture, made the seaventeenth day of Januarie, in the year of our Lord one thousand six [hundred fifty and eight*], between Nicholas Cossen, Esq. High Sheriffe of the County of Cornwall, of the one parte, and the Maior [and Free Burgesses of] the Burgh of East Looe, in the said Countie, of the other parte, witnesseth, that the said Mayor and [Burgesses have] authorized, nominated, elected, and chosen, and do hereby authorize, nominate, elect, and chuse John Kendall, Esq. [to be Burgess] for the said Burgh in the Parliament to be holden at the Cittie of Westminster the seaven and twentieth [day of] Januarie, and to doe and consent unto all such things wch there in the said Parliament, by com'on consent, shall be [ordained].

---

  * The words between crotchets, being defaced in the original, are supplied from the other indenture.

Witness whereof to one parte of the said Indentures the said High Sherife, and to the other parte the said Mayor [and Burgesses have] putt their handes and seales the day and year first above written.

Nicho. Read.	Edward Dobbins.
Philip Pope.	John Hoskins.
Jn°. Natt.	Peter Coode.
Thomas Collings.	William Pope, Mayor.
William Egar.	Walter Pris.
Richard Hickes.	William Ambrose.
John Hickes.	Tho⁸. Clements.

[The original is in the Tower of London.]

This Indenture, made the seaventeenth day of Januarie, in the year of our Lord one tho[usand six hundred] fifty and eight, betweene Nicholas Cossen, High Sherife of the County of Cornwa[ll, of the one] parte, and the Mayor and Free Burgesses of the Burrough of East Looe, in the [said County], of the other parte, witnesseth, that the said Mayor and Burgesses have authorized, nominated, [elected, and] chosen, and do hereby authorize, nominate, elect, and chuse John Buller, Esq. to be Burgess [for the said] Burrough in the Parliament to be holden at the Cittie of Westminster the seven and twentieth day of January . . . . and to doe and consent unto all such things which there in the said Parliament by com'on consent [shall be] ordained. In witness whereof to one parte of these Indentures the said

High Sheriffe, and to the other the said Mayor and Burgesses, have putt their handes and seales the day and year first above [written].

Nicho. Reed.	Edward Dobbins.
Philip Pope.	John Hoskins.
John Natt.	Peter Coode.
Thomas Collings.	William Pope, Mayor.
William Egar.	Walter Pris.
Richard Hickes.	William Ambrose.
John Hickes.	Thos. Clements.

[The original is in the Tower of London.]

COPY OF RECORD OF SESSIONS CONCERNING LOOE BRIDGE.

Cornub'. s's.

Memorandum quod ad Generalem Sessionem Pacis D'ni Regis, ten'dam apud Bodmin, in et pro Comitatu pr'd', septimo die Octobris, anno regni D'ni n'ri Caroli Sec'di, Dei gra' Anglie, Scotie, Francie, et Hib'n'e Regis, Fid' Defensoris, &c. vicesimo . . . . . John Coryton, Barron' Walter Moyle, Milit', et aliis sociis suis Justic' . . pr'd'co concernand' necnon ad div'sas felonias, transgressiones, et alia mat . . . . Comitatu perpetrat' audiend' et terminand' assigna' venit Nich'us Glyn . . . unus Justic' d'ti D'ni Regis ad Pacem in Com' p'd'to conservand' assigna . . . necnon, &c. et super visum suis p'sent' q^d quidam pons vocat' Looe Bridg jacens super aquam vocatam . . . inter Burgos de East Looe et West Looe, in Com' p'd'to, in varia pla . . . est ruinosus et in maximo decussu ob defectum rep'acionis. Ita quod legei dic' D'ni Regis in per supra vel ultra pontem p'd'c'm absque magno periculo ire . . . aut transire non valent ad . . . nocumentum omni' leg' . . . . . p'd'tum c . . . . . trans et ultra pontem p'd'ct'm trans' . . . . . Et q^d Inhabitantes de alter' Burg' de East Looe et West Looe eundem pontem de jure . . . . et reparare debent ut consueverunt. Et super hoc postea scil. ad Generalem Sessionem Pacis d'ti Dom' Regis tentam apud Bodmin, in et pro Com' pr'd' decimo-quarto die Julii, anno regni D'ni Regis, nunc, &c. vicesimo-sexto, coram Joh' Carew, Baronett' John' . . . Bar^o, Waltero Moyle, Mil', et aliis, . . . Justic' dic' D'ni Regis ad Pacem in Comitatu pr'd' conservand': necnon ad diversa felon', transgressiones, et alia malefacta in eodem Com' perpet^r audiend' et terminand' assignatis, venerunt Inhabitant' de Burg' de East Looe et West Looe in prop' person' suis coram Justic' . . . . auditum presentamenti priori et eis legitur. Que lect' et audire . . . superior imposit' allocat' . . . . se volint ind' acquitare dicunt q^d ip'i pontem pr'd't'm jure reficere vel reparare non debent. Et de hoc ponunt se sup' pri'um. Et Robertus . . . . Gen' qui in hac parte sequitur pro Dom. Regis similiter [Here the copy is much obliterated]. A Jury was sworn to try the facts; and their verdict was as follows: . . . . dicunt supra sacrum suum q^d Inhabitantes Burg' pr'd' de

East Looe et West Looe pr'd' reparare non debent, sed q^d idem pons reparari debet ut consuevit p^r Com' pr'd'; super quo visus est p^r Cur' hic intellectis omnibus et singulis premissis matur'sq' deliber' inde precis habita consideration' est per Cur' hic, &c. q^d Inhabitantes Burg' pr'd' de East Looe et West Looe de presentamento pr'd' ac de om'ibus content' eunt sine die.

> Concordat' cum Record. Exam' p' me
> Thom. Horwell, Cler' Pac' Com'
> pr'd' Deputatus.

Cornwall to wit.

At the General Quarter Sessions of the Peace of our Sovereign Lord the King, held at Liskeard, in and for the said County, the sixteenth day of July, in the eighth year of the reign of our Sovereign Lord George the Second, by the grace of God of Great Britain, France, and Ireland King, Defender of the Faith, and so forth, before John Glanvill, Richard Eliot, John Williams, Francis Gregor, Jeffery Morth, John Saltren, George Dennis, Esquires, and others their Companions, Justices of our said Sovereign Lord the King, assigned to keep the peace in and for the said County, and to hear and determine divers felonies, trespasses, and other misdemeanors committed within the said County;

Complaint being made unto this Court, by the Inhabitants of the Boroughs of East Looe and West

SESSIONS RECORD CONCERNING LOOE BRIDGE. 259

Looe, in this County, that the Bridge situate between the said Boroughs, com'only called Looe Bridge, is now ruinous and in decay; and it appearing unto this Court, upon the oaths of John Clubb, of East Looe aforesaid, Gentleman, aged sixty-three years and upwards, Peter Jewell, of West Looe aforesaid, Mariner, aged seventy-seven years or thereabout, and Thomas Gourd, of the same, Mason, aged forty-one years or thereabout, now examined in open Court, that the said Complaint is true; and that the said Bridge hath, for the space of forty-five years last past and upwards, been repaired at the charge of this County, when and as often as it wanted repair during that time. And there being no proof now given or offered to this Court that the said Bridge was ever repaired at any other expence than that of the said County, it is thereupon ordered by this Court, to prevent any danger that may happen to his Majesty's subjects that may have need that way to travel, that Mr. Alexander Hambly, one of the present Surveyors of the Bridges within the said County, do, upon notice of this order, forthwith cause the said Bridge to be put into sufficient repair at the charge of the said County. But it doth not appear unto this Court that any notice hath been given to any person or persons, in behalf of the said County, that the said Complaint was intended to be made in this Sessions. For which reason this County is at liberty to controvert any future charge of repairing of the said Bridge, except what is before directed.

By the Court,

WELCH, Deputy Clerk of the Peace of and for the County aforesaid.

OTES OF BODRIGAN'S GRANT.

To all faithfull Christian People to whom this p'sent writinge shall come, Otes of Bodrigan, Knight, Lorde of Pendrym and Loe, sendeth greetynge in our Lorde, &c. Know, your Universitie, that where certain contentions hathe byn moved betwene Henr' of Lyme, John Hadmore, John Dyala, Adam German, Nicholas of Lornocke, Thom's Fontaine, Roger Delamonde, Reginald Chappman, John Symon, Thomas Froste, Walter of Lyme, John Vigros, and Richard Sockemore, then Reve and Maior of the said towne, and all other Burgises of Loe, of th'one p'tie, and we the foresaid Otes of the other p'tie; upon the which certain p'ts . . . . . upon us by the foresaid Burgeses made by divers places in our Mannor of Pendrime, and also of rent of xx*l.* by the foresaid Henr' of Lyme, John Hadmore, &c. and all other Burgises aforesaid, appropreat and against us, to our disinheritance in the towne of Showta Consulate [*].

---

[*] I do not know why this place was then so called. The place goes by the name, at present, of Shutta, and probably took its

Nevertheless, the foresaid Henr' and all Burgess aforesaid have more attentively besought us that of foresayde trespasses we should mercyfully dyspence with them and the l're . . . . . our deede of Luce Vossall and Philippe of Bodregan, our ancestors . . . . . shoulde to them confirme. We therefore, for the healthe of our soles, and all our ancestres, favoreing the Petition of the said Burgises, have seen the Deede of the said Luce and Philippe, in these wordes: — Know ye, all men that be present and to come, that I, Luce Russell, Ladye of Pendryme, with th' assent and consent of Henr' of Bodrigan, myne only sonne, have given and graunted to all our Freemen of Loe, and of the Showta, all our lands in the townes of Loe and of the Showta, by these bounds: that is to saye, from a certaine stone that is called Paine Rocke, by Kykyshiere * theire, towards the Est upon the Sea,

---

name from the shoot of water there. There is a place at Shutta called Shutta Ball; and a field above it is called by that name. Whether there ever was any military work here, tradition does not say. In towns the appellation of Ballium was given to a work formed with palisadoes, and sometimes masonry, covering the suburbs, but in castles was the space immediately within the inner wall.

* There is no place of this name or like it at present. I cannot make out its derivation. There is a place near Paiu Rock (Pedn or Pen, the High or Head Rock) called Little Island; but, being part of the main land, cannot correctly be called an island. Probably the name has been transferred to this spot from a little island which might have been near to it, and now swallowed up or destroyed by the sea.

and so by the edge of the gardens of Loe, of old tyme diked, unto the corner of the gardyns of Walter of Lyme, next the garden of John Markistone, our Conventionarie of Pendryme, togather with one gardyn which is called Pollingshire, which conteyneth in itself, without the bandes afforesaied, xx perches of lande; and so from the garden of the foresaid Walter, by ye old dikes, until the King's highe waie, which leadeth from Loe towards our mannor of Pendryme, and so by the King's highwaie descendynge to the dike of our p'ke, the which is called the Lorde's P'ke, towarde the Northe, with all the lands within the same p'ke; and so from the corner of the foresaid p'ke, by the bank, lyneally discendynge unto the corner of the garden of Thom's Le Tailor, in the towne of the Shoute; and from the foresaid corner, or going upp against the Est, includynge all the whole p'ke of Thomas Tailor, in the towne of the Shoute; and from the foresaid corner of the p'ke, lineally descendyng towards the garden of Henr' of Lyme; and so by the dike of the foresaid garden, includynge all the Hill parke of John Diala, unto the greate way of the Shoute; and from thence, including all gardens of the Shoute agaynst the West p'te, unto the Sea. To have and to hould all the foresaid lande to the foresaid men, and to their heires, of us and of our heres, freely, quietly, and to inherit for ever; and the same, with their appurt's, without challenge or contradiction of us or of our heires, to give and to sell whensoever and to whomsoever they will. Yielding, therefore, unto us and to our heires, by the yere Өγ of silver at the feast of Easter. We graunt also to the foresaid men that the relief of a full whole Ⱳenre, that is to say, of a one fourth p'te of an acre of every which lande do not pass, xxx pence. We graunt also that the foresaid men and their heires to be quitt and discharged of all tallages and aied, as Burgeses of other boroughs of Cornwall. And the' to have the rent of all censors of the foresaied towne, and all other profitts, and to the help of thir rent aforesaid, so that we or our heires be not bounde the' to tax. And that the Reve or Maior of the foresaied towne be by common election yerely to be chosen, and after the whole yere to be amoved. We will that the Court of the foresayde townes to be holden theire from fortnight to fortnight by the Mondaye; and the plees of the foresaied townes be brought forth and . . determined by the said Burgises. And that no foreiner may have tavrne within the foresaied townes, unless he be in the libertye and companie of them of the same townes. In witness whereof to this p'sent wryttinge we have putt to our seales; theis witnesses, Richarde Corviens, Ric. de Kyliarde, Angowe de Tregarricke, William the son of Baldwin, Tristram le Kessel, Robert Crocherde, Robert de Lewcott, John de Arewood, Wymond of Heize, and many others. We the foresaied Ottes will, for us and our heires, that the foresaied Henr' of Lyme and John Hadmore, &c. and all the Burgess of the sayed townes, and their heiris, be our free Burgises. And that thei maie have free burgess in the townes aforesaied, with all thinges which to the lib'itie of a free borough app'teynethe, in as mouche as in us is, and as the foresayde date above beareth wytnesse. And the foresayed Henr' of Lyme, John Hadmore, &c. and for all other our Burgess of the foresayde townes of Loe and of the Showta, for their confirmation and their trespasses to be pacifyed, we will, for us and for our heires, that all other l'res, deedes, and writtinges, to us and to our ancestres made before the date of this present writtinge by any of the ancestres of the foresayed Otes our Lorde. And yff the' hereafter maie be founde, that all be made voied, and had for noughte, that for souche this our graunte, and the confirmation of this p'sent writtinge, maie for ever take strengthe to the same writtinge, made after the manner of chirographe, as with myne owne hande, as well as the seal of the foresaid Otes our Lorde, as the seale of Henr' of Lyme, John Hadmore, &c.; togath[r] also with the common seale of the Burgess[s] of the townes aforesayed, interchangeably be put. To this witness Lord William of Bodreans, Henr' of Campe Arnulphe, John of Carminow, Knyghte, John de Frandi, Anglo de Fursdon, Rob[t] Hamblie, Richard de Landon, Herb'te de Shevioke, John Cl'ico, and many others. Dated at Loe, the Fridaie the feaste of St. Peter ad Vincula, the yere of the raigne of Edwarde the son of Kynge Edwarde the xiiij[the], * &c.

This copy is indorsed thus:

| Lowe & Showta Le Charter ib'm. | Transcript' p' Copia' inde xix die Octob' a⁰ xxiij R' nu'c viz. p[r] qu'md'm Ric'uTrethenack d⁰ viz. xxiij Re ... 8⁰. | Which signifies, Transcribed by the Copy thereof the 19th Oct[r] in the 23d year of the reign of the now King, to wit, by RichardTrethenack. |

EUSTACIUS DE GRENVILL'S GRANT TO HIS MEN OF SHETE † [SHOWTA OR SHUTTA AFORESAID].

Sciant presentes et fut', q[d] ego Eustaci' de Grenvill dedi et concessi, et tradidi, et hac presenti carta mea confirmavi, om'ib's homi'b's n'ris de Shete totam t'ram meam eju'de' ville ad feodfirmam habendam et tenendam eis et he'dib's suis de me et he'dib's meis imp'petuu' lib'e quiete integre et plenarie, cu' om'ib's p'tine'tiis suis in bosco plano in viis semitis in pratis pasturis in aquis molendinis in exitib's

---

* This deed was made in the 14th year of the reign of Edw. II.

† Messieurs Lysons, in their *Magna Britannia*, have given a list of Cornish manors, mentioned in various records, the situation of which they could not ascertain; among them is Shete (probably this place), which in the thirteenth of Edward IV. belonged to Ph. Coplestone.

et introitib's in eschaetis et in om'ib's aliis aisiamentis, reddendo inde annuatim mi' et he'dib's meis qu'ordecim marcas argenti ad duos anni t'rminos, scil't ad festum S'c'i Michael' septem marcas, et ad festum S'c'i Thome Ap'li septe' marcas, p' om'i serv'c'o et exacc'one ad me et ad he'des meos spectantib's. Salvo s'vitia . . . . . . videlicet quantum p'tinet ad t'ciam p'tem feodi unius militis. Salvo et m' et he'dib's m'is relevia d'ca t're, scil't ad qu'ntita'em duar' parti'm redditus illius, scil't qui relevia dabit cum forte contig'it. Salvo et si ego v'l he'des n'ri capti fuimus de guerra p'd'ci homines mei adjuvabu't nos ad corp' n'r'm redimendu' de p'sona et delibandu', et hoc q°uscunq' capti fuim's, q^d Deus avertat. Prete'a auxil'm mi' facient ad filiu' meu' milite' faciend'. Istud idem facient he'dib's mi's. Et et'm auxili'm michi facient ad filiam meam maritandam. Similit' istud idem facient he'dib's meis. Et sciendu' est q^d si forte int' p'c'os homines meos aliq' fut' contencio v^l discordia que p' ip'os non possit ad concordiam reduci, ip'i ad me et ad he'des meos accedent tam ad D'num eor' et ibide' coram nob' debent concordari, et illa mis'c'dia erit mei et he'd'm meor'. Et si forte aliquis ali' mihi et he'dib's meis aliquam fecit querelam de pred'c'is homi'b's meis, et coram me v^l he'dib's meis p'bari possit q^d ip'i homines mei in hoc delig'rint, ego et he'des mei exinde emendac'onem capiem'. Prete'a cum forte aliquis eor' decesserit, v^l feodu' compleverit, pred'c'i homines mei he'dem et t'ram suam eum p'tin' et catalla sua custodient p' conciliu' amicor' predicti he'dis, et heres ipse erit sub custodia p'pinq'oris amici sui, et p'd'ci homines facient m'et he'dib's meis s'vicim illius t're. Cu' v° p^{d}cus heres tal' sit etatis q^d deb'at t'ram ten'e, se'd'm consuetudinem Regni, predic' homines mei pred'c'am t'ram cum p'tin' et catalla pred'ca he'di restituent in eod'm statu v^l in meliori quo ip'i t'ram illam et catallam receperunt. Pred'c'i v'o homines mei ad om'ia presc'pta firmit' tenenda ponent tenementu' suu' in plegiu'. Ego v'o Eustacius et he'des mei warrantizabim^s pred'c'is hominib's m'is et he'dib's suis totam p'd'cam t'ram de Shete cu' p'tin' cont' om'es gentes. Et ut hæc mea Donac'o concessa ratè et firmè p'maneat p'sentem cartam sigilli mei apposic'one duxi roborandam. Hiis Testibus Jordano Abbate de Dureford, Will'o de Shorewell, Will'o de Lalilia, Elija filio ejus, Thoma de Ho, Germano de Ranville, Rob'to de Berling, Hereb'to de Tere, Will'o de Linford, Nichol' de Langardle, Rad. Gulthope, Henr' de Chalverille, Ric' de la Bere, Will'o de Thewantenere, et al'.

Seal.

This deed is without a date; but by the writing is supposed to have been granted about the reign of King John. It is beautifully written, but very difficult to transcribe. Some of the words may be mistaken by the transcriber.

268   APPENDIX.

Gilbert, in his History of Cornwall, under the title of "Lord Grenville," speaks of a Sir Eustace de Grenville, supposed to have been a nephew of Robert, second son of Rollo the first Duke of Normandy, who attended Richard I. in his expedition into Normandy, and for his services was, with William Marshall, Earl of Pembroke, Richard Earl of Clare, and Hugh de Nevil, excused from paying centage. In the sixteenth of John he was Constable of the Tower of London, and, following the example of several of his ancestors, was a great benefactor to the Abbey of Netley, in Buckinghamshire, founded by his ancestor Walter Gifford.

This, most probably, was the person who made the above grant.

The revenues of the Bodies Corporate of East and West Looe are not great, and are generally applied to repairs of the streets, quays, &c. &c. and entertainments at the corporate meetings, at which each Corporation invites the Members of the other, so that between them there are several grand dinners in the course of a year. At these entertainments, after "The King and Royal Family" are drank, the next toast is, "The Two Looes," and then, "Two Looes" a second time [*]. Each of the Boroughs has

---

[*] During the late Revolutionary War a learned D. D. was present at one of these entertainments, and when "Two Looes"

a very large and elegant China punch-bowl, which was given to them by Admiral Sir Joseph Knight†, who was a native of East Looe. And East Looe has three other elegant China bowls, two of them holding four gallons each, presented to them by the late John Buller, Esq. Each of these bowls has an inscription, " To the worthy Electors of East Looe, Health and Prosperity;" on the opposite side, under Mr. Buller's arms, " JOHN BULLER, of East Looe, Esq.;" and a view of Looe, taken from Borlase's History of Cornwall, with Mr. Buller's arms, beautifully enamelled, on its side. When Mr. Buller sent these bowls from India, he also sent a large present of arrack in another vessel to the Electors, which, unfortunately, was captured by a French privateer, just

---

was given he began to think why such a toast should be pronounced, and with three cheers. Upon " Two Looes" a second time being given, with three cheers, he rose up, and begged to be informed of the cause of the toast, stating that he was aware he should be fined a bumper for making the enquiry; but as he had not heard of any victory over the French, he wished to know the particulars of what had occurred at " Toulouse" to deserve such toasts and cheering!

† Admiral Sir Joseph Knight was born in East Looe, in a house still in existence, and now belonging to Mr. Edw. Speare. He first went to sea, as I have been told, with a Capt. Wilshman, of Looe, as a cabin-boy of, I fancy, a merchant-ship. When our late King (George III.) visited Portsmouth, in June 1773, Capt. Joseph Knight then commanded the Ocean, and, being senior Captain in the Fleet at Spithead, had the honour of knighthood conferred upon him by the King on the 24th of June; and he had afterwards the honour to kiss his Majesty's hand upon the

as it had reached the English coast. It is a common saying in Cornwall, that no business can be done without good eating and drinking; and I think the Looers are not behind their neighbours in this respect; and that it is not a modern practice may be shewn from a bill of one of their entertainments at a Law Court for East Looe, on the 25th of October 1725, as follows *literatim*:

	£.	s.	d.
To 60 Bottells of Claret	4	10	00
To 28 Bottells of Shurey	2	16	00
To 6 Bottells of Canary	0	15	00
To 115 Quarts of Alle	1	08	09
To Eatables in all	5	00	00
Carried forward	£14	09	09

quarter-deck under the Royal Standard. Sir Joseph died in the year 1775, and was buried in Harwich Chapel, Essex, where a monument bears this inscription:

To the memory of
Sir JOSEPH KNIGHT,
Rear-admiral of the White.
Descended from an antient family in Cheshire,
born in Cornwall;
he served his King and Country for more
than half a century
with loyalty, disinterestedness, and fortitude.
Obiit 8 September 1775, ætatis 66.
And of Dame PHILIPINA his wife, daughter
of Anthony Deane, Esq. of this county;
a zealous friend, instructive companion,
and excellent parent.
Obiit 20 July 1799, ætatis 72.

APPENDIX.

	£.	s.	d.
Brought forward	14	09	09
To 6 Doz. of Lemons - -	0	12	00
To 7 Quarts of Brandy - -	0	14	00
To 5½ of Sugg^r - - - -	0	07	04.
To Tobacco - - - - -	0	02	00
To Horse Meate - - - -	0	02	06
The Totall	£16	07	07

Such an entertainment would now cost (1819) little less than seventy pounds.

As the Borough of East Looe is in the Parish of St. Martin's, it may not be improper to insert in this work the following transactions which have taken place in the said Parish, and in which East Looe is in some degree concerned.

In Dei no'i'e, Amen. We whose names are subscribed, haveing received a Commission, dated the three and twentieth daye of July in the yeare of our Lord God 1663, from the Reverend Joseph Martyn, Doct^r of Laws, Commissary Generall to the Right Reverend Father in God Seth, by Divine permission, Lord Bishop of Exon, for the placeing and assigning of Seats in the Parish Church of St. Martin's by Looe, within the s^d Diocess of Exon, and being all mett togather at the Parish Church the second daye of September 1663, and haveing here taken into consideration the conveniency of seating the Parishioners of the s^d Parish according to their quality, paym^{ts}, and fittest p'portions, have, for the conservation of order, peace, and decency, with the general consent of the said Parrishioners, ordered the same, and do hereby make a Certificate thereof: and taking into consideration an Agreement, made the 17th day of November in the 43^d yeare of Queen Elizabeth, for the Division of the said Parish Church between the Corporation of East Looe and the rest of the Parishioners, we do consent that the same shall be ratified and continued as it was before, the Church being equally divided between them, the one halfe to the Parish, the other halfe to the Corporation, according to their usuall bounds: and for the seating of p'rticular persons in both respectively, we do agree that it be as hereafter followeth:

The Parish are seated as followeth } ... Names ... Seats. ...

The Corporation of East Looe are placed and seated as followeth } ... Names ... Seats. ...

[The names and seats are added; but it is useless to insert them.]

Provided, that whereas the two former seats in the East side of the South isle are above mentioned to be in the right of Mr. Mayow. It is concluded between the Townde and the s^d Mr. Mayow, that if the s^d Mr. Mayow can make out his peculiar right to all the seats of that rowe in the s^d isle, that his exceptance of the saide two seats for the p'sent shall be no p'judice to him as to the title. And in cause the saide Mr. Mayow do not make out clear right to all the saide seats in the s^d rowe, that then they shall be in the disposal of the Towne.

Subscribed and consented to the daye and year above written, by us,

    RICHARD LANGSTON.   WILLIAM SCAWEN.
    WALTER CONNING.   WALTER LANGDON.
              ROB. HANCOCKE, Rect^r.
              JOHN HILL, Churchwarden.

The 30th day of April in the year of our Lord 1666.

> Hereafter followeth a Note of such anchant Customs as hath bin used within the Parish of St. Martin's, as well in time past as this present and time out of minde observed and kept.

Ar^t. 1. The Parishners of the said Parish ought to have, by thare custom, of thare Parson or his Proctor under him, a Bull alwaie remaininge upon the Gleab of the Parsonage of St. Martin's aforesaid, for the necessary use at all times when occasion shall sarve.

Ar*t*. 2. Item, our custom is, that if any within the said Parish abow two cows in his keeping, the same ought to bring tything witch according to the place accustomed, unless they can agree otherwaie with the Parson or the Proctor for the same. And he that hath but one or two cows in his keeping to pay but a penny for a cow, as by the custom hath been heretofore held.

Ar*t*. 3. The Parishioners aforesaid are to anser Parson or his Proctor a peney for every calf killed, and a halfpeney for every calf reared, according to the custom.

Ar*t*. 4. The Parishners aforesaid ought, by thare anchant custom, to bring, on St. Mark's day, thare tything lambs to the accustomed place in time; and if any man within the said Parish hath but seven, then the Parson or his Proctor ought to have one; and if any have under the number of seven lambs, he ought to pay at the next Easter then following, to the Parson or his Proctor, a farthing for every lamb, according as in time past.

Ar*t*. 5. For every man inhabiting within the said Parish, according to the number of his sheep, ought to pay the tenth flice of wool, and to bring it to the place accustomed, as in time past.

Ar*t*. 6. For our tything corn we ought, by our anchant custom, to tithe it at the time of curing, unless we can agree with the Parson or his Proctor for the same; but if they cannot agree for the same, the Owner or Tailer thereof are to give warning, in open Church, when they carry, whereby the tenth shock or the tenth sheef is to be left for the Parson or Proctor may be saved; and after the same is so tythed and left, it is to be taken away in the space of three days after.

Ar^t. 7. The tythe of hay, after the first raking, the Parson or his Proctor ought to have, unless the Owners have or can agree for the same.

Ar^t. 8. If thare be any cyder made within the Parish, the Parson or his Proctor ought to have two pence for every such hogshead of cyder of the Owner, according to the custom.

Ar^t. 9. Tything honney is to be brought by the Owner to the place accustomed, for the Parson or his Proctor, according to the anchant custom.

Ar^t. 10. The Owner of every mill within the s^d Parish is to pay at Easter to the Parson or his Proctor two shillings for every such mill.

Ar^t. 11. And for every small dutey, as his ripe beans, the' must be tythed according to the quantity; and for herbe gardens, every Owner is to pay for every such garden to the Parson or his Proctor one penny yearly at Easter; and pigs and geese to be paid when the' become due, as in times past hath been accustomed.

Be it known to all men, by these presents, that I, Stephen Medhopp, Parson of the Parish of St. Martin's, and we, the Parishioners of the said Parish, whose names are under written, doe acknowledge that this award with us written was done with the consent and good liking, made by Richard Carew and John Wrey, Esquirse, and was don with the consent and good liking of us all. In witness whereof we have subscribed our names.

    STEPHEN MEDHOPP, Rector.
    JOHN LANGSTON.
    JOHN IVEY.
    JOHN HOSKING.
    HENRY CHUBB.
    JOHN ANDREWS.
    JOHN KNIGHT.

MAYOR-CHOOSING DAYS.

The following Table may be of service; it shews the Days of the Mayor-choosing at East Looe, from the year 1800 to the year 1899.

	1800	1828	1856	1884	Sept.
					22
	1	29	57	85	14
	2	30	58	86	27
	3	31	59	87	19
B	4	32	60	88	10
	5	33	61	89	23
	6	34	62	90	15
	7	35	63	91	28
B	8	36	64	92	19
	9	37	65	93	11
	10	38	66	94	24
	11	39	67	95	16
B	12	40	68	96	28
	13	41	69	97	20
	14	42	70	98	12
	15	43	71	99	25
B	16	44	72	—	16
	17	45	73	—	8
	18	46	74	—	21
	19	47	75	—	13
B	20	48	76	—	25
	21	49	77	—	17
	22	50	78	—	9
	23	51	79	—	22
B	24	52	80	—	13
	25	53	81	—	26
	26	54	82	—	18
	27	55	83	—	10

It appears, from the Table, that in the period of 28 years the Mayor-choosing Day falls twice on the 10th, 13th, 16th, 19th, 22d, 25th, and 28th; and once on the 8th, 9th, 11th, 12th, 14th, 15th, 17th, 18th, 20th, 21st, 22d, 24th, 26th, and 27th.—A new order takes place after the year 1899, on account of the year 1900 not being a leap year in the Gregorian style. D. G. *Tredrea*, Sept. 1812.

APPENDIX.

A VIEW of the VOLUNTEER ARMY of GREAT BRITAIN *in the Year 1806; designed to commemorate the great and united Spirit of the* BRITISH PEOPLE, *armed for the Support of their antient Glory and Independence against the unprincipled Ambition of the* FRENCH GOVERNMENT.

ROYAL CORNWALL VOLUNTEERS.

	Men.		Uniforms.
Crinnis Cliff Battery - - - - -	120	— Captain Joseph Dingle - - -	1
Fowey Artillery - - - - -	180	— Captain William Browne - -	2
Helstone Infantry - - - - -	60	— Captain John Rogers - - -	2
Killigrew Cavalry - - - - -	56	— Captain H. P. Andrews - -	3
Launceston Infantry - - - -	285	— Lieutenant-colonel Thomas Phillipps	4
Looe Artillery - - - - -	70	— Captain Thomas Bond - - -	2
Maker Artillery, First Company -	121	— Captain William Little - -	2
Ditto Second Company -	90	— Captain William Vallack - -	2
Loyal Meneage Infantry - - -	574	— Lieutenant-colonel James Passingham	5

Carried forward 1556

	Men.		Uniforms.
Brought forward	1556		
Mountsbay First Regiment of Infantry	569	Lieutenant-colonel Rose Price	5
Ditto Second ditto ditto	418	Lieutenant-colonel Richard Hichens	6
Ditto Artillery	215	Major John Davis	2
Pendennis Artillery	573	Lieutenant-colonel Isaac Burgess	7
Penryn Infantry	418	Lieutenant-colonel George C. George	8
Penwith Cavalry	105	Major Lord De Dunstanville	9
Royal Redruth Infantry	103	Captain Henry Noal	5
St. Ives Infantry }	378	Lieutenant-colonel James Halse	6
Ditto Artillery }			7
St. Mabyn Infantry	92	Captain Francis J. Hext	10
Breage Infantry	113	Captain John Tregear	5
East Cornwall Troop	44	Captain Rt. Hon. Reginald Pole Carew	11
St. Germans Cavalry	40	Captain Lord Eliot	11
North Cornwall Infantry	630	Lieutenant-colonel Wrey Ians	4
East Cornwall Infantry	1073	Lieutenant-colonel Lord Eliot	5
Loyal Meneage Cavalry	136	Major Vyell Vyvyan	11
Carried forward	6463		

APPENDIX.

	Men.		Uniforms.
Brought forward	6463		
Portreath Artillery	94	— Captain W. Reynolds	2
Roseland Infantry	348	— Lieutenant-colonel Francis Gregor	5
Royal Stannary Artillery	1113	— Lieutenant-colonel Thomas Tyrwhitt	2
Truro Infantry	344	— Lieutenant-colonel Thomas Warren	5
	8362		

The effective force of the Volunteer Army of Great Britain in the year 1806 was

$\left\{\begin{array}{l}\text{Cavalry } 31,771 \\ \text{Infantry } 328,956 \\ \text{Artillery } 10,133\end{array}\right.$

Total 370,860.

A MERRY TALE.

I have now nearly exhausted my subjects. As a faithful Historian, however, I cannot help inserting the following story, which I have seen in print, for the mere purpose of gravely contradicting the slurs which are thereby intended to be imposed on one or other of the two Looes. Similar jokes have been made on other Cornish Boroughs, but all of them create more mirth than mischief, whatever their authors intended. This story is printed at the end of an old edition of Æsop's Fables, and runs thus:

" A MERRY STORY.

" Having been conversant with birds and beasts, I will add one true story thereon, which demonstrates that stupidity and ignorance possess some human souls to such a degree, that they seem to have no more knowledge than the beasts that perish.

" In the reign of Queen Elizabeth, a fellow who wore his hat buttoned up on one side, and a feather therein, like a tooth-drawer, with the rose and crown on his breast for a badge, had obtained a licence from the then Lord Chamberlain, to make a show of a great ape about the country, who could perform many notable tricks; and by going to markets and fairs, his master picked up a great deal of money.

The ape usually rid upon a mastiff dog, and a man beat a drum before him. It happened that these four travellers came to a town called Loo in Cornwall, where, having taken an inn, the drum beat about the town to give notice, that at such a place was an admirable ape, with very many notable qualities, if they pleased to bestow their money and time to come to see him; but the towns-people being a sort of poor fishermen who minded their own employments, none of them thought it worth their while to see this worthy sight, at which the fellow being vexed, resolved to put a trick upon them whatsoever came of it, and therefore he contrives a warrant which he sends to the Mayor to this effect:

"These are to will and require you and every one of you with your wives and families, that upon sight hereof, you make your personal appearance before the Queen's Ape, for he is an ape of rank and quality, and is to visit all her Majesty's dominions, that by his converse and acquaintance with her loving subjects, he may be the better enabled to do her Majesty service in discovering their fidelity and loyalty. And hereof fail not, as you will answer the contrary at your utmost peril."

This warrant being brought to the Mayor, he sent for a shoemaker at the farther end of the town to read it, which when he had heard, he assembled his brethren the Aldermen to the Common-hall, to consult of this weighty affair. Being met, they all sate silent at least a quarter of hour, no man speaking a word, not knowing what to say; at length a young man who had never served any office said, "Gentlemen, if I might speak without offence, and under correction of the Worshipful, I would give my opinion in this matter." "Pray, neighbour, speak freely," quoth the Mayor, "for though you never yet bore any office, yet you may talk as wisely as some of us." "Then," says the young man, "I am of the mind that this ape-carrier is an insolent saucy knave, who designs to make our town ridiculous to the whole kingdom; for was it ever known that a fellow should be so audacious to send a warrant without either name or date to a Mayor of a town, who is the Queen's Lieutenant, and that he and his brethren, their wives and children, should be all commanded to appear before a jackanapes; therefore, my counsel is that you take him and his ape, with his man and his dog, and whip the whole tribe of them out of the town, which will be much for your reputation and credit." At which words, a grave Alderman, being much disturbed, replied, "Friend, you have spoken little better than treason; remember it is the Queen's Ape, and therefore be careful what you say." "You speak true, brother," quoth the Mayor. "I wonder how that saucy fellow came into our company; pray, friend, depart; I think you long to have us all hanged." The young man being put out of doors, "Well now, brethren," says the Mayor, "what is to be done with this troublesome business?" "Marry," quoth another old senior, "we may see by the feather in his cap, and the badge he wears, that he is the Queen's man, and who knows what power a knave may have at Court, to do poor men in the country an injury? therefore, let us e'en go and see the Ape, it is but two-pence apiece, and no doubt the Queen will take it well, if it come to her ear, and think that we are very civil people to show so much duty to her Ape; what may she imagine we would do to her bears if they should come hither; besides 'tis above two hundred miles to London, and if we should be complain'd of and fetched up by pursivants or messengers, I'll warrant it would cost us at least ten groats a man, whereas we now come off for twopence apiece." This wise speech was though so pertinent, that the whole drove of townsmen with their wives and children went to see the Ape, whom they found sitting on a table with a chain about his neck, to whom Mr. Mayor put off his hat, and made a leg to show his respect to the Queen's Ape; yet pug let him pass unregarded; but Mrs. Mayoress coming next in a clean white apron with her hands laid upon it, she, to shew her breeding, makes a low curtsie to him; and pug, like a right courtier, though he did not mind the man, yet, to shew his respect to the woman, put out his paw to her, and made a mouth; which the woman perceiving, "Husband," quoth she, "I think in my conscience the Queen's Ape mocks me;" whereat pug made another wry face at her, which Mr. Mayor observing, grew very angry, cry-ing, "Thou sirrah ape, I see thy sauciness, and if the rest of the courtiers have no more manners than thou hast, I am afraid they have been better fed than taught; but I'll make thee to know, before thou goest out of town, that this woman is my wife, an antient woman and a midwife, and one that for her age might be thy mother;" and then going in a rage to the door, where the ape's tutor was gathering in his pence, "Sir," says he, "do you allow your ape to abuse my wife?" "No, by no means," quoth the fellow. "Truly sir," quoth the Mayor, "there be sufficient witness within that saw him make mops and mows at her, as if she were not worthy to wipe his shoes." "Sir," said the fellow, "I will presently give him severe chastisement for his impudence;" and thereupon taking his whip, and holding Jack by the chain, he gave him half a dozen smart lashes, that made pug's teeth chatter in his head like virginal jacks; which Mr. Mayor espying, runs to the fellow, and holding his hand, cried out, "Enough, enough, good Sir, you have done like a gentleman; let me intreat you never to give correction in your wrath; and pray, Sir, when the play is done, be pleased to come along with your ape to my house, and both of you take a small supper with me and my wife."

DISTANCES OF PLACES FROM LOOE.

LAUNCESTON.

	Miles	Miles
To Liskeard	8	
Launceston	19	
Total	—	27

TAVISTOCK.

To Liskeard	8	
Callington	8	
Tavistock	8	
Total	—	24

FALMOUTH.

To Fowey	9	
St. Austell	7	
Truro	13½	
Falmouth	12	
Total	—	41½

EXETER, through Ashburton.

To Plymouth	15	
Ivy Bridge	11½	
Brent	4	
Ashburton	9	
Chudleigh	9	
Exeter	10½	
Total	—	59

	Miles	Miles

EXETER, through Totness.

To Ivy Bridge	-	-	-	-	26½	
Totness	-	-	-	-	12	
Newton Bushel	-	-	-	8	
Exeter	-	-	-	-	15	
				Total	—	61½

BATH.

To Exeter, as before, through Ashburton	59	
Collumpton	-	-	-	12	
Wellington	-	-	-	12	
Taunton	-	-	-	-	7	
Bridgwater	-	-	-	-	12	
Piper's Inn	-	-	-	-	10½	
Wells	-	-	-	-	10½	
Bath	-	-	-	-	20	
				Total	—	143

BRISTOL.

To Wells as before	-	-	-	123	
Bishop's Chuc	-	-	-	12	
Bristol	-	-	-	-	7	
				Total	—	142

PORTSMOUTH.

To Exeter as before	-	-	-	59	
Honiton	-	-	-	-	16	
Axminster	-	-	.	-	10	
Bridport	-	-	-	-	9	
Dorchester	-	-	-	-	15	
Blandford	-	-	-	-	16	
				Total	—	125

APPENDIX.

	Miles	Miles
Brought over	—	125
Winborne	10	
Ringwood	9	
Southampton	20	
Botley	10	
Fareham	8	
Portsmouth	8	
Total	—	190

PENZANCE.

To Truro as before	29½	
Redruth	8	
Penzance	18	
Total	—	55½
From Looe to Bodmin		16
Looe to Lostwithiel		12
Looe to St. Germans		9
Looe to Polperro		3

PLYMOUTH to FALMOUTH.

The two ways by Liskeard and Looe compared.

LISKEARD way.

To Liskeard	18	
Lostwithiel	12	
St. Austell	9	
Truro	13½	
Falmouth	12	
Total	—	64½

Looe way.

	Miles.	Miles.
To Looe	15	
Fowey	9	
St. Austell	7	
Truro	13½	
Falmouth	12	
Total		56½

Looe way consequently nearer by eight miles.

Looe to London.

	Miles.
To Axminster as before	87
Crewkerne	13
Yeovil	10
Sherborne	5
Shaftsbury	15
Salisbury	20
London	83
Total	233

Looe to London another way.

	Miles.
To Plymouth	15
Exeter	46
Honiton	16
Axminster	10
Bridport	9
Dorchester	15
Blandford	16
Woodyeat's Inn	11
Salisbury	11
Carried over	149

		Miles.	Miles.
Brought over		149	
Andover	- - - -	18	
Whitchurch	- - -	7	
Basingstoke	- - -	12	
Hartford Bridge	- - -	10	
Bagshot	- - - -	10	
Staines	- - - -	10	
Hounslow	- - - -	7	
London	- - - -	9	
	Total	—	232

ADDENDUM TO THE ACCOUNT OF ST. NEOT AND ST. NEOT'S CHURCH, PAGE 194.

"There was (says Capgrave[*]) a certain King of the West Angles, and of Kent, Eudulphus[†] by name, more disposed to acts of pious liberality than to worldly ambition. He was a zealous defender of

---

[*] Capgrave, Nova legenda Angliæ, fol. 239, edit. Lond. 1516. Capgrave was a canon of St. Augustin, and a distinguished writer in the reign of Henry VI.; to whom and to Humphrey Duke of Gloucester several of his works are addressed. Perhaps the legendary stories related by him, being so minutely copied in the windows of St. Neot's church, will afford a presumption that the painting was executed at the time when his Lives of the English Saints were in fresh repute.

[†] Ethelwolf.

the Church against all its enemies, and gave largely of his substance both to it and to the poor. God had regard to these his good works, and blest him with a son named Neotus. This youth of royal birth received every advantage that could be derived from the best education, and gave early marks of his contempt for the vanities and cares of this world, chusing rather to be a servant in the house of his God than to indulge in the luxury and splendour of earthly palaces. He therefore became a monk in the house of Glastonbury, while Dunstan was abbot there. Here he was soon distinguished for his pious exercises and severities, and for the miracles he performed in casting out devils and healing the sick. Numbers resorted to him from all parts, both for the cure of bodily complaints and for instruction in their spiritual concerns. He was endowed with every Christian virtue, eminent for his learning, eloquent of speech, discreet and intelligent in giving counsel, and of countenance truly angelic; but in stature he was another Zacchæus, insomuch that he was obliged to be mounted on an iron stool whenever he performed mass [*]. Being made sacrist of

---

[*] The Saint is not represented in the windows of St. Neot's church as lower of stature than any of the other figures; yet there is a tradition in the parish no less ridiculous than the story here related by Capgrave. The inhabitants shew a stone, opposite to the South porch, on which St. Neot is said to have stood whenever he was disposed to go into the church to his

the church, a certain great man knocking hastily while he was locked alone in it, Neotus ran to open the door to him. He found himself too short to reach up to the lock of the door, when lo! by divine energy the lock moved downward from its place, and stopped opposite to the girdle of the saint.

"After some time, being wearied with the concourse of people which resorted to him at Glastonbury, he was, by divine impulse, directed to seek a retirement in the remote province of Cornwall. He therefore directed his steps Westward, accompanied only by one adherent named Barius, whom he had made acquainted with his design, and who remained faithfully attached to him till the hour of his death. The same Providence which had moved him to undertake this journey continuing to be his guide, he arrived in safety at the spot destined for his abode*. The hermitage in which he settled is about ten miles distant from the monastery of St. Petroc, in

---

devotions, and from thence to have thrown the key towards the church door, not being able from the ground to reach to the lock. The key of course found its way into the key-hole, and opened the door for him. The stone in question was evidently the foundation of an antient cross, such as in popish times were always placed opposite to the South porch in every churchyard.

* The abbey of Glastonbury having a cell of monks at Lemain, opposite Looe Island, possibly St. Neot might have paid them a visit, and might have been one of the causes of his coming into Cornwall.

Cornwall *; and, taking its name from this holy man, is now called by the people of the country Neotstoke. It is a spot abounding in wood, well watered with various clear streams, and not far distant from the sea †. Having spent seven years here in great sanctity, he resolved on taking a journey to Rome, where he was honourably received by Martin, at that time pope; and, after some space past with him, to their mutual edification, he returned home with the Pope's blessing, and with permission to build a monastery at this his place of retirement. Accordingly, he erected here a suitable edifice, and filled it with monks; and was thought worthy of frequent consolation from angelic visitors. Near the spot on which his monastery stood there was a spring of clear water, which in the driest seasons never failed ‡. In it this man of God perceived there were three fishes; but not presuming to touch them till it should be revealed to him for what purpose they were placed there, an angel appeared, to

---

* This is a mistake; the meaning must be that Neotstowe is about ten miles distant from Petrocstowe, or Padstow, not from the monastery of St. Petroc at Bodmin.

† About twelve miles.

‡ This beautiful spring, with a rill issuing from it, that constantly supplies the neighbouring village with water, is yet to be seen at the foot of a steep wood. About fifty years since a very large and spreading oak, which grew almost horizontally from the bank above, and over-shadowed the well, was cut down by the tenant of the estate for repairs.

acquaint him that every day, or as often as he should find occasion, he might take one, and one only, of these fishes for his use, leaving the other two untouched. This condition being observed, he was assured that on his next return to the well he should always find three fishes, as at the first. It happened, soon after this, that our Saint was afflicted with a grievous disorder, and unable, for some days, to take any sustenance. Barius, his faithful and affectionate servant, being alarmed at his long abstinence, went to the well, and caught *two* fish, which he cooked in different ways, boiling one and broiling the other, and brought them to his master in a dish. The good Saint instantly took alarm, and enquired with much earnestness from whence these two fish came. Barius, with honest simplicity, told him that he had taken them from the well, and had drest them in different ways, hoping that if one did not suit his sickly palate, the other might.

"Then said the Saint, 'Why hast thou done thus? In opposition to an express command hast thou presumptuously ventured to take from the well more than one fish at a time?' He then commanded his trembling servant instantly to carry back the two fishes to the well; and throwing himself prostrate upon the floor, he continued in prayer till Barius, returning, acquainted him that the two fishes, after having been drest, were now in the well, alive, and active, and disporting in the water as usual. Neotus then commissioned him to go again, and catch one fish only, and to dress that for his use; which his order being complied with, no sooner had he tasted of the fish than he was instantly restored to perfect health.

"Afterwards it befell that the oxen belonging to the monastery were stolen; and for want of them the servants of the holy monks could not plough their grounds. Then behold! many stags from the adjoining woodlands, forgetting their savage nature, came and offered their necks to the yoke, and continued obediently to perform all the labours necessary for the support of the monastery until the robbers who had carried off the oxen, hearing of this miracle, brought them back to Neotus, and, expressing their repentance, framed their future lives by his counsel. It is said that, from that day to the present, these deer, and all that are descended from them, are marked with white wherever they were touched with the yoke or by the harness. "But this," says the grave historian, "as I will not venture positively to affirm, so neither will I presume to deny it, or to doubt of the divine power to perform so great a miracle."

"It happened, also, that this same servant of Heaven, standing in the well, in which he was daily wont to repeat the whole Psalter throughout, a hind, whom the dogs were pursuing, broke from the wood adjoining, and running towards him, fell at his feet, nor could it by any means be brought to rise till he had assured it of protection and security. The dogs presently after advancing towards it in full cry were checked and reproved by Neotus; on which they immediately turned tail, and fled hastily away from their prey. The huntsman, beholding this wonder, fell prostrate before the Saint, and took upon him the habit of a monk in the priory of St. Petroc; in which priory his horn is preserved as a memorial of this adventure.

"During the residence of Neotus in this place, his brother Alfred, afterwards King of the West Saxons, came to him to intreat his blessing and instruction. Neotus readily conferred upon him both; and training him in good learning, and forming his mind to prudence and virtue, he corrected the evil dispositions of his youth; and this he did with a degree of freedom and boldness which, by the nearness of his blood, he was entitled to exercise. The same Alfred, when he came afterwards to the throne, betrayed some symptoms of a proud and tyrannical temper; for which he was sharply reproved by our Saint, who instructed him in the duties of a Sovereign, and foretold his future humiliation and sufferings, as also his glorious deliverance from them; adding, withal, that he himself should shortly go the way of all flesh. He died, accordingly, soon after, in the odour of sanctity, at this his monastery of Guerrirstoke; and the earth that covered his grave, when mixed with any liquid, was sovereign in all disorders both of men and cattle.

The history of Alfred's troubles is well known. When his fortune was at its lowest ebb, Neotus his brother appeared to him in a vision, comforting him with the promise that he should not only overcome his pagan foes, but should likewise convert them and their leader to Christianity; and that, in the seventh week after Easter, he would again appear to him, and would in person lead him and his troops to victory. This his promise he faithfully performed; and on the appointed day he was plainly seen by Alfred and all his army leading them against the Danes, whom they defeated, and who, with their King, Guthrun, were prevailed upon to embrace the Christian faith.

"Barius, after this, removed a part of Neotus's relics to Enolvesburi, in the county of Huntingdon. Lewina, lady of Enolvesburi, fearing the incursions of the barbarians, caused them again to be removed from thence to Croyland, of the abbey at which place her brother, Orketellus, was superior. It being doubted, in after times, whether any relics of this Saint were really deposited at Croyland, the abbot ordered wax candles to be lighted, and breaking open, with great reverence, the chest wherein it was reported they lay, there issued from it a most fragrant and delicious smell; and in it were found the crown of the skull, with the bones of the shoulder and breast, and of the hips and shins, being all that Lewina had sent thither. These bones Henry, then abbot, removed from the spot where they before were, and placed them under an altar erected in the church of Croyland to the honour of St. Neot."

Such is the account given by Capgrave of Neotus. If he had, in truth, any share in forming the character of Alfred, or in inducing him to found or restore the University of Oxford, he was deserving of a better historian than the monkish panegyrists. Leland adds credit to both these facts. "Many," he says, "write that he was nearly allied by blood to the great Alfred, and lived in close intimacy with him, and was of great use and comfort to him during his deprest state in the isle of Athelingey. He is also believed to have induced him to rebuild the English School at Rome, founded by King Ina, and augmented in its revenues by Offa; and from the same pious zeal for learning and religion to have prevailed on him to found the new schools at the ford of Isis." Mr. Hals, in the papers he has left, says, that "St. Neot, younger son of Ethelwolfe, King of the West Saxons, built and endowed Neotus College in Oxford, which was afterwards pulled down and new built by William Long, alias de Wykeham, Bishop of Winchester, 5 March, 1379, and called by him New College."

Since the preceding work was nearly finished at the press, a friend has pointed out to me the Rev. Mr. Gorham's "History of Eynesbury and St. Neot's, Huntingdonshire, and of St. Neot's, Cornwall;" in the Preface of which elegant work Mr. Gorham thus speaks of the Patron Saint of those places:

"From the more immediate subjects of local Antiquities some little digression has been made (in chapter II. section 1.) to the Biography of the SAXON SAINT whose name is perpetuated in that of the town. The very obscure and contradictory information which is to be obtained from either antient or modern Writers respecting ST. NEOT might alone be considered as a sufficient reason for an enquiry into the accuracy or falsehood of preceding statements. Since the time of Camden and of Wood, the simple authority of those truly great names has been a ready passport (with less diligent Writers) for assertions derived from MSS. of suspected authority, or from records of doubtful age. *One* learned modern Writer* has, indeed, pursued

---

* The late Mr. Whitaker; Life of St. Neot, edit. 1806.

a line of independent investigation; but, in his eccentric (however original) volume, fable is perpetually intermingled with fact, and dogmatical assertion substituted for modest enquiry. A strict scrutiny into the unsustained positions to which allusion has just been made necessarily leads to their rejection. The materials for a Biography of NEOT thus become reduced to a few simple facts; and we are constrained to awake from the pleasing delusion, by which the events of his life have been closely connected with a remarkable period of British Annals. If the criticism in pp. 20—26, and in pp. 41—44, be correct, he will no longer appear in the venerable character of "The first Theological Professor at Oxford;" dispensing his pious instructions to that Infant University: nor will he be encircled with the fictitious glory which imagination has shed around " the oldest Brother of Alfred the Great;" renouncing the ambitious bustle and splendid occupations of the Court for the devotional retirement and self-denying services of the Cloister. What is lost, however, in *effect* is gained in *accuracy;* the threads of a false association having been withdrawn, the tissue of History may possibly have been deprived of some gaudy colours; but her dress exhibits a more becoming (though less ostentatious) texture.

"These criticisms respecting the Life of NEOT naturally led to some notice of the obscure CORNISH VILLAGE (see p. 29) which was his principal abode;

— the sylvan retreat, where, as a Hermit, he dwelt in his mossy cell; — the secluded valley, where, as an Abbot, he founded his Monastery and erected his Collegiate Chapel."

In Chapter V. of his work Mr. Gorham has given a Sketch of the Topograph of St. Neot's Parish in Cornwall; with a more particular view to the description of its beautiful Church, dedicated to ST. NEOT.

Having thus finished my work, I beg to apologize to the reader for every imperfection he may find in this little sketch. It was begun and ended by me as an amusement to myself; but as some parts of it may give information, and perhaps some little pleasure to others, I can see no reasonable ground for withholding it from the public. I acknowledge I have not been very methodical. Now and then you catch a view of one or other of the Boroughs, and then lose it; but as the work is so small, perhaps this mode may be the best I could have pursued, and it strongly strikes me as being like the Looes themselves. Every ten steps you take in their vicinity give you a change of scenery, which is certainly more pleasing than a continued view of the same objects from the same position. The shifting of the scenery in a walk round Looe may be almost compared to the rapid changes of the kaliedoscope.

INDEX.

A.
Anstis, John, Garter, 177.
Antiquity of Looe, 1.

B.
Ballast, 149.
Barbican, 34.
Barrows, 88.
Barton, derivation of, 176.
Bathing-machine, 30.
Battern Cliffs, or Cleaves, 116.
Beach, Sea, 30.
Beer, derivation of, 176.
Beville, Sir W. anecdote of his servant, 156.
Bindown Hill, 118.
Bodrigan, Otho de, 89.
——— grant or charter, 260.
Bolt, 98.
Botelet, 188.
Bray, 183.
Bridge, 8, 114.
——— record concerning, 256.
Brining, or luminous appearance of the sea, 83.
Buller, Sir Edward, 174.
Burgesses, Capital, 4.
——— Free, 4.

C.
Cage for Scolds, 59.
Calais, fleet before, 95.
Canal, 143.
Celts, 69.
Chapel at East Looe, 10.
——— Lamain, 61.
Cheese Wring, 195.
Churchend, 35.
Clickitor Rocks, 218.
Cold Harbour, 34.
Conduit at East Looe, 213.
Conger Douce, 84.
Corn Trade, 84.
Corporation of East Looe, 2.
——— of West Looe, 63.
——— revenues, how applied, 268.
Cornwall, Duchy of, 56.
Courtenay, Francis, 42.
Crafthole, 117.
Cromlech at Trethevye, 216.
Curiosities, natural and artificial, within a ride of Looe, 192.

D.
Divining-rod, 141.
Dodge, Rev. Richard, 154.

Doniert's or Dungerth's monument, 197.
Dosmery Pool, 192.
Down, inclosure of the, desireable, 72.
Downderry Cliffs, 116.
Drakewall's mine, 119.
Druids, account of, 213.
Druidical basins, 205.
Ducking-stool, 60.
Dulo, 46.

E.

Earthquake, 141.
East Looe. See Looe.
Eddystone Lighthouse, 101.
Election, indentures of, 246.
Encroachment of the sea, 101.

F.

Fairs, 142.
Fishing and Fish, 124.
Fishery of Looe River, 176.
——— Pilchard, 74.
Fleets, before Calais, 195.
——— Combined, 245.
Foreigners, 39.
Fortifications of East Looe, 24, 33.
Fowey, 119.
Foys-Fenton, 151.
Freemen, 39.
Fresh water, 223.

G.

Gentlemen's seats near Looe, 153.
George of Looe, ship, 88.
Giant's hedge or mound, 64.
Glynn farm, 181.
Gorham, Rev. Mr. extract from his History of St. Neot's, 299.
Grenville's, Eustace de, grant to his men of Showta, 265.
Ground-plot of East Looe, 33.
Guildhall at West Looe, 59.
Gumb's (Daniel) house, 203.

H.

Health of the Looes, 30.
Heartseeds, 130.
High water, 147.
——— tides, 147.
Hills at Looe, 45.
——— in Cornwall, 118.
Hingston Hill, 118.
Honor of Wallingford, 56.
Horestones, 62.
Houses, 32.
Hurlers, 195.

I.

Imports, 88.

K.

Kayne. See St. Kayne.

INDEX.

Kelp, 130.
Keverel, 184.
Keynsham, 219.
Killigarth, 156.
Kilmarth, 209.
Kilminorth, 164.
Kippiscombe Lane, 120.
Knight, Adm. Sir Joseph, 269.

L.

Langdon, Rev. Walter, 21.
Law Court bill, 270.
Lemain, 60, 292.
—— Chapel, 61.
Longstone, 117.
Looe, antiquity of, 1.
—— curiosities within a ride of, 192.
—— River, fishery of, 176.
—— ship George of, 88.
—— health of, 30
—— Island, 25.
—— longitude and latitude of, 150.
—— limits of the Port of, 225.
—— Hill, prospects from, 110.
—— resemblance between and Weymouth, 150.
—— Bridge, Sessions records at, 256.
—— scenery about, 96.
—— Tokens, 94.
—— Corporation, merry tale concerning, 281.

Looe, high water at, 147.
—— and Weymouth, 150.
Looe, East, 1.
—————— Corporation of, 2.
—————— Chapel at, 10.
—————— Conduit at, 213.
—————— Ground-plot of, 33.
—————— Situation of, 45.
—————— Fortifications of, 24, 33.
—————— Members of Parliament for, 228.
—————— Mayors of, 233.
—————— Population of, 145.
—————— Town Seal of, 89.
—————— Walks, 96.
Looe, West, 60, 113.
—————— Guildhall, 59.
—————— Members of Parliament for, 237.
—————— Mayors of, 242.
—————— Mill, 71.
—————— Shuta Spring, 223, 224.
—————— Teverbin's grant to, 51.
—————— Town Seal of, 50.
—————— Description of, 60.
—————— incorporated, 63.
—————— Down, 64.
—————— Walks, 113.
—————— Corporation of, 63.
—————— Population of, 146.
Lostwithiel, 119.
Lugger's Cove, 124.
Lydcott, 184.

x

M.

Macarmick, Gen. Wm. 191.
Maiowe, Philip, 21.
Maker Camp and Barracks, 111.
────── Tower, 112.
Markets, 142.
Martin's, St. See St. Martin's.
Martin, St. Bishop of Tours, 24.
May-pole, 37.
Mayors of East Looe, 233.
────────── West Looe, 242.
Mayor-choosing Days from 1800 to 1899, 277.
Medhope, Rev. Stephen, sen. 22.
────────────────── jun. 23.
Members of Parliament for East Looe, 228.
────── West Looe, 237.
Midmain Rock, 61.
Mill, West Looe, 71.
Millendreath Beach, 98, 115.
Monuments, 20.
Morval, 179.

N.

Natural History, 129.
Neot, St. See St. Neot's.
Nicholas, Major, 191.
Nicolas, Nicholas Harris, 191.

O.

Otho de Bodrigan, 89, 260.
Ore, 132.

P.

Parliamentary representation of Cornwall in Oliver Cromwell's time, 6.
Pelynt, or Plint, 162.
Pennyless Bench, 37.
Peterels, 130.
Petty, Sir William, 7.
Pilchard Fishery, 74.
Places, distance from, 142.
Pleady, 115.
Plymouth, distance from, 111.
Polgover, 184.
Polperro, 122.
Polvellan, 70, 174.
Population, 145.
Portbigham, 50.
Port, annexed to the Duchy, 57.
Portlooe, 173.
Port of Looe, 225.
Portnadler Bay, 61.
Post, General, 145.
Purpura, 126.

R.

Ramehead, 97.
Redgate, 196.
Representation of Cornwall in Oliver Cromwell's time, 6.
Rides, 115.
Riots, 84.
River, 46.
────── Fishery, 176.
Roads, 141.
Roman Roads, 64.

INDEX.

S.

Salubrity, 30.
Samphire, 129.
Scenery about Looe, 96.
Schools, 25.
Scolds, cage for, 59.
Sea-bathing, 30, 144.
— excursions, 122.
— weeds, 129.
— fences against the, 148.
— pinks, 129.
Seaton, 116.
Sessions record about Looe Bridge, 256.
Sharp Torr, 207.
Shells, 129.
Shoot at West Looe, 223.
Shutta, or Shoota, 49.
Signal Posts, 113.
Situation, 1, 150.
Slow-worm, 130.
St. Cleer Well, 215.
St. German's Beacon, 117.
St. Kayne, 14.
St. Kayne's Well, 218.
——————— Verses on, by Mr. Southey, 221.
St. Martin, Parish of, 18.
——————— antient customs in, 273.
——————— seats in the Church of, 272.
St. Mary in the Marsh, 49.
St. Neot's Church, 192.
——————— legend of, 291.
Stones, Druidical circle of, 121.
Storms, violent, 135, 149.
Streets, 32.
Suit in the Exchequer, 39.

T.

Table Land, 100.
Tale, a merry, concerning Looe Corporation, 281.
Talland, 60, 153.
Thunder storms, 132.
Tides, 147.
Tokens, Looe, 94.
Toup, Rev. Jonathan, 18.
Town Seal of East Looe, 89.
——————— West Looe, 50.
Towns ventilated, 115.
Trade, 73.
Tradesmen's Tokens, 94.
Trecothick West Indiaman lost, 154.
Tregarrick, 162.
Trelawny family, 159.
——————— Bp. Sir Jonathan, 11.
Tremodart, 185.
Trenant Park, 174.
Trethevye Cromlech, 216.
Treverbin's grant to West Looe, 51.
Treworgey, 176.
Triggs, Mr. Clement, 27.

V.

Virgula Divina, 141.
Volunteer Artillery, 36.

INDEX.

W.

Wager, Sir Charles, 165.
Walks at East Looe, 113.
Wallingford, Honor of, 57.
Water excursions, 120.
——— high, at Looe, 147.
——— fresh, 223.
Waterloo Villa, 191.
West Hundred, name from whence derived, 151.
West, Parishes in the Hundred of, their names, and number of acres in each, 152.
West Looe. See Looe.
Westnorth, 117.
Weymouth and Looe, resemblance between, 150.
Wood, submarine, 98.
Wrinkle, 117.
Wring Cheese, or Cheese Wring, 195.

EMBELLISHMENTS.

View of East Looe .... Frontispiece.
View of West Looe .... Page 59
Seal of the Corporation of West Looe, or Portbyhan........ 50
Seal of the Corporation of East Looe 89
Edystone Lighthouse 101
Edystone Lighthouse in a Storm 102
Cheesewring and Dungerth's Monument 204
Map of Gentlemen's Seats in the Neighbourhood of the Looes 189

THE END.

LONDON: PRINTED BY JOHN NICHOLS AND SON,
25, PARLIAMENT STREET.